POPULATION AND ETHNO-DEMOGRAPHY
IN VIETNAM

POPULATION AND ETHNO-DEMOGRAPHY IN VIETNAM

KHONG DIEN

National Center for Social Science and Humanity
Institute of Ethnology
Hanoi

SILKWORM BOOKS

This publication was made possible by a grant from SIDA.

ISBN 974-7551-65-9

First published in 2002 by
Silkworm Books
104/5 Chiang Mai–Hot Road, M. 7, Chiang Mai 50200, Thailand
E-mail: silkworm@loxinfo.co.th
Website: www.silkwormbooks.info

Cover photograph by Nguyen Duy Thieu
Set in 10 pt. Palatino by Silk Type
Printed by O. S. Printing House, Bangkok

CONTENTS

LIST OF PHOTOGRAPHS

1. A Muong House, Da Bac district, Hoa Binh province (Khong Dien)
2. An old Muong woman, Ngoc Hoi district, Kon Tum province (Nguyen Duy Thieu)
3. A Muong girl, Mai Chau district, Hoa Binh province (Doan Dinh Thi)
4. An old Tho woman, Quy Hop district, Nghe An province (Nguyen Duy Thieu)
5. Bana men drink alcohol (ruou can), Konchro district, Gia Lai province (Nguyen Duy Thieu)
6. A Bru woman, Huong Hoa district, Quang Tri province (Nguyen Duy Thieu)
7. Kho Mu women, Thuan Chau district, Son La province (Doan Dinh Thi)
8. A Ta Oi girl, Huong Hoa district, Quang Tri province (Nguyen Duy Thieu)
9. A Gie-Trieng woman (the Gie group), Dac Lay district, Kon Tum province (Nguyen Duy Thieu)
10. Gie-Trieng women (the Trieng group), Dac Lay district, Kon Tum province (Nguyen Duy Thieu)
11. A Khang house, Muong La district, Son La province (Khong Dien)
12. A Brau woman, Sa Thay district, Kon Tum province (Nguyen Duy Thieu)
13. A Mnong grave and funerary statues, Buon Don district, Dac Lac province (Khong Dien)
14. Researchers from the Institute of Ethnology (Hanoi) and Hmong people, Tuan Giao district, Lai Chau province (Doan Dinh Thi)
15. Hmong girls, Sa Pa district, Lao Cai province (Nguyen Duy Thieu)

37. A Gia Rai long house in Ea Hleo district, Dac Lac province (Khong Dien)
38. A Gia Lai woman, Ea Hleo district, Dac Lac province (Khong Dien)
39. An Ede girl on the outskirts of Buon Ma Thuot town, Dac Lac province (Nguyen Duy Thieu)
40. Ede girls in Krong Buc district, Dac Lac province (Khong Dien)
41. Worship sorcerers of the Cham people following Brahmanism in Phuoc Huu Commune, Ninh Phuoc district, Ninh Thuan province (Khong Dien)
42. Folkdance of the Cham people in Phuoc Huu Commune, Ninh Phuoc district, Ninh Thuan province (Khong Dien)
43. A Raglai woman in Phuoc Dai Commune, Bac Ai district, Ninh Thuan province (Khong Dien)
44. The Phu La women (the Xa Pho group) in Tuan Giao district, Lai Chau province (Doan Dinh Thi)
45. A Phu La woman (the Han group), Bac Ha district, Lao Cai province (Nguyen Duy Thieu)
46. The La Hu children, Muong Te district, Lai Chau province (Khong Dien)
47. The Cong women, Muong Te district, Lai Chau province (Nguyen Duy Thieu)
48. A Si La woman, Muong Te district, Lai Chau province (Khong Dien)
49. The Lo Lo women in Meo Vac Commune, Meo Vac district, Ha Giang province (Khong Dien)
50. The Festival of the Kinh (Viet) people in Vinh Bao district, Hai Phong City (Khong Dien)

All photographs were taken in the 1990s

FOREWORD

This book studies the ethno-demographic situation in Vietnam, focusing mainly on the last few decades. The analysis is based on population censuses, annual statistics from both central and local government offices, as well as data collected from ethnological and ethno-sociological field visits. It is hoped that the systematic presentation of these materials will help policy makers and managers as they formulate policies and make plans for ethnic minorities and the population of Vietnam as a whole.

The Vietnamese edition of this book was published by the Hanoi Social Sciences Publishing House in 1995. The English edition of this book was translated by Mrs Nguyen Thi Hue and checked by Dr Andrew Hardy. The author revised and supplemented some data based on the Vietnam Population Census which was conducted on 1 April 1999, including the ethnic minorities' rankings in terms of linguistics, ethnic distribution, which were detailed down to the provincial level, and the population of each ethnic minority in decreasing order was noted.

On the occasion of the publication of this English edition, I would like to express my sincere thanks to the SIDA fund of Sweden; Dr Claes Corlin and Dr Wil Burghoorn, Göteborg University, Sweden; Mrs Nguyen Thi Hue and Dr Andrew Hardy; Silkworm Books and the readers of the earlier version is this book who provided me with material and psychological support as well as funding, translation, and permission to publish this book.

This is the first book in English about ethno-demography in Vietnam. Certainly it is not complete, and the comments of the readers will be greatly appreciated.

Khong Dien

INTRODUCTION

The link between social sciences and natural sciences has grown considerbly in the past century. For several decades now, stimulated by developments within the natural sciences, some social sciences have been seeking new research methodologies, most of them using mathematically sophisticated statistical methods.

New research methodologies have gradually been developed and applied in economics and history, permitting social scientists to move from the description of events to more rigorous forms of categorization and the development of descriptive formulae.

Ethnography, which has long been considered to belong to the science of history, has the task of documenting various events in different ethnic groups and uncovering the process of their development over time. Moreover, it is characterized by its geographic focus upon specific territories. It is, for example, difficult to explain changes in ethnic features if attention is not also paid to research into the environmental circumstances in which people live and work. Similarly, the characteristics of the natural environment cannot be considered self-evident, but should be viewed in relation to the lives of the local residents. While natural conditions cannot determine the process of social development, they do have a significant impact on humans, their selection of tools and their means of production, as well as their influence on traditional production practices.

The traditional methods which have been widely applied so far in ethnological research—the basic tools of direct observation and description—have been incomplete with regard to new knowledge and ethnological phenomena in all their complexity.[1] As a consequence, it is necessary to develop new sciences. One such new science is ethno-geography, which is an inter-disciplinary science arising out of the meeting between ethnology and geography. A key sub-component of ethno-geography is ethno-demography, which obviously links ethnology with demography.[2]

Although demography and ethnology have been closely linked to one another since the last decades of the nineteenth century, the development of the two disciplines has not been even. While ethnologists were still focusing on exotic or "primitive" ethnic groups (e.g. tribes), demographers were showing increasing interest in developed ethnic groups. Later on, when ethnologists began to study modern ethnic groups, demographers expanded their field to include less-developed countries. In recent years, these differences in interest have begun to diminish. Today, both ethnology and demography share similar research methodologies and agendas. To be more precise, ethnological research methods have been applied widely by demographers.

The primary task of ethno-demography is to identify the ethnic composition of the population of a certain country and a certain region. This requires ethno-demographers to identify the population of the nation and of each ethnic group, and study changes in the composition of different ethnic groups and the nation over time. To accomplish this, ethno-demography analyses basic demographic indicators (birth, mortality, marriage structure, migration, etc.) of an ethnic group and a nation or a certain territorial region. Ethno-demography aims to identify the relationship between these indicators and their economic, cultural and social features. For example, the birth rate is often closely linked to attitudes towards marriage in general, marriage age in particular and preferred number of children, as well as other psychological characteristics and customs of an ethnic group. On the other hand, the mortality rate is primarily related to economic and social development concerns such as work and leisure habits, diet, and health-care practices. Morality data also shed light on a range of other social customs such as taboos, funerals, and child-raising practices.

In ethno-demography, there are two research trends; one relates to in-depth research on demographic issues and the other to in-depth research on ethnic groups. The present project favours the second trend.

At present, the issue of "ethnicity" is a critical one, particularly in countries and/or regions where political boundaries do not coincide with ethnic boundaries. The disparity between boundaries has sometimes led to serious territorial disputes. For this reason, more research on the composition of different ethnic groups, their distribution, location, and other demographic features is required.

More generally, population growth is an increasingly urgent concern. In 1950 the world population was recorded at 2.5 billion; by 6.30 A.M. on 11 July 1987, a boy named Mategegaspa, in the former Yugoslavia, was counted as the five billionth citizen of the world. So, in only twenty-seven years, the world population has doubled. Currently, it is increasing by an average of 92.6 million people every year. Today, the highest population growth figures are recorded in Asia, Africa, and Latin America.

Population statistics cannot explain social structure or social change; the population size and density do not determine the nature of social organization, but population size does greatly affect the speed with which a society develops. Additionally, population size and density may promote or check social development in a variety of ways.

Population growth is a condition for boosting material production, but only up to a certain point. The contradiction between the rate of population growth and the level of social and economic development is, in many cases, the result of redundancy. In other words, overpopulation and excess labor place additional pressures on production and often give rise to conflicts and/or migration within and between territories.

The above problems are not a new phenomenon. In ancient Greece and Rome, people understood that the population should be limited in order to maintain the existing standards of living. In his book *An Ideal Nation* Plato proposed that the nation's population should be limited by force. According to him, marriage should only be allowed with state approval. Only men between the ages of 30 and 35 should be allowed to have children. Like Plato, Aristotle advocated the constitutional regulation of population growth and proposed that men should marry at the age of 37. He was concerned that unchecked birth-rates would give rise to new citizens being born without access to land for tilling. These landless citizens would first fall into poverty and then into crime.[3]

The founders of Marxism were also very concerned about population issues and considered studies concerning population to be the primary task of economic, political, and social research of a nation or territory. Karl Marx wrote, "When we consider any country politically and economically, we often start with research on the population of that country. It seems that it is the correct method to start in practice with realities and specific things. Therefore, the science of political economy should start with the population. That is the starting point, basis, and the subject matter for the entire process of social production."[4] From this perspective, any sharp change in the population of a nation—whether it is an increase or a decrease—reflects a turning point in the economic, social, and cultural development of that nation. This, in turn, subsequently shapes the direction of that nation's history.

In Vietnam the population increased very slowly from the beginning of the Christian era until the nineteenth century. Over nearly twenty centuries, the population increased by only five million—the average population growth rate being 0.65%. During the eighty years of French colonial occupation the Vietnamese people suffered appalling exploitation. Although the birthrate had by then increased, mortality rates were correspondingly high and the annual population growth rate for this period was therefore only 1.3%.

Vietnam declared its independence on 2 September 1945. However, the legacy of harsh exploitation, first by the French colonialists and then by Japanese soldiers occupying the country at the end of World War II, helped produce the worse famine in the history of the nation. The 1945 famine claimed the lives of nearly two million people. This was followed by the nine year war of resistance against the French colonialists who returned to reclaim control of Vietnam. The war ended with the liberation of the North (the territory north of the seventeenth parallel), but it had cost tens of thousands of lives. For this reason, the average population growth rate was only 1.5%. This period, in which the country remained divided, was then followed by the war of resistance against the United States, which again saw millions of lives lost in the struggle for national independence. Nevertheless, in this period, and in the years that followed the country's reunification in 1975, the population growth rate increased rapidly. In only twenty-two years (1955–1977), the population of the country doubled from 25 million to 50 million, reaching an average annual growth rate of 3%.

Although the State has issued many resolutions and directives concerning population and family planning, the actual results have not been as hoped. In recent years, the annual national population growth rate has remained at 2.2%, which is higher than the average rate of developing countries in general.

MAP 1   ADMINSTRATIVE MAP OF VIETNAM

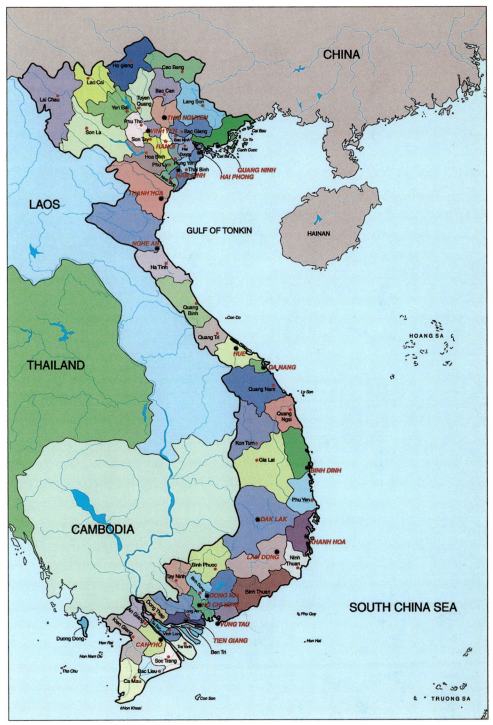

MAP 2   ETHNO-LINGUISTIC GROUPS

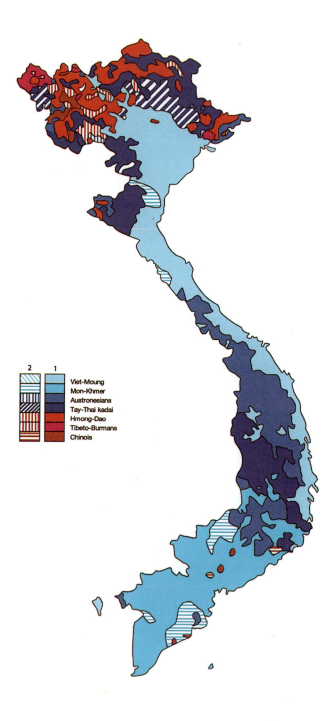

2	1	
		Viet-Moung
		Mon-Khmer
		Austronesians
		Tay-Thai kadai
		Hmong-Dao
		Tibeto-Burmans
		Chinois

1. A Muong house, Da Bac district, Hoa Binh province (Khong Dien)

2. An old Muong woman, Ngoc Hoi district, Kon Tum province (Nguyen Duy Thieu)

3. A Muong girl, Mai Chau district, Hoa Binh province (Doan Dinh Thi)

4. An old Tho woman, Quy Hop
district, Nghe An province
5. Bana men drink alcohol (*ruou can*),
Konchro district, Gia Lai province

6. A Bru woman, Huong Hoa
district, Quang Tri province

7. Kho Mu women, Thuan Chau
district, Son La province

8. A Ta Oi girl, Huong Hoa
district, Quang Tri province

9. A Gie-Trieng woman (the Gie group), Dac Lay district, Kon Tum province

10. Gie-Trieng women (the Trieng group), Dac Lay district, Kon Tum province

12. A Brau woman, Sa Thay district, Kon Tum province

(next page)
11. A Khang house, Muong La district, Son La province (top)
13. A Muong grave and funerary statues, Buon Don district, Dac Lac province (middle)
14. Researchers from the Institute of Ethnology (Hanoi) and Hmong people, Tuan Giao district, Lai Chau province (bottom)

15. Hmong girls, Sa Pa district, Lao Cai province

16. Hmong women, Bac Ha district, Lao Cai province

17. Hmong women and children, Muong Lay district, Lai Chau province

18. Blacksmith, a traditional profession of the Hmong people, Mai Chau district, Hoa Binh province

19. Welcoming a bride to her husband's house, the Yao (the Quan Chet group) Da Bac district, Hoa Binh province (Khong Dien)

20. Yao women (the Thanh Y group), Hoanh Bo district, Quang Ninh province

21. Offerings in *cap sac*
(kwa tang) ceremony of
the Yao people, Da Bac
district, Hoa Binh
province (Khong Dien)
22. A Yao woman (the
Red Yao group), Sa Pa
district, Loa Cai province
(Nguyen Duy Thieu)

23. A Tay girl (the Ngan group), Quang Hoa district, Cao Bang province (Khong Dien)

24. A Tay girl, Bac Ha district, Lao Cai province (Nguyen Duy Thieu)

25. Tay women, Hoa An district, Cao Bang province (Nguyen Duy Thieu)

26. A rice field belonging to the Tay, Quang Hoa district, Cao Bang province (Doan Dinh Thi)

27. Nung girls, Quang Hoa district, Cao Bang province (Doan Dinh Thi)

29. A Giay woman, Sa Pa district, Lao Cai province (Nguyen Duy Thieu)

28. Nung girls, Hoa An district, Cao Bang province (Nguyen Duy Thieu)

30. Thai children, Thuan Chau district, Son La province (Doan Dinh Thi)

32. A Thai woman, Muong La district, Son La province `(Nguyen Duy Thieu)

31. Thai children, Thuan Chau district, Son La province (Khong Dien)

33. Vietnamese ethnographers and Thai women in Thuan Chau district, Son La province (Doan Dinh Thi)

34. A Thai waterwheel for husking rice, Thuan Chau district, Son La province (Khong Dien)
35. Thai waterwheels for irrigating highland fields in Thuan Chau district, Son La province (Khong Dien)
36. A highland market for ethnic groups living in the northwest of Vietnam (Khong Dien)

37. A Gia Rai long-house in Ea Hleo district, Dac Lac province (Khong Dien)
38. A Gia Lai woman, Ea Hleo district, Dac Lac province (Khong Dien)

39.   An Ede girl on the outskirts of Buon Ma Thuot town, Dac Lac province
(Nguyen Duy Thieu)

40. Ede girls in Krong Buc district, Dac Lac province (Khong Dien)

41. Priests of the Cham people following Brahmanism in Phuoc Huu commune, Ninh Phuoc district, Ninh Thuan province (Khong Dien)

42. Folk dance of the Cham people in Phuoc Huu commune, Ninh Phuoc district, Ninh Thuan province (Khong Dien)

43. A Raglai woman in Phuoc Dai commune, Bac Ai district, Ninh Thuan province (Khong Dien)
44. The Phu La women (the Xa Pho group) in Tuan Giao district, Lai Chau province (Doan Dinh Thi)

45. A Phu La woman (the Han group), Bac Ha district, Lao Cai province (Nguyen Duy Thieu)
46. La Hu children, Muong Te district, Lai Chau province (Khong Dien)

47. Cong women, Muong Te
district, Lai Chau province
(Nguyen Duy Thieu)
48. A Si La woman, Muong
Te district, Lai Chau
province (Khong Dien)

49. Lo Lo women in Meo Vac commune, Meo Vac district, Ha Giang province
(Khong Dien)

50. The Festival of the Kinh (Viet) people in Vinh Bao district, Hai Phong city
(Khong Dien)

CHAPTER I

ETHNIC COMPOSITION

L YING at the crossroads of Southeast Asia, Vietnam has long been the place of residence and interchange between different tribal and ethnic groups of various linguistic and cultural backgrounds. Since Vietnam was founded, and throughout their struggles against foreign invaders, Vietnamese people of different ethnic backgrounds have shared a tradition of patriotism, mutual love, and assistance. This shared past has formed the basis for uniting a diverse community of more than fifty ethnic groups and ensuring the rights and obligations of all groups in relation to each other within a unified nation. The ethnic minorities are entitled to use their own languages and to maintain their distinct identities by practicing their traditional customs and cultures.[1]

One of the factors influencing the composition and development of the ethnic groups is their ethno-demography. Studying the processes of ethno-demography entails the use of precise and detailed statistics on ethnic groups, especially those statistics derived from censuses and statistical yearbooks from the central and local levels of government. However, statistical yearbooks in Vietnam have not generally included ethnic indicators, and censuses are also rare. Over the past thirty years, Vietnam has carried out five censuses, but only two were conducted on a national scale and only the 1989 census included specific ethnic indicators. In this book, therefore, we confine ourselves to statistical data from the national level and/or the local level. We also use data collected from ethnological, sociological and demographic surveys conducted in certain parts of the country to supplement the statistical data mentioned above.

Comparison, analysis and explanation of the ethno-demographic data would not be feasible without the application of consistent scientific methodologies regarding the definition and classification of ethnic groups. For this reason, we shall briefly present the principles behind the definition and classification of ethnic communities used by both Vietnamese and foreign ethnologists.

I. PRINCIPLES OF CLASSIFICATION OF ETHNIC COMMUNITIES

1. GENERAL CONCEPT

First, let us examine the concepts of ethnic community and nationality. Most of the ethnologists from the former Soviet Union considered "ethnic community" to be synonymous with "ethnic group." Some, however, argued that the concept of ethnic community is broader, and denotes a group comprising many different minorities which share similar types of cultures and languages.[2] Nevertheless, all agreed that ethnic communities may be defined according to typical characteristics, such as:

Living in a certain region. Territory is a basic material condition for the formation of ethnic communities. It was held that even groups speaking different languages and expressing different cultural forms may become united over time by sharing a territorial region and its natural conditions. In reality, however, many communities such as the Jews and Gypsies (Digan) live in many different countries and regions even very far from each other, but still maintain a sense of belonging to the same ethnic group.

Speaking the same language. It may be argued that linguistic communities tend to cohere.[3] Language is not only a medium for communication, but also provides the means for the development of cultural and spiritual life. Language is therefore perhaps the most important feature of an ethnic group.[4] At the same time, it is important to note that language is not a definitive criterion for the demarcation of ethnic groups either. Today, many groups speak two or three different languages, and different ethnic groups may share the same language, such as French, English, or Spanish.

Cultural features. Culture evolves in a group over time and hand in hand with its history. It is handed down over the generations and contributes to the richness and diversity of mankind's experience. The important question is whether an ethnic group really is the inheritor of its culture, and whether it continues to develop that culture in a

2

creative and progressive way. This dynamic definition is preferable to discussions of whether they live in the same style of house, utilize the same pattern of clothing, or wear the same hats.

SINCE, as noted above, different groups may share a language, but not the same cultural features, our definition of an ethnic group considers specific cultural features in conjunction with language. Together, they constitute a separate cultural identity.

Ethnic awareness or consciousness. This is a decisive factor in defining an ethnic group. It is self-awareness or self-identity, far more than the material conditions which may give rise to ethnic grouping, which ultimately defines an ethnic group. Although the community may be divided territorially, its culture disintegrated, and its mother tongue lost, ethnic consciousness may persist.

In addition to the above definitions of ethnic community, some argue that the economy should be considered a key factor. Others deny this, regarding it as leading to a simplification of the relationship between the economy and the ethnic group.[5] While economic issues are very important and necessary for the emergence of an ethnic community, they are generally not useful for identifying ethnic groups since an "economic community" often does not coincide with an "ethnic community." An economic community emerges first through the interaction of different territorial communities and a national community. It does not arise from within the ethnic group itself, but from a complicated series of inter-relationships and interactions within a nation.[6] In short, economic relationships do not always signal an ethnic community. When a territorial relationship is broken, economic relationships may dissolve while ethnic relationships continue.[7]

Psychological features are also mentioned by some authors. However, in his book *Ethnic Groups and Ethnology*, the academic Y. V. Bromlei strongly opposes all attempts to explain ethnic difference in terms of psychology. He argues that psychological differences are relative between groups, not absolute, and he suggests that differences also exist within any particular social group.[8]

According to V. I. Kozlov, the psychological characteristics of an ethnic group have to do with the people's awareness of natural and social events. When a nation is beset by class differences, each class will tend to develop particular psychological features and different manners of behavior. Therefore the author proposes that in looking at ethnicity one should concentrate not upon the psychological community, but upon the existence of certain typical psychological features of the ethnic group as they appear through shared cultural activities and social life.[9]

In the early 1980s, scientists from the former Soviet Union were engaged in discussion about national psychology, and the debate was published in *Soviet Ethnology Magazine* (Nos. 2, 3 and 4, 1983). On this issue, A. F. Dashdamirov stated that the spiritual life of the community is governed by its economic, territorial and linguistic features, and is shaped according to the impact of the historical development of the nation. Specifically, it is moulded by the unique features of its own history, the socio-cultural development of the ethnic group, and the typical traditions and achievements of the group in terms of its spirituality, philosophy, aesthetics, ideology, culture, science, education, psychology, and so on. In other words, culture, psychology, and national consciousness are not the sum total of the factors by which a community may be distinguished from other ethnic groups, but they are contributing factors, which reflect the lives of its members.[10]

This discussion was furthered by Y. V. Bromlei, who expressed the opinion that some contributors to philosophical and historical newspapers and books denied the reality and existence of psychology common to ethnic communities, and characteristics common to ethnic groups. They argued that there is no such thing as a common psychology. Of course in the capitalist world, the exploiters and the exploited were quite different in terms of social position within production systems, in society, and in ethical values. There was a very complicated system of psychological characteristics. However, according to Y. V. Bromlei, within this complex system, there exists a community of psychological attributes. The presence of two cultures in the capitalist nation does not contradict the existence in it of a certain cultural community.[11]

According to V. P. Levkovich, various non-ethnic factors, such as class and social structure, have an impact on the formation of ethnic similarity—an important element for the development of ethnic consciousness. The opinions of different groups and strata may cross-cut ethnic divisions. Conversely, ethnic groups which are united in terms of class may share many other similarities. In other words, economic streamlining may lead to other forms of conformity.[12] It may therefore be concluded that while psychology is an important factor to consider in relation to ethnic groupings, its significance remains open for discussion.

A further feature which is discussed in relation to the definition of

4

ethnic groups is that of endogamy (intra-marriage). In an article published in the *Soviet Ethnology Magazine*, Y. V. Bromlei proposed that the concept of ethnic group should be broadened so that an ethnic group should be considered a community distinguished by internal affinal bonds. Affinal bonding should then be included as one of the most important criteria defining an ethnic group.[13] Elsewhere this author has stressed that endogamy is a major factor creating stability within ethnic groups. Mixed marriages between ethnic groups are held to rupture the groups' boundaries.[14] V. I. Kozlov similarly posits ethnic endogamy as a practice of key importance for ensuring reproduction of the group and accounts for its persistence as a distinct entity over time. However, we should consider endogamy to be a feature rather than a cause of an ethnic group, since it is not the sole defining characteristic.[15]

So, in general, some of the criteria by which ethnic groups are to be defined are agreed upon. Others require further consideration and clarification. In particular, the question of what term should be used to refer to ethnic groups is not simple. Some French authors, when writing about ethnic groups, including those in Vietnam, have used the term "ethnic groups," while American ethnologists have tended to prefer "ethnic minorities," or "ethnic minority groups." The ethnologists of the former Soviet Union often used the term *narod* to refer to groups, whether they were of majority or minority status.[16]

2. VIEWPOINTS OF VIETNAMESE ETHNOLOGISTS

IN the past, many Vietnamese and foreign authors made contributions to the ethnology of Vietnam, although many of the works published only appeared in the late nineteenth and early twentieth centuries. French authors described single ethnic groups (A. Azema and R. Henri,[17] Bonifacy[18]), all the ethnic groups, in a particular region (E. Diguiet,[19] H. Maitre[20]), or ethnic groups in all regions (G. Maspero,[21] D. Rozarie[22]). But the first constructive debates on the criteria used to define an ethnic group only started at the beginning of the 1960s. Following some field surveys in north Vietnam, and discussions with key members of ethnic minority groups who had migrated from the south to the north, ethnologists decided to organise a symposium in August 1960 in Hanoi. Most of the reports were then published in the *Ethnological Review* of the former Central Committee for Ethnic Groups. These reports included papers by Vuong Hoang Tuyen,[23] Mac Duong,[24] La Van Lo,[25] Hoang

Thi Chau and Nguyen Linh.[26] This symposium clarified many questions concerning the criteria for defining ethnic groups. However, the symposium was unable to agree upon the basic factors necessary for a standard definition by which groups should be distinguished.[27]

In 1968, the Institute of Ethnology was established under the Vietnam Committee for Social Sciences. This committee is now known as the National Center for Social Science and Humanities. One of the Institute's tasks (and perhaps its key task) during the initial period after its foundation was defining the composition of different ethnic groups living within Vietnam. The Institute dispatched many teams to various parts of the country from the 17th parallel northwards to collect data. In 1973, the Institute, together with other departments under the Central Committee for Ethnic Groups and the Faculty of History at Hanoi University, organized two symposia in Hanoi to discuss the definition of ethnic groups. The results were then published in the *Ethnological Bulletin* No. 1, 1972 and No. 3, 1973 and also in *Ethnological Review* No. 1, 1974 and in the book *The Issue of Defining the Composition of Ethnic Minorities in Northern Vietnam*.[28] The sections below provide a summary of the key opinions of some of the ethnologists who participated in this historical event.

According to Be Viet Dang, an ethnic group should be considered the basic unit for defining ethnic composition. Furthermore, the ethnic community was considered to be a broader concept and the local sub-group a narrower one. The ethnic community or group may be considered a group of variable stability, formed historically in relation to a common residential area, economic activities, language and cultural characteristics. The group also shares a common name.

After noting the importance of territory for the origin and evolution of the ethnic community, the author explains that territory cannot be considered the foremost criterion for defining ethnic groups in northern Vietnam. The same applies to ethnic characteristics, since these, the author continues, also cannot be used as definitive of the ethnic composition of groups. The remaining criteria, then, are language, cultural activities, and ethnic consciousness, which remain the key criteria for defining ethnic groups in Vietnam.[29]

Researchers at the Institute of Ethnology, which held two follow-up workshops in June and November 1973, generally agreed with this viewpoint.[30] At the initial workshop, Hoang Hoa Toan discussed how groups which live far apart experienced their commonality when they met, and understood themselves to be part of a single group. Lam Xuan Dinh drew attention to the population sizes of groups. He contended that even small populations may meet the criteria for constituting an ethnic group. As a consequence, Dang Nghiem Van and Trieu Huu Ly argued that a group's name should be respected, while Bui Khanh The proposed that the written form of the name should correspond to the group's own literary customs.

At the second workshop, researchers participated in another heated discussion. Nguyen Duong Binh pointed to the complexity of the relationships between any ethnic group and its local sub-groups. The speaker proposed a careful and scientific study of this relationship which would be indispensable for the definition of the composition of ethnic groups in Vietnam.[31] Hoang Hoa Toan reiterated that the three criteria of language, culture, and ethnic/national consciousness are all important, but stressed the last. He wrote, "Taking national consciousness as the important criterion for defining the composition of an ethnic group is a scientific issue of great practical significance."[32] Lam Thanh Tong, after presenting some issues relating to the ethnic composition in Laos, agreed with these three criteria, but disagreed with those researchers who laid special stress on the criteria of ethnic consciousness. He argued that since the ethnic groups in our country are immersed in a capitalist system, each group is often subdivided into several smaller local groupings which develop their own characteristics. There is consequently a danger that local groups will be mistaken for distinct ethnic groups if careful studies are not undertaken.

In contrast, Hoang Thi Chau and Nguyen Linh considered the task of defining ethnic composition to be secondary, and associated it with the taking of censuses, which is also known as "defining the boundaries of ethnic groups." But such censuses, mainly done by administrative authorities in cooperation with relevant scientific agencies, frequently create more confusion. For example, local authorities have been known to name local sub-groups in ways which do not correspond to groupings defined on the basis of linguistic surveys. For these reasons, the role of ethnologists is crucial in defining ethnic groups, as is the role of linguists.

As Trieu Huu Ly pointed out at the workshop, the name a group uses to define itself expresses a sense of pride, unity, and ethnic consciousness. He also stressed that the origin and historical development of the ethnic group must be given consideration.[33] Finally, Trieu Huu Ly held that the criteria for defining ethnic composition should be linked to the historical characteristics of Vietnam. He proposed that in addition to the three criteria proposed above, another one should be added, specifically the origin, the formation and the development of the ethnic group.

Bui Khanh The, after pointing out the importance of the language as a key criterion in defining the composition of ethnic groups, proposed that when defining the names of ethnic groups to make a new list, it was necessary to conduct a linguistic analysis to determine whether the names reflect linguistic, historical and/or social characteristics of the group. He cited the debate over the various names of the "Muong," the "Tay Hat," and the "O Du" to make his point. Lam Xuan Dinh, on the other hand, proposed that ethnic language replace tribal language, as all the ethnic groups are equal.[34]

II. COMPOSITION OF ETHNIC GROUPS IN VIETNAM

MUCH has been written about ethnic groups in Vietnam, ranging from monographs to histories, field surveys, and maps. However, even into the middle of this century, no complete list of the ethnic groups in Vietnam had been constructed. The terminology used to classify ethnic groups and the tables listing the number and sizes of ethnic groups varied between authors. Researchers tended to use the tools and perspective of their own professional specialization to make generalizations about ethnic composition. For instance, geographers focused on residence patterns tend to favor the principles of migration in order to differentiate local groups. Linguists have been more concerned with linguistic relationships. In the late 1950s, a reasonably complete and detailed list of ethnic groups in Vietnam was published in the book *Ethnic Minorities in Vietnam*, by La Van Lo, Nguyen Huu Thau, Mai Van Tri, Ngoc Anh, and Mac Nhu Duong, from the ethnology research group of the Central Committee of Ethnic Minorities. A copy of the table as it appeared in this book is presented in Table 1.

According to these authors, then, Vietnam has sixty-four ethnic groups, with sixty-three of these belonging to three linguistic families: the Sino-Tibetan, Mon-Khmer, and Malayo-Polynesian. The Tay-Thai, Meo-Yao, and Lac-Viet are included in the Sino-Tibetan linguistic family. (Later linguists and ethnologists regrouped these within the Malayo-Polynesian linguistic family.) However, some confusion is evident. For instance, the Mang and some Xa groups were inappropriately included in the Tibeto-Burman linguistic family, and May and Ruc were included in the Mon-Khmer family. There were also problems with the definition of ethnic groups. Nevertheless, this

Table 1: List of Ethnic Minorities in Vietnam[35]

A. THE SINO-TIBETAN LINGUISTIC FAMILY

1. The Tibeto-Burman Group

No.	Ethnic group	Population	Distribution
1	U-Ni	4,969	- Lao Cai, Sin Ho, Muong Te (Thai-Meo autonomous region)
2	Co-Sung	1,511	- Muong Te (Thai-Meo autonomous region).
3	Kha Pe, Kha To	189	- Muong Te (Thai-Meo autonomous region)
4	Mang-U	641	- Muong Te (Thai-Meo autonomous region)
5	Xa including Xa Khao, Xa Cau, Xa Xip, Xa Pho, Xa Kha in Zone 4.* They are also called Tinh in Ba Thuoc region.**		- Scattered in the Thai-inhabited regions, mostly in Thuan Chau, Song Ma, Tuan Giao, Muong La, Mái Son, Muong Lay, Muong Te (Thai-Meo autonomous region); Tuong Duong (Nghe An)
6	Co Cho***	118	- Muong Te (Thai-Meo autonomous region)
7	Chi- La***	64	- Muong Te (Thai-Meo autonomous region.
8	Lo Lo	2,138	- Bao Lac (Cao Bang), Dong Van (Ha Giang)
9	Pu-Piao	359	- Dong Van (Ha Giang)

2. The Sino-Tay language group
   a. The Tay linguistic line

No.	Ethnic group	Population	Distribution
10	Thai–there are two main branches: Black Thai and White Thai. In Zone 4, they are also called Tay Deng, Tay Muoi, Tay Khang, Tay Pong, Tay Hat, Man Thanh, Hang Tong.	344,628	- Concentrated in the Thai-Meo autonomous region and the uplands of Thanh Hoa and Nghe An provinces.
11	Lao	3,448	- Song Ma, Phong Tho, Than Uyen (Thai-Meo autonomous region)
12	Lu	1,254	- Sin Ho, Phong Tho (Thai-Meo autonomous region)

*Zone 4 was the military code name for the north-central region of Vietnam, stretching from Thanh Hoa south to Quang Tri. The term is still commonly used and will appear throughout the remainder of this book.

**According to some ethnologists the Xa Khao (Zin Muong Te) and Xa Pho languages are based on Sino-Tibetan characters, while Xa Cau and Xa Khao (in Muong La) are of the Mon-Khmer language group.

***Further studies and defining are needed.

a. The Tay linguistic line (cont.)

No.	Ethnic group	Population	Distribution
13	Tay, often called Tho. In Hai Ninh region they are called Phen, but Tay is the most appropriate name.	437,019	- In all northern highlands and midlands from the left bank of the Red River to the Bac Bo (Tonkin) Gulf; the largest number live in Lang Son, Cao Bang, Bac Can, Tuyen Quang, Ha Giang, Thai Nguyen and Yen Bai provinces.
14	Nhang, also called Giay		- Mostly in Bat Xat, Muong Khuong, Bao Thang (Lao Cai); Dong Van (Ha Giang), Phong Tho (Thai-Meo autonomous region)
15	Nung, including the following branches: Nung Phan Sinh, Nung Chao, Nung Tung Xin or Xuong, Nung Loi, Nung Qui Rin, Nung An, Nung Ink, etc.	270,810	- Living among the Tay, but mostly concentrated in the Vietnam-China border provinces: Lang Son, Cao Bang Ha Giang, and in Bac Giang.
16	Cao Lan	27,209	- Mostly concentrated in Tuyen Quang
17	Pa Di (further defining)	533	- Muong Khuong (Lao Cai)
18	Tu Di (further defining)	663	- Muong Khuong, Bac Ha (Lao Cai)
19	Thu Lao	528	- Muong Khuong, Bac Ha (Lao Cai)
20	Chung Tra (further defining)	180	- Vi Xuyen (Ha Giang)
21	Phu La (further defining)	1,634	- Muong Khuong, Bat Xat, Bac Ha (Lao Cai), Hoang Su Phi (Ha Giang))

b. The Han (Chinese) linguistic line

No.	Ethnic group	Population	Distribution
22	Xa Phang, of Han origin-Yunnan	7,227	- Tua Chua, Xin Ho, Muong Te (Thai-Meo autonomous region) Lao Cai, Ha Giang
23	Quy Chau, of the Han of Quy Chau origin		- Bao Lac (Cao Bang), Phong Tho (Thai-Meo autonomous region)
24	San Chi	6,824	- Quang Yen, Hai Ninh
25	San Diu, also called Trai Hoa, of Han origin, also called		- Mostly in Thai Nguyen, Tuyen Quang, Hon Gai, Hai Ninh
26	Hac Ca, Ngai	80,538	- Mostly in Hai Ninh, some in Quang Yen, Hon Gai, Cao Bang, Lang Son

b. The Han (Chinese) linguistic line (cont.)

No.	Ethnic group	Population	Distribution
27	Meo: including following five main branches: White Meo, Flowery Meo, Red Meo, Black Meo, Sua Meo	182,474	- Mostly in Dong Van (Ha Giang) Lung Phin, Xi Ma Cai, Pha Long, Muong Khuong (Lao Cai); Tua Chua, Ta Sin Thang, Than Uyen, Tram Tau, Lang Nhi, Phu Yen, Dien Bien Phu (Thai-Meo autonomous region).
28	Man: also called Giao, including the following branches: Man Tien, Man Quan Chet, Man Son Dau (also called Man Lo Gang), Man Coc Ngang, Man Dai Ban, Man Lan Ten, Man Quan Trang	177,900	- Scattered in northern uplands and midlands provinces and uplands of Thanh Hoa province. Most live in Ha Giang, Tuyen Quang, Cao Bang, Lao Cai, Yen Bai and Son La (Thai-Meo autonomous region).
29	Co Lao (further defining)	549	- Vi Xuyen, Hoang Xu Phi (Ha Giang)
30	La Chi (further defining)	3,169	- Hoang Xu Phi (Ha Giang), some in Bac Ha (Lao Cai)

3. The Lac-Viet Group

No.	Ethnic group	Population	Distribution
31	Muong: in Mai Da also called Ao Ta, in Quang Binh called Nguon, Sach, in Quy Chau in Zone 4 called Tho	366,738	- Along the stretch of land from Yen Bai, through Phu Tho, Son La, Son Tay, Ha Dong, Hoa Binh, Ninh Binh to the uplands of Thanh Hoa. In Quang Binh, live the Nguon and the Sach who have the same origin as the Muong.
32	Dan Lai: also called Li Ha or Ha Do	632	- Con Cuong, Tuong Duong, (Nghe An)

B. THE MON-KHMER (KHO ME) LINGUISTIC FAMILY

1. The Xo Dang (Sedang)-Ma Puoc Group*

No.	Ethnic group	Population	Distribution
33	Puoc	3,658 •	- Van Chan, Yen Chau, Song Ma, Muong Te, Mai Son (Thai-Meo autonomous region)
34	May	904	- Quang Ninh and Tuyen Hoa (Quang Binh)

* The names of these ethnic minorities are used for the whole group as they have the most commonly used language in each region. The Xa Cau and Xa Khao Muong La in the Thai-Meo aotonomous region also belong to this group. (See the Xa in the Han (Chinese) Tibeto-Burman linguistic at the beginning of this table.)

1. The Xo Dang (Sedang)-Ma Puoc Group (cont.)*

No.	Ethnic group	Population	Distribution
35	B'ru	855	- Quang Ninh, Bo Trach (Quang Binh)
36	Khua	892	- Tuyen Hoa (Quang Binh)
37	Ruc	189	- Tuyen Hoa (Quang Binh)
38	Van Kieu	23,000	- Western Quang Tri and Quang Binh provinces
39	Toi Oi	6,000	- Upland of Quang Tri
40	Kha Tu	20,000	- Ben Hien, Ben Giang (Quang Nam)
41	Stieng	20,000	- Gi Rinh and Tay Ninh
42	Gie	18,000	- Northern Dac Glay (Kon Tum) to Ben Giang (Quang Nam)
43	Ve	12,000	- Ben Giang (Quang Nam)
44	Cham (during the war of resistance they were often called "Cham Re" to distinguish them from the Cham or Chiem Thanh in Ninh Binh Thuan. "Re" is the name of a tributary of Tra Khuc River).	90,000	- Son Ha, Minh Long, Ba To (Quang Ngai), An Lao (Binh Dinh)
45	Xo Dang (Sedang): including the following branches: To Dra (thin forest), Kmrang (old forests), Duon, Hre, Cor (also called Ta Cor), Ha Lang, Ka Dong	80,000	- Scattered throughout the mountainous region of Kon Tum, Western Quang Nam and Quang Ngai provinces
46	Ba Na: including the following branches: Ba Na Con Tum, Golar, Do Lang, Bo Nam, Ala Cong, To Lo	99,000	- Around Kon Tum provincial capital, eastern and southern Kon Tum high plateaus stretching to southwestern Binh Dinh province
47	Mnong: including the following having branches: Kil, Gar, Rlam, Dip, Bu Dang, Di Pri, Bunor, Preh, Nong	40,000	- On Lang Biang high plateaus, southwestern Dac Lac high plateaus
48	Lat	-	- Eastern and northern parts Sre group (Gi Rinh)
49	To Lop: also called Nop		
50	Co Don	10,000	
51	To La	-	
52	La Gia	-	
53	Ro Ngao	6,000	- In north-western Kon Tum provincial town

* The names of these ethnic minorities are used for the whole group as they have the most commonly used language in each region. The Xa Cau and Xa Khao Muong La in the Thai-Meo aotonomous region also belong to this group. (See the Xa in the Han (Chinese) Tibeto-Burman linguistic at the beginning of this table.)

2. The Khmer Group

No.	Ethnic group	Population	Distribution
56	Khmer (Southern)	450,000	- In western and southeastern Nam Bo. Mostly in Soc Tang, Tra Vinh, Rach Gia, Bac Lieu, Vinh Long, Chau Doc and Ha Tien province.

C. MALAYO-POLYNESIAN LINGUISTIC FAMILY
1. The E De, Gio Rai-Raglai Group*

No.	Ethnic group	Population	Distribution
57	Gio Rai: including the following branches: Hdung, Hbau, Arap, To-Buan	160,000	- In Playku high plateau
58	E De: including the following branches: Kpa, Adham, Ktul, Dlie, Rue, Blo, Mdhua	120,000	- In Dac Lac High plateau
59	Bih		- In south-western Buon Ma Thuot
60	Chu Ru	40,000	- Tay Ninh province
61	Raglai		- From Khanh Hoa to northern Binh Thuan provinces
62	La Oang: also called Noang		- In north-western Binh Thuan

2. Cham Group

No.	Ethnic group	Population	Distribution
63	Cham: including Chiem Thanh, also called Cham Pa. In the areas near Phan Ri provincial town, there is a group of Cham mixed with Kinh and called Kinh Cuu	45,000	- In the plain of Phan Rang, Tuy Phong, Phan Ri, Phan Thiet in Ninh Thuan and Binh Thuan provinces
	TOTAL	3,298,546	

* The names of these ethnic minorities are used for the whole group as these ethnic groups have the most commonly used language in each region.

was a magnificent pioneering work of systematization and its results provided the scientific bases for the census of 1 March 1960, covering northern Vietnam.

In the 1960s and early 1970s, some projects on ethnic groups in Vietnam were published by authors such as Vuong Hoang Tuyen, Mac Duong, La Van Lo, Dang Nghiem Van, Cuu Long Giang Toan Anh, Be Viet Dang, Bui Van Kin, Dang Nghiem Van, Ha Van Vien-Ha Van Phung.[36] However, most of their works focused on one specific ethnic group or a few ethnic groups in a particular region. By 1973 scientists had not yet produced a comprehensive list of ethnic groups in Vietnam (see Table 2).

Comparing the two lists from Tables 1 and 2 we can see that although the ethnic groups are classified as falling into three linguistic families, in Table 2 some the Mon-Khmer languages are placed in the

Table 2. List of Ethnic Groups in Vietnam, listed according to language[37]

I. THE AUSTRO-ASIATIC LANGUAGE FAMILY	23. Xre	II. THE SINO-TIBETAN LINGUISTIC FAMILY
	25. Stieng	
1. The Viet-Muong Group		*1. The Tibeto-Burman Group*
1. Viet		
2. Muong	*3. The Tay-Thai (Tai) Group*	45. Ha Nhi
3. Tho		46. La Hu
4. Chut	28. Lao	47. Phu La
		48. Lo Lo
2. The Mon-Khmer Group	30. Tay	49. Cong
5. Khang		50. Si La
6. Kho Mu	32. Cao Lan-San Chi	
7. O Du		*2. The Chinese (Han) Group*
8. Xinh Mun	34. Phu La	
9. Mang		51. Hoa
10. Bru	36. Thuy	52. San Diu
11. Pa Co (Ta Oi)		53. Tu Di
12. Ca Tu	*4. The Meo-Yao Group*	
13. Gie		III. THE MALAYO-POLYNESIAN LINGUISTIC FAMILY
14. Ve	38. Yao	
15. Treng		
16. Xo Dang	40. Tong	54. Gia Rai
17. Ha Lang		55. E De
18. Co	*5. Other linguistic groups*	56. Cham Hroi
19. Hre (Cham Re)		57. Raglai
20. Ba Na	42. Co Lao	58. Chu Ru
21. Mo Nong		59. Cham
22. Ma	44. La Ha	

14

Malayo-Polynesian family. In the Austo-Asiatic language family, apart from the Mon-Khmer group, there are also the Viet-Muong, the Tay-Thai, the Meo-Yao and other linguistic groups (the Ka Dai group). In Table 2, there are only fifty-nine groups, while in Table 1 there are sixty-four (including the Kinh, i.e., the ethnic Vietnamese).

The names of ethnic groups included in Table 1 that do not appear in Table 2 are: Xa, Co Cho, Pa Di, Thu Lao, Xa Phang, Dan Lai-Ly Ha, May, Khua, Ruc, Van Kieu, Lat, To Lop, Co Don, To La, La Gia, Ro Ngao, Bih, La Oang, Cao Lan and San Chi.[38]

The names of some ethnic groups which have newly appeared in Table 2 include: Tho, Chut, Khang, Kho Mu, O Du, Ha Lang, Co, Thuy, Pa Then, Tong, La Ha, Kong, Cham Hroi, Cao Lan-San Chi, Co Ho.

Ethnic groups which have been listed in both tables, but under changed names include: U Ni → Ha Nhi, Co Sung → La Hu, Kha Pe → Si La, Mang U → Mang, Chi La → Si La, Lu → Lu , Nhang → Giay, Chung Tra → Bo Y, Qui Chau → Pu Na, Kha Tu → Ca Tu, Cham → Hre, Man → Yao, Puoc → Xinh Mun.

The listing in Table 2, as noted, is the result of ethnological research and of the symposia held in 1973. This material provided the basis of the two censuses. The first was begun on 1 April 1974 in the north, while the second was initiated on 5 February 1976, in the south (see annexes 2 and 3). So, some changes may be noted in the list between the census from north Vietnam in 1960 and that in 1974. Apart from this, some of the small groups have been combined into larger groups: Hoa + Xa Phang = Hoa; May + Sach + Ruc + Arem + Mang Lieng = Chut; Khua + Tri + Ma Cong = Bru; Tay Pong + Dan Lai-Ly Ha + Keo + Mon + Cuoi + Ho = Tho.

To prepare the 1979 general census for the entire country, the Vietnam Committee for Social Sciences, together with the Committee for Ethnic Groups of the Party Central Committee, submitted a joint report on research results to the Prime Minister. This was in accordance with Directive No. 83/CD of the Council of Ministers on the coordination of research for the definition of ethnic composition of ethnic groups in Vietnam.

On 2 March 1979, the General Statistics Office, with the authorization of the Government, made Decision No. 121–TCTK/ PPCD. This provided an official list of ethnic groups in Vietnam which could be used as the basis for the general census, and included statistical information from the central and local levels of government (see Table 3).

Table 3. List of Ethnic Groups in Vietnam[39]

No.	Ethnic groups	Other names	Distribution
1	Kinh (Viet)	- Kinh	- In the whole country
2	Tay	- Tho, Ngan, Phen, Thu Lao, Pa Di	- Cao Bang, Lang Son, Ha Tuyen, Bac Thai, Hoang Lien Son, Quang Ninh
3	Thai	- Tay, Tay Khao (White Thai) Tay Dam (Black Thai) Tay Muoi, Tay Thanh (Man Thanh) Hang Tong (Tay Muong) Pu Thay, Tho Da Bac	- Son La, Nghe Tinh, Thanh Hoa, Lai Chau, Hoang Lien Son, Ha Son Binh, Lam Dong provinces
4	Hoa (Han)	- Trieu Chau, Phuc Kien, Kwangtung, Hai Nan, Ha, Xa Phang	- Ho Chi Minh City, Hanoi, Hau Giang, Hai Phong, Cuu Long
5	Khmer	- Cur, Cul, Cu, Tho, Viet of Mien origin, Khmer Krom	- Hau Giang, Cuu Long, Kien Giang, Minh Hai, Ho Chi Minh City, Song Be, Tay Ninh provinces
6	Muong	- Mol, Mual, Moi,* Moi Bi, Ao Ta (Au Ta)	- Ha Son Binh, Thanh Hoa, Vinh Phu, Hoang Lien Son, Son La, Ha Nam Ninh
7	Nung	- Xuong, Giang, Nung An, Phan Sinh, Nung Chao, Nung Loi, Qui Rin, Khen Lai	- Cao Bang, Lang Son, Ha Tuyen, Bac Thai, Hoang Lien Son, Quang Ninh, Ho Chi Minh City, Lam Dong
8	Hmong	- Meo, Flowery Meo, Green Meo, Red Meo, Black Meo, Na Meo, White Man	- Ha Tuyen, Hoang Lien Son, Lai Chau, Son La, Cao Bang, Lang Son, Nghe Tinh
9	Yao (Dao)	- Man, Dong, Trai, Xa, Diu Mien, Kiem Mien, White Quan, Red Yao, Quan Chet, Lo Gang, Yao Tien, Thanh Y, Lan Ten, Dai Ban, Tieu Ban, Coc Ngang, Coc Mun, Son Dau, etc.	- Ha Tuyen, Hoang Lien Son, Cao Bang, Lang Son, Bac Thai, Lai Chau, Son La, Ha Son Binh, Vinh Phu, Ha Bac, Thanh Hoa, Quang Ninh
10	Gia Rai	- Gio Rai, To Buan, Ho Bau, Hdrung, Chor	- Gia Lai-Kon Tum
11	Ngai	- Xin, Le, Dan, Khach Gia	- Quang Ninh, Cao Bang, Lang Son
12	E De	- Ra de, De, Kpa, Adham, Krung, Ktul, Dlie, Rue, Blo, Epan, Mdhur,** Bih	- Dac Lac, Phu Khanh
13	Ba Na	- Golar, To Lo, Gio Lang, Y Lang, Ro Ngao, Krem Rol, Con Kde, Ala Cong, Kpang Kong, Bo Nam	- Gia Lai-Kon Tum, Nghia Binh, Phu Khanh

* The name the Thai call the Muong.
** Mdhur is a middle group between Ede and Gia Rai, the group in Cheo Reo self-registered as Gia Rai.

No.	Ethnic groups	Other names	Distribution
14	Xo Dang	- Xteng, Hdang, Todra, Mo Nam, Ha Lang, Ca Dong, Kmrang, Con Lan, Brila, Tang	- Gia Lai-Kon Tum, Quang Nam-Da Nang
15	San Chay (Cao Lan-San Chi)	- Cao Lan, Man Cao Lan, Hon Ban, San Chi (also called Son Tu and never includes the San Chi group in Bao Lac and Cho Ra)	- Bac Thai, Quang Ninh, Ha Bac, Cao Bang, Lang Son, Ha Tuyen
16	Co Ho	- Xre, Nop (Tu Lop) Co Don, Chil,* Lat (Lach) T'rinh	- Lam Dong, Thuan Hai
17	Cham (Cham)	- Chiem Thanh, Hroi	- Thuan Hai, An Giang, Ho Chi Minh City, Nghia Binh, Phu Khanh
18	San Diu	- San Deo, Trai, Trai Dat, Man Quan Coc	- Bac Thai, Vinh Phu, Ha Bac, Quang Ninh, Ha Tuyen
19	Hre	- Cham Re, Chom, Kre, Luy	- Nghia Binh
20	Mnong	- Pnong, Nong, Pre, Bu Dang, Di Pri, Biat, Gar, Ro Lam, Chil	- Dac Lac, Lam Dong, Song Be
21	Raglai	- Raclay, Rai, Noang, La Oang	- Thuan Hai, Phu Khanh
22	Stieng	- Xa Dieng	- Song Be, Tay Ninh
23	Bru-Van Kieu	- Bru, Van Kieu, Mang Cong, Tri, Khua	- Binh Tri Thien
24	Tho**	- Keo, Mon, Cuoi, Ho, Dan Lai, Ly Ha, Tay Pong, Con Kha, Xa La Vang***	- Nghe Tinh, (Nhu Xuan) Thanh Hoa
25	Giay	- Nhang, Dang, Pau Thin, Pu Na, Cui Chu****	- Hoang Lien Son, Ha Tuyen, Lai Chau
26	Co Tu	- Ka Tu, Cao, Ha, Phuong, Ca Tang*****	- Quang Nam-Da Nang, Binh Tri Thien
27	Gie-Trieng	- Dgie, Tareh, Giang Ray, Pin, Trieng, Treng, Ta Rieng, Ve, La Ve, Ca Tang	- Quang Nam-Da Nang, Gia Lai-Kon Tum
28	Ma	- Chau Ma, Ma Ngan, Ma Xop, Ma To, Ma Krung	- Lam Dong, Dong Nai

* Chil is a local group of Mnong, a group in the south living mixed with the Co Ho which calls itself the Co Ho.

** Tho here is different from the Tho also called the Tay in Viet Bac, the Thai in Da Bac and the Khmer in the Mekong River Delta.

*** Xa La Vang: the name of many ethnic groups leading nomadic life along the border.

**** Cui Chu (Qui Chau) has a branch living in Bao Lac (Cao Bang province) mixed with the Nung and listed as the Nung.

***** Ca Tang: the common name of many ethnic groups in the mountainous region of Quang Nam-Da Nang province close to Laos. It is necessary to differentiate this common name from the separate name of each ethnic group.

No.	Ethnic groups	Other names	Distribution
29	Kho Mu	- Xa Cau, Mun Xen, Pu Thenh, Tenh, Tay Hay	- Nghe Tinh, Son La, Lai Chau, Hoang Lien Son
30	Co	- Cor, Col, Cua, Trau	- Nghia Binh, Quang Nam-Da Nang
31	Ta Oi	- Ta Oi, Pa Co, Pa Hi (Ba Hi)	- Binh Tri Thien
32	Cho Ro	- Do Ro, Chau Ro	- Dong Nai
33	Khang	- Xa Khao, Xa Sua, Xa Don, Xa Dang, Xa Hoc, Xa Ai, Xa Bung, Quang Lam	- Lai Chau, Son La
34	Xinh Mun	- Puoc, Pua	- Son La, Lai Chau
35	Ha Nhi	- U Ni, Xa U Ni	- Lai Chau, Hoang Lien Son
36	Chu Ru	- Cho Ru, Chu	- Lam Dong, Thuan Hai
37	Lao	- Lao Boc, Lao Noi	- Lai Chau, Son La, Thanh Hoa, Hoang Lien Son
38	La Chi	- Cu Te, La Qua	- Ha Tuyen
39	La Ha	- Xa Khao, Khla, Phlao	- Lai Chau, Son La
40	Phu La	- Bo Kho Pa, Mun Di Pa, Xa Pho, Pho, Va So Lao, Pu Dang	- Hoang Lien Son, Lai Chau
41	La Hu	- Khu Xung, Co Sung, Kha Qui	- Lai Chau
42	Lu	- Lu, Nhuon, Duon	- Lai Chau
43	Lo Lo	- Mun Di	- Cao Bang, Lai Chau, Ha Tuyen
44	Chut	- Sach, May, Ruc, Ma Lieng, Arem, Tu Vang, Pa Long, Xo Lang, To Hung, Cha Kui, Tac Cui Umo, Xa La Vang	- Binh Tri Thien
45	Mang	- Mang U, Xa La Vang	- Lai Chau
46	Pa Then	- Pa Hung, Tong	- Ha Tuyen
47	Co Lao		- Ha Tuyen
48	Cong	- Xam Khong, Mong Nhe, Xa Xeng	- Lai Chau
49	Bo Y	- Chung Cha, Trong Gia, Tu Di, Tu Din	- Hoang Lien Son, Ha Tuyen
50	Si La	- Cu De Xu, Kha Pe	- Lai Chau
51	Pu Peo	- Ka Peo, Pen Ti Lo Lo	- Ha Tuyen
52	Brau	- Brao	- Gia Lai-Kon Tum
53	O Du	- Tay Hat	- Nghe Tinh
54	Ro Mam		- Gia Lai-Kon Tum

According to the 1979 listing, Vietnam has 54 ethnic groups. This means that some changes have occurred since the listing of 1974 (Table 2), and they can be generalized as follows:

1. The merger of two "ethnic groups" into one:
   - Gie + Trieng = Gie-Trieng
   - Tu Di + Bo Y = Bo Y
   - Cham + Cham Hroi = Cham
   - Xo Dang + Ha Lang = Xo Dang
   - Xre + Co Ho = Co Ho
   - Pu Na + Giay = Giay
   - Thuy + Pa Then = Pa Then
   - Tong + Yao = Yao

2. The designation of new ethnic groups:
   - Ngai (dividing Hoa into two ethnic groups Hoa and Ngai)
   - Cho Ro
   - Brau
   - Ro Mam

3. The correction of incorrectly named or designated ethnic groups:
   - Pa Co = Ta Oi
   - Ca Tu = Co Tu
   - Cao Lan-San Chi = San Chay
   - Meo = Hmong

Research developments up until 1979 had, then, made some progress, but this was just the beginning. This is partly due to the fact that the ethnic composition of Vietnam, as of the world in general, is not static. It is not easy to establish whether a group constitutes a distinct ethnic community or is part of a larger ethnic community, or whether it is simply a sub-group distinguished by dint of territorial affiliation. There are also many factors which stimulate changes such as boundary demarcation, assimilation, or splitting of ethnic groups at different periods of time. Sometimes scientific grounds for distinguishing ethnic communities are lacking. Some researchers have tried to selectively interpret the material, while the political and/ or economic interests of those under study have certainly influenced research outcomes in other instances.

While twenty years ago, people in Vietnam often talked about merging ethnic groups or creating closer relationships between ethnic groups, the tendency has moved in the opposite direction today. Now, many local sub-groups within an ethnic group wish to split off and form their own "tribe" or group. For example, the Nguon, a sub-group of the Kinh (ethnic Vietnamese), the Dan Lai-Ly Ha, Tay Pong groups of the Tho ethnic group, the May, Ruc and Sach of the Chut ethnic group, the Thu Lao and Pa Di of the Tay ethnic group, the Cao Lan and San Chi of the San Chay ethnic group, the Hroi of the Cham ethnic group and the Van Kieu of the Bru ethnic group have all advocated taking this direction. Let us look at each of these cases in turn.

- The Nguon group in Quang Binh province, as noted in the list of ethnic groups by La Van Lo et al. (Table 1), is classified as a local sub-group of the Muong ethnic group. During a field trip made by a group of ethnologists in August 1973, a study was made of family annals of some of the clans. From this it was established that the Nguon were originally a branch of the Kinh people from Thanh Hoa and Nghe An provinces. They moved down to Quang Binh in the fourteenth and fifteenth centuries as part of the process of southward expansion and development of the country.[40] Throughout the exchanges and discussions brought about by the field trip, the people and local authorities acknowledged themselves as Kinh. However, at present, as part of a process of socio-economic and ethnic development, both the local people and the authorities want to split the Nguon into a separate ethnic group.

- In 1973, the Tho group was simply defined as an ethnic group (see Table 2). But in fact, the Tho group is made up of the following sub-groups: Keo, Mon, the Cuoi groups in Nghia Dan, Tan Ky, Quy Hop districts, the Dan Lai-Ly Ha in Con Cuong district and the Tay Pong in Tuong Duong district in Nghe An province. The Dan Lai-Ly Ha group now comprises more than five hundred people in the Chau Khe municipality of Con Cuong district, and the Tay Pong group comprises more than three hundred people living in the Tam Hop municipality, Tuong Duong district. These groups want to separate into their own respective groups. At the same time, some of those living in Thanh Hoa and Nghe An provinces, who previously considered themselves to be Kinh, Tay or Muong, have recently registered themselves as Tho. For example, in the 1979 population census, no Tho were registered for the Nghia Dan district (Nghe An province), whereas in 1989 the registered population of Tho was 17,399.

- The Chut ethnic group was formed through the amalgamation of several groups, including May, Ruc, Sach, Arem and Ma Lieng. Two of these, the May and Ruc, were previously considered independent ethnic groups (see Table 1). In discussions with a team of ethnologists in August 1973 and at a subsequent conference held in Quang Binh province on the composition of ethnic groups (October 1973), representatives of these groups acknowledged themselves to be from the Chut ethnic group. On the basis of linguistic and cultural data, scientists agreed that the Chut were an ethnic group belonging to the Viet-Muong Linguistic group.[41]

- The Bru ethnic group is found in the western upland regions of three provinces (Quang Binh, Quang Tri and Thua Thien-Hue) and live in several sub-groups. These include the Khua, Tri, Ma Cong, and Van Kieu. These groups share a single, common origin. Over time they moved to new regions to earn a living, and were forced to settle in different rural communes. This historical process gave rise to the distinct sub-groups named above. Nevertheless, they shared many common linguistic features (both in syntax and phonetics) and cultural characteristics. Moreover, they refer to themselves as Bru. Interestingly, the term Bru is also used to describe the ethnic groups belonging to the Mon-Khmer linguistic group in the northern Truong Son Range. In 1973, these groups were listed as a single Bru or Bru-Van Kieu group, although the Van Kieu have long wished to be called the Van Kieu ethnic group.

Concerning this ethnic group, there is also a sub-group of Ba Hi now living in the western part of Quang Tri and Thua Thien-Hue with a population of less than four hundred. The census for the southern provinces carried out in 1976 revealed that some twenty people living in Huong Hoa district, Quang Tri province, registered themselves as Van Kieu, while those living in A Luoi, Thua Thien-Hue, registered themselves as Ta Oi. Some expressed the desire for Ba Hi to be recognized as a group in its own right. So in the list of ethnic groups of Vietnam compiled in 1979, the Ba Hi were listed as part of the Ta Oi ethnic group. Later, some proposed that they should be listed as part of the Bru-Van Kieu group.[42]

- The Ta Oi live close to the Bru in the south. The Ta Oi consist of several local groups, such as the Pa Co, Ba Hi, and Ta Uot (also known as Ca Tua or Can Tua). This group used to be called the Pa Co, which is closely linked to the name of some heroic fighters during the war of resistance against the United States. However, this name does not cover the other two sub-groups in this ethnic group. The question is complicated further by a second consideration, that some people still wish to categorize the Ca Tua (or Can Tua) as belonging to the Co Tu ethnic group, who are still living close to the Ta Oi ethnic group in southern Vietnam.

- The Gie-Trieng ethnic group is made up of three groups (see Tables 1 and 2). These are the Gie, the Trieng, and the Ve. These sub-groups can all understand and speak each other's languages and they share many cultural features. In 1978, a symposium was held in Pleiku, Gia Lai-Kon Tum province (now Gia Lai and Kon Tum provinces). This was organized by the Gia Lai-Kontum People's Committee in co-operation with the Vietnam Committee for Social Sciences and the Central Committee for Ethnic Groups.[43] The conference came to the conclusion that the Gie, the Trieng and the Ve groups are, in fact, one ethnic group with the name of Gie-Trieng.

- The conference participants also concluded that the Xo Dang (Sedang) ethnic group is composed of the Ha Lang, Ca Dong, and Ro Ngao. Shortly after the proceedings, differences in opinion over both conclusions re-emerged.

- The Co Ho ethnic group primarily lives in the central highlands province of Lam Dong, and it consists of six sub-groups with various levels of social and economic development.[44] The largest group is the Xre, who are chiefly involved in wet-rice cultivation. These people live in most of the districts of Lam Dong province. After the Xre come the Co Ho, the Nop, the Co Don, the Chin and the Lat. The lists of ethnic groups (see Tables 1 and 2) show that the Co Ho and the Xre were previously considered to be distinct ethnic groups. Meanwhile, the people of the Chin and Lat groups as well as the local authorities of Lam Dong province wish to seek a review of the question of their separation from the Co Ho community, into two distinct ethnic groups.

- The Ta Mun group live in the southern province of Song Be. Earlier listings grouped the Ta Mun as part of the Stieng, and indeed Ta Mun is an alternative name for Stieng and does not refer to a local group.[45] In 1987, M. B. Kruikov from the Soviet Moscow Institute of Ethnology (now in the Russian Federation) and Tran Tat Chung from the Institute of Ethnology (Hanoi) carried out a field survey in Lam Dong and Song Be provinces. On the basis of their comparative study of the kinship systems of some of the groups, they concluded that the Ta Mun group (of five hundred people) in Binh Long district, Song Be province, was not a part of the Stieng group, but belonged instead to the Cho Ro ethnic group, which has been influenced by Khmer culture. However, the authors have yet to publish their opinions regarding whether or not Ta Mun constitute an ethnic group.[46]

- The Tay ethnic community currently comprises several sub-groups, including the Pa Di, the Thu Lao, and the Tho (in Da Bac district, Hoa Binh province). According to Ngo Duc Thinh, the Pa Di group were named by the Han (Chinese) and might be derived from the name Bach Di or Bach Y. The group is of Thai origin, but appears to be merging with the Nung Din or Tay. Therefore, the ethnic identity of the group needs to be decided by the Pa Di themselves.[47]

In a later article, Ngo Duc Thinh concluded that the Pa Di are in fact a local Tay group.[48] According to Ngo Duc Thinh and Chu Thai Son, the Thu Lao group is now in the process of assimilating into surrounding groups. Yet this group continues to maintain its identity in terms of history, linguistics, and culture, and its members have a strong awareness of being a Thu Lao group. These factors help us distinguish them from the Tay.[49] According to Be Viet Dang, the language used by the Thu Lao, although it shares some features with the Tay-Thai languages, also possesses some special characteristics which are closer to the Nung Din. The Thu Lao have very close ties with the Nung Din sub-group (of the Nung ethnic group) in several areas, but in terms of ethnic relationships they consider the Tay in Bac Ha (Lao Cai province) to be their kin.[50]

In the 1972 publication *Contributions to Research on Hoa Binh Province*, the Tho group of Da Bac district, Hoa Binh province, was listed as a distinct ethnic group.[51] According to Chu Thai Son and Nguyen Chi Huyen, the Tho in Hoa Binh acknowledged themselves as *Phua Tay* (Thai ethnic group) or as *Con Tay Don* (the White Thai). After analyzing their ethnic characteristics and comparing these with the criteria for definition of ethnic groups in Vietnam, the authors concluded that, "We can easily recognize the Thai ethnicity of the Tho inhabitants of Da Bac district (Hoa Binh) using any criteria."[52] However, in recent population censuses, the Tho people registered themselves as Tay.

- The San Chay ethnic group comprises the Cao Lan and San Chi groups. Many articles have been published in Vietnam and overseas about these two groups. Most of the French authors consider the Cao Lan as belonging to the Yao ethnic group. Other authors have listed them in the Tay-Thai group, and a few authors have listed the Cao Lan as part of the Han (Chinese) linguistic group. However, most authors from France, Vietnam, and from the former Soviet Union, hold that these two groups share a great deal and may therefore be considered a single ethnic group.[53]

Nguyen Nam Tien conducted a number of studies on these two groups in the provinces of Quang Ninh, Lang Son, Ha Bac, Thai Nguyen, and Tuyen Quang. He found similarities in traditional ceremonies concerned with sowing and harvesting rice, the arrangement of villages, interior decoration of homes, womens' clothing, and life-cycle customs concerning birth, marriage, and death. The author concluded that in every cultural respect, in historical terms, and in regard to their ethnic self-awareness, these two groups were one and the same. Only their respective languages remained as a sort of barrier between them. Interestingly, both groups used the same language for worship and prayer, especially during the ritual for taking the soul of the dead back to its native land. For this reason, the author defined the Cao Lan and the San Chi as a single ethnic group named Cao Lan-San Chi ethnic group.[54] Nevertheless, the composition of these two groups of people still remains an open question which deserves further research and discussion.

- The Bo Y ethnic group was created by merging the Tu Di and Bo Y (see Tables 1 and 2). The Tu Di speak Han (Chinese). In the first half of the eighteenth century, they separated from the Bo Y group in Do Van district, Guizhou province, China, and moved south to live in Muong Khuong, Lao Cai province. Another, larger section of the group also migrated south and settled in Quan Ba, Ha Giang province. Because of the later migration of the larger group, it still retains its original language and name, the Bo Y, which belongs to the Tay-Thai linguistic group. According to Chu Thai Son, although this group is scattered throughout various administrative regions of the country, it should keep the single official name of Bo Y.[55]

- The Cham ethnic group was also formed by a merger of the Cham Hroi from southern Binh Dinh and those from the northern part of Phu Yen. The Cham have a long history in both Vietnam and elsewhere in Southeast Asia. The Cham Hoi itself was formed by a process of natural integration between the Ba Na (in Van Canh, Binh Dinh province and Dong Xuan, Phu Yen province), the E De (in Son Hoa, the Hinh River in Phu Yen) and those of the Cham who remained after most of them had migrated south in earlier centuries. It is clear here that this was the result of a complex and diverse multi-lingual and multi-cultural process. In the Van Canh and Dong Xuan regions, people use both the Cham and Ba Na languages in their daily communication, and sometimes they even mix them.[56] One of the groups is characterized by a matrilineal structure, while the other is patrilineal. Consequently, members of one and the same family may register themselves as members of different ethnic groups, and it is even possible for the same person to consider him/herself, in some circumstances, to belong to the Cham, while in others as belonging to

24

the Ba Na. In spite of these difficulties it is still appropriate to list the two groups as a single ethnic group named Cham.

In the pages above, we have discussed some of those ethnic groups which have given rise to controversy, in terms of both theory and practice. We believe that there will be further cases in the future which give rise to similar problems and which will require careful consideration. This is extremely important, and close co-operation between researchers and administrators at all levels is therefore required in order to settle each controversy rationally (on a case-by-case basis), and to respect local peoples' ethnic consciousness.

CHAPTER II

THE DISTRIBUTION OF POPULATION AND ETHNIC GROUPS

I. THE DISTRIBUTION OF POPULATION

ACCORDING to the 1990 statistical yearbook, Vietnam had a population of 66,233,300, with an average density of 200 persons per square kilometer. Vietnam's population, like that of many other countries, is unevenly spread between the mountains and the plains. Uneven distribution of inhabitants may also be found between the north and the south, the deltas and inland plains, the urban and rural areas, the lowlands and uplands. More than three quarters of the population live on the lowland plains, which make up less than one quarter of the country's land area. By contrast, the mountainous regions and high plateaus, which cover three quarters of the country's total land area, contain only one quarter of the population (see Table 4).

Similarly, the Red River Delta covers an area of only 12,466.1 sq km, but has a population of 13,024,900, with an average density of 1,045 persons per sq km. On the other hand, the eleven mountainous northern provinces cover an area of 93,500 sq km, but have a population of only 7,057,200, with an average density of 75.5 persons per sq km. The four Central Highlands provinces have an area of 55,568.9 sq km, but their population is only 2,596,700, with an average density of 47 persons per sq km. These disparities become more startling when population densities are measured by province. Thai Binh province, for instance, has a population density of 1,098 persons per sq. km, Lai Chau province has 26 persons per sq km, while Kon Tum province has only 22 persons per sq km. The mountainous province of Bac Thai (now Thai Nguyen and Bac Kan) has an average population density of 163 persons per sq. km and Lam Dong province has 66 persons per sq km.[1]

Table 4: Population and population density for selected provinces

No.	Provinces	1921*		1979**		1990***	
		Population (persons)	Density	Population (persons)	Density	Population (persons)	Density
1	Ha Giang	70,743	7	367,240	63	475,600	82
2	Cao Bang	132,232	27	477,400	56	581,200	69
3	Lang Son	134,815	22	482,100	59	624,300	76
4	Son La	35,209	8	485,300	33	703,300	49
5	Thai Binh	855,825	548	1,489,300	1,002	1,673,500	1,098
6	Thanh Hoa	1,243,800	224	2,519,800	226	3,081,100	276
7	Quang Nam	675,400	203	1,521,900	127	1,793,400	149
8	Tay Ninh	92,686	20	679,900	169	811,100	201
9	Ben Tre	270,879	176	1,034,100	464	1,241,600	552

* Yves Henry. 1928. *Document Demographique*, pp. 9–12.
** According to *Statistical Year Book 1980*. Hanoi, 1981. pp. 391–392.
*** According to *Statistical Year Book 1990*. Statistical Publishing House, Hanoi, 1992. p. 5–6.

Although these differences seem marked, they are less so than they were a few decades ago. For example, the three provinces of Thai Binh, Lang Son, and Cao Bang differed greatly in 1960. At that time, Thai Binh had a population density 23.4 times higher than that of Lang Son and 30.9 times higher than that of Cao Bang. In 1990 the figures were 14.4 times and 15.9 times, respectively.[2]

II. THE DISTRIBUTION OF ETHNIC GROUPS

OF the fifty-four ethnic groups, only four—the Kinh, the Hoa, the Khmer, and the Cham—live predominantly on the plains, the coastal regions and in the midlands. These ethnic groups practice wet rice cultivation (except for some Hoa people). The remaining fifty ethnic groups live predominantly in the mountainous regions, many of them practicing shifting cultivation (also known as slash and burn or swidden farming).

In the northern mountainous region, the Red River may be considered to mark the border between the Tay and the Nung ethnic groups on the one side, and between the Thai and those groups speaking Mon-Khmer languages on the other. Thirty-one of the fifty-four ethnic groups live in this region, and they belong to seven or eight language groups, from two or three linguistic families. Along the Vietnam-China border live the Tibeto-Burman groups, and the Mon-Khmer people live along the Vietnam-Lao border.

At present, ethnic groups commonly live in close proximity to one another, and this will be explained in greater detail in the next section. However, a study of residential patterns allows us to differentiate between the residential areas of the Tay, who often settle in lowland valleys and in the foothills, from the Nung, San Chay, and San Diu. These latter ethnic groups migrated to Vietnam relatively late. As a result, they tended to settle in hilly or mountainous regions, which are less fertile than the lowlands. The Yao similarly live in the midland areas, while the Hmong have settled in the highlands.

The most notable feature of the ethnic groups living in the northern highland areas is that they are so widely distributed. Each ethnic group is represented in several communes and districts. Of the 109 districts in the eleven northern mountain provinces, fifty-nine (54% of the districts and provincial towns) have inhabitants from more than ten ethnic groups (see Table 5).

Table 5: The number of districts and ethnic groups living there (1989)

No.	Provinces	Number of Districts	Districts having less than 10 ethnic groups	10 ethnic groups	11 ethnic groups	12 ethnic groups	13 ethnic groups	14 ethnic groups	15 ethnic groups
(1)	(2)	(3)	(4)	(5)	(6)	(7)	(8)	(9)	(10)
1	Ha Giang	10	1	2	1	4	1	0	1
2	Tuyen Quang	6	0	1	1	1	1	1	1
3	Cao Bang	13	11	2	0	0	0	0	0
4	Lang Son	11	6	3	0	1	0	0	1
5	Son La	10	3	1	3	1	1	1	0
6	Lai Chau	8	1	0	0	0	0	3	4
7	Lao Cai	9	1	0	5	2	1	0	0
8	Yen Bai	8	2	1	2	2	1	0	0
9	Bac Thai	12	5	1	2	1	1	0	2
10	Quang Ninh	12	11	1	0	0	0	0	0
11	Hoa Binh	10	9	0	0	1	0	0	0
	Total	109	50	12	14	13	6	5	9

Compared with the 1979 census, the number of districts and provincial towns in 1989 in which more than ten ethnic groups were represented had increased by thirty.

The districts in which more than fifteen ethnic groups are represented include: Bac Quang (sixteen ethnic groups), Yen Son (sixteen), Huu Lung (sixteen), Phong Tho (fifteen), Sin Ho (sixteen), Dien Bien (sixteen), Tuan Giao (seventeen), Dong Hy (sixteen) and

Thai Nguyen City (fifteen): None of these areas, which cover several hundred square kilometers, is populated by only a single ethnic group. There are also very few communes (less than 3%) in which only a single ethnic group is represented. There is, however, a large number of communes in which three or four ethnic groups are represented (see Table 6).

On average, each commune had a population of some 2,668 in 1979, or 3,282 in 1989. In Quang Ninh province alone, because of the substantial size of its communes, the average population for a single commune was 4,360 in 1979, and 4,619 in 1989 (see Table 7).

Table 6: Residential situation of ethnic groups (1979)

No.	Provinces	Number of com- munes in province	Number of communes with						
			1 ethnic group	2 ethnic groups	3 ethnic groups	4 ethnic groups	5 ethnic groups	6 ethnic groups	7 ethnic groups
(1)	(2)	(3)	(4)	(5)	(6)	(7)	(8)	(9)	(10)
1	Ha Tuyen	303	3	25	64	64	63	49	35
2	Cao Bang	223	8	37	52	64	38	19	5
3	Lang Son	224	1	25	77	86	29	5	1
4	Lai Chau	149	10	28	40	25	24	7	15
5	Hoang Lien Son	342	9	68	96	64	41	28	36
6	Bac Thai	250	–	–	3	24	76	44	103
7	Son La	197	7	30	59	52	22	10	17
8	Quang Ninh	172	19	40	29	29	29	16	10
9	Hoa Binh	205	2	114	59	17	8	3	2
	Total	2,065	59	367	479	425	330	181	224
	(%)	100.00	2.87	17.86	23.31	20.68	16.06	8.81	10.9

Table 7: Average population of a commune (unit: person)

No.	Province	1979	1989
1	Ha Tuyen (former)	2,582	3,238
2	Cao Bang	2,151	2,533
3	Lang Son	2,163	2,728
4	Lai Chau	2,161	2,899
5	Hoang Lien Son (former)	2,275	3,000
6	Bac Thai (former)	3,260	4,055
7	Son La	2,608	3,533
8	Quang Ninh	4,360	4,619
9	Hoa Binh	2,454	3,184
	Average	2,668	3,309

Another feature of this distribution pattern is the fact that the ethnic groups tend to be scattered across many communes. For example, the Tay are represented in 1,385 communes in the region, the Nung in 988 communes, the Yao in 938 communes, the Hmong in 745, communes and the Thai in 439 (according to 1989 statistics). The Tay, the Nung, and the Yao, and a few other ethnic groups such as the Muong, the San Diu, and the San Chay, live distributed in the mountainous areas of the midland region. The Thai, the Muong, and the Hmong live in a long stretch of country extending as far as Thanh Hoa and Nghe An provinces in what is known as the former Zone 4. In these two provinces, each ethnic group keeps to its own area, each living at a different altitude. Going from east to west, that is from the lowlands to the highlands, the groups found first are the Kinh, then the Tho, the Muong, and finally the Thai. In the highest region are the Kho Mu and the Hmong.

Nghe An may be considered to demarcate the southern extent of the traditional distribution of the ethnic minority groups of northern Vietnam. Although the ethnic groups of the Mon-Khmer linguistic group may be found right down as far as the provinces in the southernmost part of the country, those residing in the north differ from those in Quang Binh province in the south. In the past, for example, Ha Tinh had no ethnic minority groups. The region from the Ngang Pass to Song Be and Dong Nai provinces in the south, was regarded by ethnologists as a separate region, called the Truong Son-Tay Nguyen region (the Central Highlands).

Truong Son-Tay Nguyen is a distinct region in geographical, ethnological and historical terms. Apart from ethnic groups which speak the Viet-Muong languages, such as the Kinh and the Chut, and some groups such as the Tay, the Nung, the Thai, the Muong, and the Yao which migrated recently to the area, the region contains nineteen other ethnic groups, referred to as local ethnic groups. Ethnic distribution maps clearly show that the ethnic groups belonging to the Malayo-Polynesian family live in the central area, with most of them concentrated in the east, close to the coastal plains. Proceeding from north to south the following ethnic groups are recorded:

The Mon-Khmer group in the northern Truong Son Range includes the Bru, the Ta Oi, and the Co Tu. They live in villages consisting of ten to thirty traditional-style houses, often round or shaped like the bird's nest. The ethnic groups are arranged in a circle around the communal house, with its common yard where poles are located for use in killing buffaloes. According to traditional rules, and like those of other groups, the top beam of the roof of one house must not be in line with the main roof of another house.

The Mon-Khmer groups found in the central Truong Son Range include the Gie-Trieng, the Xo Dang, the Co, the Hre, the Ba Na, the Ro Mam, and the Brau. These groups live in the northern part of Tay Nguyen (Central Highlands) and in the western parts of some of the northern central coastal provinces. The topography here is quite complicated. There are some high mountain peaks, such as Ngoc Linh and Ngoc Pan, and some mountain ranges running from the northwest to the southeast. This region is sharply divided by the upper streams of several major rivers which flow down to the coastal plains. As a result, transportation is very difficult. For this same reason, cultural interaction between the different ethnic groups living within this region, as well as with those residing outside of it, has been limited until recently. The ethnic groups here, whether Ba Na, Xo Dang, or Gie-Trieng, live in hamlets called *play*. Groups living together with the Co Tu have been influenced by their circular village structure. But farther down, however, the shape of the villages is different and is highly dependent upon local topography.

In the middle of the Mon-Khmer group in the central and southern parts of the Truong Son Range are groups which speak Malayo-Polynesian languages. These are the Gia Rai, the E De, the Cham, the Raglai, and the Chu Ru. These groups may be distinguished by the profound importance of the matriarchal system, which persists to the present as an influential part of daily life. Villages and hamlets tend to be large and houses are arranged in strictly even parallel rows.

The ethnic groups consitituting the Mon-Khmer group in the southern Truong Son Range (also called the southern Tay Nguyen group) include the Mnong, the Co Ho, the Ma, the Stieng, and the Cho Ro. Here the village (known as *buon* or *bon*) may take any of a rich variety of forms, and no clear rule or patterns are evident.

Relative to the ethnic groups of northern Vietnam, those of the Truong Son-Tay Nguyen region tend to be more distinctly concentrated in certain areas. Three or four decades ago, the boundaries between ethnic groups, between groupings of ethnic groups, and even between villages of the same ethnic group, were fairly clear. This was due to the local topography, which is very inaccessible, making travelling and market-oriented trade in commodities very difficult. As a result, people practised subsistence agriculture. Moreover, traditional social life put a high value upon "neighborliness," communal unity, and kinship. The village was the highest level of social organization, and the villagers knew of no other form. In addition, the educational level of the villagers was low and their scientific knowledge poor. Consequently, catastrophes such as crop failure, epidemics, death, and forest fires were considered to be the work of evil spirits and ghosts. Disputes have often arisen within and between villages as each blamed the other for "causing disasters." Sometimes this has led to an entire hamlet uprooting and migrating to another, distant place.

The boundaries around ethnic groups, villages, and hamlets that were considered sacred were even more strictly respected. Over the past several decades, however, the impact of the war and demands for increased production have led to increasing contact between ethnic groups, and boundaries between them have started to dissolve. This has led to greater integration in terms of residence patterns,[3] particularly with regard to the Kinh and local ethnic groups. Less than half a century ago, the Tay Nguyen was populated largely by local ethnic groups. By 1979, the Kinh population there was 836,831, and by 1989 it had risen to 1,607,555. In 1989, the Kinh represented 70% of the population in Dac Lac province, and 76.1% in Lam Dong province.[4] The Nung, the Tay, the Yao, and the Thai, who have long lived in the northern provinces, have more recently begun to migrate southwards to areas such as the Tay Nguyen region and southeastern Vietnam (see Table 8).

Table 8: Population of some ethnic groups from the north in Tay Nguyen and nearby provinces

No.	Provinces	Tay		Nung		Thai		Muong	
		1979	1989	1979	1989	1979	1989	1979	1989
1	Gia Lai-Kon Tum	277	2,149	163	2,061	411	945	225	348
2	Dac Lac	491	10,903	624	18,594	1,596	3,153	3,301	5,275
3	Lam Dong	4,842	6,605	5,816	8,491	2,968	3,731	0	188
4	Thuan Hai	2,170	3,213	1,297	1,687	0	57	115	78
5	Dong Nai	3,739	8,303	6,799	10,927	136	482	2,055	2,562
6	Song Be	95	1,904	183	2,453	68	195	113	290
	Total	11,614	33,077	14,882	44,213	5,179	8,563	5,809	8,741

Currently, ethnic groups are becoming increasingly mixed. In part, this is due to the free migration of ethnic minority groups from north Vietnam into this region, but is also related to profound economic changes within the industrial, agricultural, and forestry sectors.

The distribution of ethnic groups in the country is discussed below in order of language:

1. The Kinh ethnic group: According to archaeological, historical, and ethnological data, the northern midlands, the Red River Delta, and the northern central region are known to have been inhabited since the Stone Age. The Lac-Viet (ancestors of the Viet-Muong people of the early third century B.C.), together with the Tay-Nung people, founded the kingdom of Au Lac under the leadership of Thuc Phan, who proclaimed himself King An Duong Vuong. The ancient Viet in the Red River Delta were often acknowledged in old history books, such as that by Thuy Kinh Chu, as the people who cultivated rice in harmony with the tidal system by using irrigation. After a long process of taming nature, which offered an ecological environment that was both favourable and harsh at the same time, they created a complete dike and irrigation system.[5] The residential areas were often concentrated in blocs along the rivers and main transport routes.

From these areas, places where rivers converge, the Kinh people started a process of migration. The evolution of their history shows how they expanded into neighboring regions and later on towards the south, even to the Truong Son-Tay Nguyen region.

This took place for the following reasons:

- Rapid population growth and demographic densities, limited land, and a lack of resources, particularly during times of crop failure.

- People were mobilized by the authorities of different feudal dynasties to be soldiers and mandarins.

- People sought refuge to avoid persecution whenever an insurrection or coup d'etat failed. Most notable were the leaders and children of the Mac dynasty, many of whom gradually assimilated with different ethnic groups, changing their ethnicity in the process.

- People were forced to perform hard labor or to serve in the army. In particular, they had to build mines and plantations during the years of colonial rule (late nineteenth and early twentieth century).

- People also went to participate in the construction and development of a new culture and economy in the uplands and mountainous regions under the new Socialist government.

Thanks to policies promoting land clearance to create "new economic zones," the Kinh population in the mountainous provinces has increased dramatically in recent decades (see Table 9).

Table 9 shows that after nearly thirty years (1 March 1960 to 1 April 1989), the number of Kinh in the northern mountainous provinces has increased in the following proportions: Ha Tuyen 425.8%; Cao Bang 55% (by 1989 alone it had decreased by 10.4% by comparison with

Table 9: The number of the Kinh in northern mountainous provinces through three population censuses
(unit: person)

Year	Ha Tuyen	Cao Bang	Lang Son	Lai Chau	Hoang Lien Son	Bac Thai	Son La	Hoa Binh	Quang Ninh
1960	64,274	8,301	26,321	10,903	89,900	221,594	28,849	32,355	188,337
1979	261,672	26,249	75,433	71,812	357,669	567,546	98,784	162,921	683,172
1989	338,001	23,780	93,251	84,744	465,185	703,180	123,068	659,202	725,421

1979); Lang Son 254.3%; Lai Chau 677.2%; Bac Thai 217.3%; Son La 326.6%; Hoa Binh 1,937.4% and Quang Ninh 285.2%.

In the Truong Son-Tay Nguyen region, the earliest Kinh presence was recorded in the eleventh century. But the Kinh population did not increase substantially until after the fifteenth century. The policy of the feudal regimes at that time was to settle the poor in areas where they could reclaim relatively unproductive land. For example, Bui Ta Han was appointed guard to Quang Nam in 1540 (see Nguyen Duc Cung, in *Vu Man Tap Luc Thu*). The governor of Quang Ngai province in 1750, Nguyen Cu Trinh, and several of his successors, including Nguyen Cong Tru, Nguyen Khac Tuan, etc., also made plans to develop the highland areas of Quang Nam and Quang Ngai. They organized areas for use as military plantations and settlement zones to receive migrants from the plains and the north to clear land and make a living. By the end of the eighteenth century in Gia Lai province there were only seven Kinh families living in what is now An Khe town. According to documents, some four to five hundred Kinh began settling in Kon Tum province around the middle of the nineteenth century. The first Kinh villages to be founded there were Tan Huong in 1874, Phuong Nghia in 1882, Phuong Hoa in 1887 and Phuong Quy in 1892. By 1933-1934 there were some 15,000 Kinh in Kon Tum province, including An Khe town, and in 1936 there were some 32,750 in the four central highland provinces.[6]

When the young French envoy, L. Sabatier, arrived in Dac Lac province around 1912, the typical E De village style was noted to have some thatched-roof houses. By 1989, there were 228,519 people living in Buon Ma Thuot and 80.9% of these were Kinh. Similarly, in Lam Dong province in the early part of this century, Dalat was virtually deserted, with only eight to ten thatched houses and a wooden house for visitors. The population there consisted of only about a dozen people, most of whom were hunters.[7] However, by 1989, Dalat City had a population of 115,959 people, 96.7% of whom were Kinh.

Today, the Kinh are represented in all fifty-three provinces and cities throughout Vietnam, and they account for the majority of the total population. There are only eight provinces in which the population of Kinh is less than 50% of the total. These include: Cao Bang (4.2%), Ha Giang (11.21%), Lang Son (15.26%), Son La (18.04%), Lai Chau (19.35%), Hoa Binh (30.97%), Lao Cai (33.74%) and Kon Tum (43.14%).[68]

Factors such as the strong sense of community in their traditional social relationships (in villages and hamlets), their cultivation of wet rice and fishing practices, and their participation in market economic activities, have led the Kinh to settle in the plains, along rivers and streams, or along provincial/district highways. Over the past few years, however, a new tendency has emerged towards scattered settlements, whereby each family received a plot of hilly land to establish farms and forest gardens.

2. The Muong ethnic group is the name given to a group which lives in a large area of hilly and mountainous land lying between the Kinh area in the east and the Thai in the west. This region is about 350 km long and 80–80 km wide,[69] stretching from the northwestern part of Yen Bai province to Nghe An province. The area covers the whole of Hoa Binh province (397,283 people), the districts of Ngoc Lac, Thach Thanh, Cam Thuy, Ba Thuoc, Nhu Xuan, and Lang Chanh, all in Thanh Hoa province (260,904 people); Thanh Son, Yen Lap and Tam Thanh in Vinh Phu province (133,198 people); Phu Yen, Moc Chau and Bac Yen in Son La province (56,099 people); Ba Vi and Quoc Oai in Ha Tay province (19,271 people); Hoang Long in Ninh Binh province (12,721 people); Van Chan, Tran Yen in Yen Bai province (11,072 people). The Muong are represented not only in this region, but also in some southern provinces such as Dac Lac (5,275 people) and Dong Nai (2,562 people). During a thirty year period, from 1960–1989, the number of communes in which Muong were present more than doubled (see Table 10).

Table 10: The number of communes in which the Muong have been present through three population censuses, and their percentage relative to the total population of each commune

YEAR	< 20 %	21–40%	41–60%	61–80%	81–100%	TOTAL
1960	161	27	38	42	227	495
1979	668	47	71	94	121	1,001
1989	850	55	56	65	135	1,161

3. The Tho ethnic group is mainly found in Nghe An and Thanh Hoa provinces. This Tho group is distinct from the group named Tho comprised of the Tay that previously lived in the Viet Bac region. The Tho live at the crossroads between the plains and the mountains, an area which borders the Muong area in Thanh Hoa province to the northeast, the Kinh areas of Dien Chau, Quynh Luu and Anh Son districts of Nghe An province to the east and south, and the mountainous region of the Thai to the west and northwest. In terms of their origin and cultural characteristics, the Tho can be considered as having emerged and developed through relationships between the Kinh and the Muong. But they have now formed their own distinct community. Apart from the name, members of the Tho group also use various specific and localized names, such as: Nha Lang (the name used by people from the plains to refer to highlanders), Tho Lam La (the name of the former canton which now covers the communes of Nghia Mai, Nghia Yen, Nghia Minh, Nghia Lam, Nghia Nhac, Nghia Loi, and Nghia Tho in Nghia Dan district), Tho Cat Mong (which is the name of the village), Tho Quy Hop (the name of the district), Ho (the name used for Tho in Giai Xuan, Tan Xuan, and Nghia Phuc in Tan Ky district), Keo (the name used for Tho in Nghia An and Nghia Tien communes, Duong village in Nghia Quang commune, and U Rai village of Nghia Thang commune in Nghia Dan district), Cuoi (the name used for Tho in Tan Hop commune in Tan Ky district and the three villages of Lo, Rach, and Dong in Nghia Quang commune, Nghia Dan district). These names have different meanings: *Ho* is a third person pronoun (they, them); *Cuoi* means human being; *Keo* is what ethnic minorities in northern Vietnam call the Kinh; *Mon* is what the Muong call themselves. At the conference on the definition of ethnic groups, held in Cua Lo, Nghe An in September 1973, the above-mentioned groups unanimously acknowledged that they belonged to the same ethnic group, the Tho. Then, in October 1973, at a conference held in Tuong Duong, district, the group known as Con Kha (Tay Poong) from Tam Hop commune, Tuong Duong district and that known as the Dan Lai-Ly Ha, in Con Cuong district, also claimed that they belonged to the Tho.[70] However, during the 1979 population census, the Tho of Nghia Dan district registered themselves as Tay, but again registered as Tho in the 1989 census. At present, the Tho are represented in the districts of Nghia Dan (17,399 people), Tan Ky (10,723 people), Quy Hop (10,700 people), Con Cuong (1,127 people), Tuong Duong (361 people) in Nghe An province (40,015 people) and Nhu Xuan (6,758 people) in Thanh Hoa province. They are also spreading into other provinces, particularly in the northern mountainous regions where each of the provinces now has anything from a few dozen to several hundred Tho. The number of communes in which Tho are represented has been increasing rapidly (see Table 11).

Table 11: The number of communes in which Tho were represented in all three population censuses

YEAR	< 20 %	21–40%	41–60%	61–80%	81–100%	TOTAL
1960	29	4	0	3	5	41
1979	157	2	0	1	1	161
1989	218	10	10	2	1	241

The population of Tho and the number of communes in which they live have both increased, partly due to migration but also because of the intensification of ethnic consciousness of the Tho, who in the past were prepared to register themselves as members of other ethnic groups.

4. *The Chut ethnic group* is the common name given to several groups: the Sach, the May, the Ruc, the Arem, and the Ma Lieng from the northwestern part of Quang Binh province and the southern part of Ha Tinh province. Chut is the name by which these people describe themselves, and according to Nguyen Duong Binh it means "wild forestmen."[71] According to Ta Long, Chut also means rocky mountain and came to be used to refer to those who live alongside the rocky mountain range in 1973.[72] At present, the Chut population live in the communes of Dan Hoa (together with the Nguon and Bru), Thuong Hoa (together with the Nguon), and the Hoa Son commune in Minh Hoa district (1,853 people). There are also Chut living in Tuyen Hoa district (395 people) and Bo Trach district (100 people) in Quang Binh province (2,355 people). There are also some Chut people, mainly of the Ma Lieng group, living in Ha Tinh province.

According to a report published by the Quang Binh Provincial People's Committee, the population and residence pattern for the Chut by 30 June 1991, was as shown in Table 12.

The number of communes in which the Chut are present has also increased rapidly across the time period covered by the three population censuses (see Table 13).

5. **The Khmer** (Kho Me) ethnic group live mainly in the Mekong River Delta, and in the past they were therefore referred to as the Khmer Nam Bo (southern Khmer). They live in hamlets and villages

Table 12: Population and residence patterns of the Chut ethnic group in Quang Binh province

No.	Local groups	Number of hamlets	Number of households	Population
1	May	14	256	1,279
2	Sach	10	209	1,140
3	Ruc	3	51	217
4	Ma Lieng	2	41	210
5	Arem	2	10	41
6	Krai (?)	-	2	30
	TOTAL		575	2,917

Table 13: The number of communes containing the Chut through three population censuses

YEAR	< 20 %	21–40%	41–60%	61–80%	81–100%	TOTAL
1960*	3	2	0	0	0	5
1979	9	3	0	0	0	12
1989	14	1	0	0	0	15

* The data for the year 1960 are not for all ethnic Chut groups.

known as *phum*, or *soc*, which are located along the major transport routes and alluvial stretches (*giong*) along the river banks and canals. In the past the *soc* comprised virtually exclusively Khmer persons, but more recently the villages have come to include two or three ethnic groups (Khmer-Kinh; Khmer-Hoa or Khmer-Kinh-Hoa). Along the Vietnam-Cambodia border in Tay Ninh and Song Be provinces in southeastern Vietnam, the Khmer live close to or interspersed with the Cham and the Stieng. At present, the largest concentrations of Khmer are in the provinces of Soc Trang (298,263 people), Tra Vinh (245,252 people), Kien Giang (145,469 people), An Giang (71,723 people), Minh Hai (63,771 people), Can Tho (28,913 people), and Vinh Long (17,598 people). In only the ten years between 1979 and 1989, the number of communes in which the Khmer were living increased by more than one hundred (see Table 14).

Table 14: The number of communes containing the Khmer through two population censuses

YEAR	< 20 %	21–40%	41–60%	61–80%	81–100%	TOTAL
1979	919	49	39	17	1	1,025
1989	1,019	53	41	31	8	1,152

6. The Ba Na ethnic group is the third largest ethnic minority in Tay Nguyen (Central Highlands). Only the Gia Rai and the E De are larger. Ba Na is the official name of this group, which includes several local groups such as the Bang Huong, the To Lo, the Go Lar, the But, the Gio Lang, the Krem, and the Ro Ngao (a group resulting from endogamy between Ba Na and Xo Dang). At the present time the Ba Na live in a large area in northern Tay Nguyen, comprising seventy-four communes in Gia Lai province (92,750 people) and twenty-two communes in Kon Tum province (27,978 people). They are mainly concentrated in towns such as Mang Giang (41,622 people), Kon Tum provincial capital (20,846 people), Kon Chro (19,013 people), and K'Bang district (15,535 people). There are also some Ba Na scattered throughout some districts of two central coastal provinces, specifically Binh Dinh (12,704 people in twenty-one communes) and Phu Yen (2,792 people in sixteen communes). Between 1979 and 1989, the number of communes containing Ba Na increased by eighteen (see Table 15).

Table 15: The number of communes in which the Ba Na were present in two population censuses

YEAR	< 20 %	21–40%	41–60%	61–80%	81–100%	TOTAL
1979	75	10	8	7	35	135
1989	80	20	13	14	36	163

7. The Xo Dang (Sedang) ethnic group live in an area which includes Kon Tum province (61,820 people), southwestern Quang Nam-Da Nang province (22,608 people) and western Quang Ngai province (7,138 people). Their neighbors include the Gie-Trieng to the north, the Co and Hre to the west, the Ba Na to the southeast, the Gia Rai to the southwest and the Vietnam-Lao border to the west. The Xo Dang are most commonly found in the following districts: Dac To (26,145 people), Kong Plong (15,628 people), Sa Thay (7,686 people), Kon Tum provincial capital (6,770 people), Dak Glay in Kon Tum province (5,591 people), Tra My in Quang Nam-Da Nang province (21,424 people), and Son Ha in Quang Ngai province (6,233 people). There are also 4,409 Xo Dang in Dac Lac province, living mainly in Krong Bach district (3,527 people). Between 1979 and 1989 the number of communes in which Xo Dang were living increased by 21, from 81 to 102 (see Table 16).

Table 16. The number of communes containing the Xo Dang through
two population censuses

YEAR	< 20 %	21–40%	41–60%	61–80%	81–100%	TOTAL
1979	32	7	2	20	20	81
1989	51	6	1	6	38	102

Some of the local sub-groups of the Xo Dang include the Xo Teng, the To Dra, the Mnam, the Ca Dong, and the Ha Lang.

8. The Co Ho ethnic group comprises six relatively independent groups:

- The Xre (Sre), who practice wet-rice farming and constitute the largest number within the this ethnic group. There are also smaller groups, such as the Mang To and the Rien. The Xre live on the Di Linh high plateaus.

- The Nop, who are also known as the To Nop or the To La, live on the Di Linh high plateaus along the transport routes leading down to Phan Thiet.

- The Co Don group, which is made up of the La Gia sub-group, lives in the southeastern part of the Di Linh high plateaus and in the western part of the former Thuan Hai province.

- The Chil, who are of Mnong origin, are present on both the Di Linh and the Lam Vien high plateaus.

- The Lat or Lach, who are concentrated in Dalat City.

- The To Ring (T'ring), who are present in three provinces: Lam Dong (where they are mainly found in Don Duong district), Khanh Hoa and Binh Thuan.

The Co Ho are concentrated mainly in Lam Dong province (82,971 people). The number of communes which contain Co Ho increased little over the ten years between 1979 and 1989 (see Table 17).

Table 17: The number of communes in which the Co Ho were found in the two population censuses[73]

YEAR	< 20 %	21–40%	41–60%	61–80%	81–100%	TOTAL
1979	60	10	7	4	12	93
1989	69	11	7	5	14	106

9. The Hre ethnic group was once considered to be of ancient Cham origin. Because of this, the group is referred to as "Cham Re" in older books and periodicals. Although the Cham had an undeniable influence on the Hre, this is now diminishing. In its place, the influence of the Kinh on the Hre is noticeable, particularly in terms of their wet-rice cultivation practices, as well as the names used for tools, plants, and fruits. Hre has now become the official name for this group. However, according to each specific locality, different groups of Hre can be distinguished. For instance, there are the Dinh people in An Lao where the Dinh River flows, the Kva people in Minh Long where the Kva River flows, the Lien people in Ba To where the Lien River flows and the Kre people in Son Ha where the Kre River is located.[74] The areas in which the Hre live are the mountainous region in western Quang Ngai province (86,375 people) and northwestern Binh Dinh province (6,128 people). There are also about 1,000 Hre people living in the eastern part of Kon Tum province. Below are the data covering the number of communes in which Hre live (see Table 18).

Table 18: The number of communes containing the Hre through two population censuses

YEAR	< 20 %	21–40%	41–60%	61–80%	81–100%	TOTAL
1979	31	3	2	7	28	71
1989	47	4	2	5	25	83

10. The Mnong ethnic group. The word Mnong (or Pnong, meaning highlander) has long been used as the name for an ethnic group. Mnong people now live mainly in Dac Lac province (46,018 people) in fifteen of the seventeen districts of the province. The largest concentrations are in the districts of Lac (18,432 people), Dak Rlap (6,686 people), Dak Nong (5,162 people), Dak Mil (5,061 people), Krong No (3,431 people), and Krong Pong (3,337 people). There are also around 10,000 Mnong people living in Song Be and Lam Dong provinces.[75] The local sub-groups of the Mnong are: the Gar, the Nong, the Kuenh, the Pre, the Prong, the Rlam, the Bu Dang, the Chil, the Bu Nor Di Bri, the Dip, the Biat, the Bu De, the Si To and the Ka. In the ten year period between 1979 and 1989, the number of communes in which Mnong people were present increased by thirty-two (see Table 19).

Table 19 shows that the number of communes with a small proportion of Mnong inhabitants (compared to the total population) is increasing. In 1989, the number of communes with a Mnong population of less than 20% was equal to the total number of communes in 1979. Meanwhile, the number of communes with higher proportions of Mnong people saw almost no increase.

Table 19: The number of communes containing the Mnong through two population censuses

YEAR	< 20 %	21–40%	41–60%	61–80%	81–100%	TOTAL
1979	32	3	6	2	10	53
1989	53	11	7	5	9	85

11. *The Stieng ethnic group* lives mainly in Song Be province (49,179 people), in the districts of Phuoc Long (15,583 people), Binh Long (14,761 people), Bu Dang (8,854 people), Loc Ninh (7,875 people), and Dong Phu (2,074 people). The Stieng are also found in Dong Nai province (764 people), and are scattered throughout the districts of Tan Phu, Xuan Loc, and Long Thanh. The Stieng have long existed as a distinct ethnic group, and are also known as the Sa Dieng, Bu Lo, Bu Dip, Bu Deh, and Bu Lach. However, the Stieng have in fact only two local sub-groups: the Bu Lo (in the upper midlands) and the Bu Deh (in the lower midlands). The number of communes in which Stieng live is small and the rate of increase is slow (see Table 20).

Table 20: The number of communes containing the Stieng through two population censuses

YEAR	< 20 %	21–40%	41–60%	61–80%	81–100%	TOTAL
1979	24	12	4	2	2	44
1989	39	8	2	3	2	54

12. *The Bru ethnic group* is concentrated in the mountainous regions of three provinces: Quang Tri (29,369 people), Quang Binh (8,045 people), and Thua Thien-Hue (609 people). The Bru consist of four local sub-groups: the Van Kieu, the Khua, the Ma Coong, and the Tri. The Van Kieu (approximately 34,000 people) are present in almost all the districts and towns of Quang Tri province, with their greatest concentration in Huong Hoa district (26,430 people) and Ben Hai (2,647 people). In Quang Binh province, the Bru live in two districts: Le Thuy (2,848 people) and Quang Ninh (1,707 people). It is worthy of note that in 1972 the US and the south Vietnam armies forced more than 2,000 people from the Van Kieu group to leave Quang Tri and

move to Dac Lac where they now number 1,688. The Khua group (approximately 3,500 people) now live in two districts: Minh Hoa and Bo Trach. The Ma Coong group (more than 2,000 people) and the Tri group (more than 100 people) live in Bo Trach district, Quang Binh province. Table 21 below shows the number of communes in which the Bru are present.

Table 21: The number of communes in which the Bru ethnic group are present, according to three population censuses

YEAR	< 20 %	21–40%	41–60%	61–80%	81–100%	TOTAL
1960*	7	1	2	3	6	19
1979	18	3	0	3	25	49
1989	33	2	1	2	25	63

*Only calculated from Vinh Linh southward

13. The Co Tu ethnic group are present throughout the mountainous region of northwestern Quang Nam-Da Nang province and southwestern Thua Thien-Hue province. They live near the Ta Oi ethnic group in the north, the Kinh in the east and the Gie-Trieng in the south and southwest. They also live close to the Vietnam-Laos border in the west, where the terrain is mountainous, densely forested, and largely inaccessible. Several decades ago in the region of Quang Nam-Da Nang, the people of this group were concentrated in only two districts, Hien (19,116 people) and Giang (8,138 people). Today, however, they are scattered throughout various districts, such as Hoa Vang, Hoi, An and Tien Phuoc. In Thua Thien-Hue province, the Co Tu are represented predominantly in the two districts of Nam Dong (6,378 people) and A Luoi (2,481 people). The number of communes in which the Co Tu are present is small and is increasing only very slowly (see Table 22).

The Co Tu have no local sub-groups, although some differentiation according to residence may be made; those living in the highlands are called Driu, those in the midlands are called Cha Lau, and those in the lowlands are called Nal.

Table 22. The number of communes in which the Co Tu are present, according to two population censuses

YEAR	< 20%	21–40%	41–60%	61–80%	81–100%	TOTAL
1979	13	1	3	5	21	43
1989	22	4	2	8	16	52

14. The Kho Mu ethnic group were late comers to Vietnam, arriving only some two hundred years ago. They live along a long stretch of land reaching from Lai Chau to Nghe An, with their main concentration along the Vietnam-Laos border. At present, the Kho Mu are concentrated largely in Nghe An province (19,441 people), though they are only present in the districts of Ky Son (13,009 people) and Tuong Duong (5,452 people). There are also 1,000 Kho Mu people living in Que Phong district. In Lai Chau province, the Kho Mu population is 11,625, scattered throughout the districts and towns of the province, but with a greater concentration in Dien Bien district (6,519 people). In Son La province, the Kho Mu are present in all districts except Phu Yen. The number of the Kho Mu for each of these districts range from twenty to four thousand people. The Kho Mu are also found in Yen Bai province (eight hundred people). They live intermingled with other ethnic groups, particularly the Thai.

Although the total population of Kho Mu is relatively small, the fact that many lead semi-nomadic lives means they can be found in many communes (see Table 23).

Table 23: The number of communes in which the Kho Mu ethnic group is represented, according to two population censuses[76]

YEAR	< 20%	21–40%	41–60%	61–80%	81–100%	TOTAL
1979	97	15	6	4	4	126
1989	102	17	6	2	3	130

The Kho Mu have been known by many names: Xa Cau, Kha Klau, Mang Cau, Tenh, Pu Thenh, Tay Hay, and Mun Sen. However, the Kho Mu people refer to themselves, and wish to be known, as Kam Mu.

15. The Ta Oi ethnic group was discussed in Chapter 1 under the heading "Composition of Ethnic Groups in Vietnam." Here, therefore, the discussion will concern their distribution in the mountainous regions of the two provinces of Thua Thien-Hue and Quang Tri only. Ta Oi was once the name used to describe the high plateau near the Vietnam-Laos border. Later, the name was applied to this ethnic group. The mass media in Vietnam, however, often refer to the Ta Oi people as the Pa Co, although this is in fact only a local sub-group of the Ta Oi. Today, the Ta Oi live side by side with the Kinh and the Bru in Quang Tri province, and with the Co Tu in Thua Thien-Hue province. In Thua Thien-Hue, for instance, the Ta Oi number 18,795 people and are present in twenty-three communes, but there is no commune that is populated by Ta Oi alone:

- In seven communes two ethnic groups are present (Kinh and Ta Oi).

- In twelve communes three ethnic groups are present (Kinh, Ta Oi, and Co Tu).

- In four communes four ethnic groups are present (Kinh, Ta Oi, Co Tu, and Bru).

In Quang Tri province, the Ta Oi number 6,994, and are present in 15 communes:

- In only one commune two ethnic groups are present (Kinh and Ta Oi).

- In thirteen communes three ethnic groups are present (Kinh, Ta Oi, and Bru).

In the provincial town of Dong Ha, there exists one commune in which five ethnic groups are present (Kinh, Hoa, Ta Oi, Bru, and Chut). Nevertheless, in many communes a substantial proportion of the population is accounted for by Ta Oi (see Table 24).

Table 24: The number of communes in which the Ta Oi ethnic group is present, according to two population censuses

YEAR	< 20%	21–40%	41–60%	61–80%	81–100%	TOTAL
1979	10	0	0	2	22	34
1989	21	0	0	4	18	43

16. The Ma ethnic group is spread mainly throughout southern Tay Nguyen. They live predominantly along the Dong Nai river basin in Lam Dong province (19,792 people), close to the Mnong in the north, to the Co Ho in the east, to the Cho Ro in the south and to the Stieng in the west.

The name Ma originates from the term *mir*, meaning terraced field. The term is distinguished from *xre*, meaning water-logged field, which is the name of a local group of the Co Ho. The local sub-groups of the Ma include the Ngan, the To, the Krung, and the Xop. In Lam

Table 25: The number of communes containing Ma through two population censuses

YEAR	< 20%	21–40%	41–60%	61–80%	81–100%	TOTAL
1979	25	2	2	1	5	35
1989	29	5	2	1	6	43

Dong province, the Ma are concentrated in the districts of Bao Loc (10,932 people), Lam Ha (2,525 people), Da Oai (2,305 people), Da Te (1,870 people), and Di Linh (1,524 people). The Ma are also found in Dac Lac province (4,286 people), concentrated mainly in Dak Nong district. In Dong Nai province there are 1,000 people, living in Tan Phu district. The number of communes in which Ma live is small, just over forty (see Table 25).

17. The Gie-Trieng ethnic group. Gie-Trieng is a compound name formed from the names of two of its three constituent sub-groups (Gie, Trieng, and Ve) and is now used as the name for the ethnic group. Of the three constituent groups, Gie is the largest. They live mainly in Dak Glay district, Kon Tum province, and the two districts of Phuoc Son and Tra My in Quang Nam-Da Nang province. In these two districts they are known as the P'nong (Pa Noong or Ba Noong), Brila, and Giang Ray. Three quarters of the Trieng group are found in Dak Glay district, Kon Tum province, while one quarter live in Giang district, Quang Nam-Da Nang province. This group of Trieng are very close to the Ta Lieng ethnic group in Laos. As for the Ve sub-group, they are only to be found in Giang district. Local people say the Ve are simply a group of Gie people who migrated from Kon Tum about one hundred years ago.

The Gie-Trieng group, then, is the largest group in Kon Tum province (20,144 people), with its greatest concentration in Dak Glay district (19,670 people). In Quang Nam-Da Nang province there are some 14,000 Gie-Trieng, of whom 10,833 are of the P'Nong group and are concentrated in the Phuoc Son district (8,847 people), Tra My (1,496 people), and Hiep Duc (759 people).[17] In Giang district there are Trieng and Ve people, together accounting for 3,008 people. In ten years, the number of communes in which Gie-Trieng are represented has increased by only nine (see Table 26).

Table 26: The number of communes in which the Gie-Trieng ethnic group is present, according to two population censuses

YEAR	< 20%	21–40%	41–60%	61–80%	81–100%	TOTAL
1979	29	1	1	2	7	40
1989	28	0	3	2	16	49

18. The Co ethnic group traditionally resided in only two districts: Tra Bong in Quang Ngai province (18,081 people) and Tra My district in Quang Nam-Da Nang province (3,007 people). More recently, Co people have begun moving into neighboring areas such as Nui Thanh, Tien Phuoc and Tan Ky. The area in which the Co live therefore adjoins the Gie-Trieng area to the north, the Kinh area to the east, the Hre to the south and the Xo Dang to the west.

The number of communes in which Co people were residing in 1989 had increased from 1979 by 17 (see Table 27). According to the 1989 census, in Nghe An province alone there were six communes in which Co lived. However, this figure is suspect.

Table 27: The number of communes containing the Co people through two population censuses

YEAR	< 20%	21–40%	41–60%	61–80%	81–100%	TOTAL
1979	12	1	0	3	12	28
1989	27	2	1	0	15	45

19. **The Xinh Mun ethnic group** formerly belonged to the Xa group and were known as the Xa Puoc. Researchers proposed that the name Puoc might refer to a particular locality, or to a group with low social status. Locals consider the name to be stigmatizing and do not acknowledge it when referring to their own group. Xinh Mun refers to highlanders. The group has two local sub-groups: Xinh Mun Da, who once lived in the Na Da hamlet in Chieng On commune, Yen Chau district, and Xinh Mun Nghet, whose ancestors once lived in Na Nghet hamlet in Xieng Kho district, Sam Nua province (in Laos).[18]

Currently, the Xinh Mun live in an area stretching from the district of Dien Bien in Lai Chau province (942 people), through Song Ma district (4,091 people), Mai Son (366 people), and Yen Chau (5,049 people) to Moc Chau (400 people) in Son La province.

The number of communes in which Xinh Mun could be found increased markedly between 1960 and 1979, although this may be accounted for by the paucity of statistics obtained in the 1960 census. In the decade between 1979 and 1989, however, the number did not increase but, on the contrary, declined (see Table 28).

Table 28: The number of communes in which the Xinh Mun were present, according to three population censuses

YEAR	< 20%	21–40%	41–60%	61–80%	81–100%	TOTAL
1960	7	0	1	2	0	10
1979	21	2	3	0	0	26
1989	21	3	1	0	0	25

20. The Cho Ro ethnic group is the result of a mixture of Kinh and Ma. The name Cho Ro, or Chau Ro, means people or group named Ro.

At present, the Cho Ro live in southern Dong Nai province (10,121 people), spread throughout the districts of Xuan Loc (6,410 people) and Tan Phu (3,099 people). They are also found in Ba Ria-Vung Tau province (3,494 people) in the districts of Chau Thanh (2,540 people) and Xuyen Loc (76 people). There are also 1,300 Cho Ro living in Binh Thuan province, mainly in Duc Linh district.

The number of communes in which the Cho Ro lived doubled in the ten years between 1979 and 1989 (see Table 29).

Table 29: The number of communes containing the Cho Ro people through two population censuses

YEAR	< 20%	21–40%	41–60%	61–80%	81–100%	TOTAL
1979	29	1	0	0	0	30
1989	61	0	0	0	0	61

21. The Mang ethnic group was, in the past, considered part of the Xa group, and was referred to by neighboring groups as Mang U, Xa Mang, and Xa O. They refer to themselves as Mang. The Mang are only present in three districts in Lai Chau province, namely Muong Te (806 people), Sin Ho (757 people), and Muong Lay (665 people). In the ten years between 1979 and 1989, the number of communes in which Mang were living decreased (see Table 30).

Table 30: The number of communes containing the Mang people through two population censuses

YEAR	< 20%	21–40%	41–60%	61–80%	81–100%	TOTAL
1979	8	1	0	1	0	10
1989	7	1	0	0	0	9

The fact that the number of communes containing Mang people decreased is accounted for by their emigration from places in which they formerly lived; the name Mang actually means "nomadic life."[19]

22. The Khang ethnic group used to belong to the Xa, and was known to other groups by various names, such as Xa Khao or Xa Don (both of which literally mean "white Xa"), Xa Xua (which means Xa who live in the gunpowder-making region) and Xa Tu Lang (meaning Xa who drink through the nose). Although the group is not large, it contains several local groups. Those which refer to themselves as Khang include Khang Dang, Khang Hoac, Khang Don, and Khang Xua. Those who refer to themselves as Hang include Ma Hang and Bu Hang. The Khang who live in Muong Te district refer to themselves as Bren.

Currently, the Khang live in two provinces. In the province of Lai Chau there are a total of 2,313 Khang people, distributed throughout the following districts: Tuan Giao (1,427 people), Dien Bien (473 people), and Muong Lay (413 people). In the province of Son La there are 1,248 Khang people, who are concentrated mainly in the district of Thuan Chau (950 people). Although the group is spread across a large area, the number of communes in which they are found is relatively small (see Table 31).

Table 31: The number of communes containing the Khang through two population censuses

YEAR	< 20%	21–40%	41–60%	61–80%	81–100%	TOTAL
1979	7	4	0	0	0	11
1989	18	1	0	0	0	19

23. The Ro Mam ethnic group is small, only slightly larger than the Brau and the O Du. Ro Mam is the name of both the ethnic group and of a former village. The Ro Mam are found in greater numbers in the neighboring countries of Laos and Cambodia. Today, the Ro Mam in Vietnam live at the crossroads of Indochina, mixing with Gia Rai in the two communes of Mo Rai (213 people) and Sa Son (9 people), both in Sa Thay district, Kon Tum province.

24. The Brau ethnic group, also known as Brao, is also very small. Brau people live in one commune together with the Xo Dang: the Bo Y commune in Sa Thay district, Kon Tum province.

25. The O Du ethnic group, as noted in the chapter on the composition of ethnic groups, are also known as Tay Hat. This group is only found in Kim Da commune, Tuong Duong district, Nghe An province, where they mix with the Kho Mu and the Thai.

26. The Hmong or Mong ethnic group is the name this ethnic community (formerly called Meo in Vietnamese) use for themselves. In China, the Hmong are called Miao. According to scientific documents and based on legends and memories of many Hmong, this ethnic group migrated to Vietnam mainly from Guizhou, China, about three hundred years ago at the earliest. Many different groups arrived in several waves. The following are the routes of their principal migrations:

- The first wave brought about a hundred households to Dong Van district, in present-day Ha Giang province. According to Chinese historians, this occurred around the end of the Ming Dynasty and the beginning of the Qing Dynasty.

- The second wave, of some two hundred households, arrived around two hundred years ago in Dong Van district as well as Bac Ha district, in present-day Lao Cai province.

- The third wave, of around 10,000 people, originating from the Chinese provinces of Gwangxi and Yunnan, arrived in Lao Cai and Lai Chau provinces between one hundred and one hundred and fifty years ago.

The question of their origins has given rise to debate and opposing views, which persist even today. Some say they are of Man origin, or belong to the Tibeto-Burman linguistic family. This group lives in the Dong Dinh Lake area or in southern Sichuan province in China. But others have put forward the hypothesis that the Hmong's origins lie farther north, and even very far in the Luong Ha region.

In Vietnam, the Hmong now consist of six groups. These include the Hmong Dau (the White Hmong), the Hmong Si (the Red Hmong), the Hmong Du (the Black Hmong), the Hmong Sua (the Mixed Hmong), the Hmong Linh (Flower Hmong), and the Na Meo (the Water Meo). The Hmong may be found in many parts of Vietnam (often in highlands of 700–800 m above sea level), in all the mountainous provinces: Ha Giang (144,064 people), Lai Chau (110,013 people), Son La (81,951 people), Yen Bai (45,110 people), Cao Bang (38,433 people), Nghe An (17,935 people), Tuyen Quang (8,418 people), Thanh Hoa (3,640 people), Bac Thai (3,433 people), Hoa Binh (2,970 people), and Lang Son (1,068 people).

The number of communes in which the Hmong are found is small by comparison with their total population. This indicates that they tend to live in concentrated patterns (see Table 32).

Table 32: the number of communes containing the Hmong through three population censuses

YEAR	< 20%	21–40%	41–60%	61–80%	81–100%	TOTAL
1960	183	55	17	23	120	398
1979	365	82	32	34	164	677
1989	474	90	46	37	155	802

27. The Yao (Dao) ethnic group. The Yao call themselves Diu Mien or Kiem Mien. Diu is pronounced in Han-Vietnamese as *Zao* (but spelled Dao) while Mien means "human." So Diu Mien means Zao, or in English Yao; Kiem Mien means "people living in the forest," a rather one-sided name which could not be used for the ethnic group as a whole.80 In the past, other names used in Vietnam for this ethnic group included Man, Dong, Trai, Xa, etc. The Yao are supposed to originate from the Man group (ancestors of the present-day Hmong and Yao) scattered along the Yangtze and Pearl Rivers in China, from 2,000 B.C.[81] They began arriving in Vietnam during the eleventh century, from various places and along various routes.

Today in Vietnam there are thirty groups of Yao. Their main groups include the Yao Tien, the Red Yao, the Yao Quan Chet (which means tight trousers), the Yao Quan Trang (meaning white trousers), the Yao Thanh Y, the Yao Coc Ngang, the Yao Coc Mun, and the Yao Len Ten.

They are scattered over a vast area in the northern mountainous and midland provinces as far as Ninh Binh. The largest numbers of Yao are found in the provinces of Ha Giang (71,676 people), Cao Bang (60,336 people), Tuyen Quang (59,121 people), Lao Cai (56,264 people), Yen Bai (52,255 people), Quang Ninh (36,177 people), Bac Thai (33,043 people), Lai Chau (30,313 people), Lang Son (21,629 people), Son La (16,860 people), and Hoa Binh (10,373 people). In the last twenty years, thousands of Yao people have migrated to Tay Nguyen and southeastern Vietnam. For this reason, the number of communes containing Yao appears high by comparison with the size of the group, and it has increased markedly (see Table 33).

Table 33: The number of communes containing the Yao through three population censuses

YEAR	< 20%	21–40%	41–60%	61–80%	81–100%	TOTAL
1960	460	145	75	38	88	806
1979	579	166	61	34	52	892
1989	703	170	72	39	51	1035

28. The Pa Then ethnic group call themselves Pa Hung. In the past, neighboring ethnic groups referred to them as Meo Lai, Meo Hoa (Flowery Meo), or Meo Do (Red Meo). They migrated to Vietnam from Than Lo in China some two hundred years ago.

Today, the Pa Then group includes the Thuy (about one hundred people) in Hong Quang commune, Chiem Hoa district, Tuyen Quang province. The area over which Pa Then are found is vast, although it covers only ten communes (and in 1979 only eight). They account for less than 20% of the population in each commune in the district of Bac Quang (where they number 2,911), Xin Man (where they number 174), Hoang Su Phi (where they number 136) in Ha Giang province, and the district of Chiem Hoa in Tuyen Quang province (where they number 430).

29. The Tay people have lived in Vietnam for a very long time. Study of historical processes regarding the evolution of ethnicity shows that one branch of the Tay merged into the Kinh ethnic group. But a number of Kinh people moved to live and work in the upland border regions, and were themselves assimilated into local Tay groups there. Tay people have different names, like Tho, Ngan, and Phen, but Tay remains the official name recognized by all groups of the Tay ethnic community. At the present time the Tay include the following local groups:

- Tho Da Bac, a group with more than 16,000 people living in the communes of Da Bac district, Hoa Binh province. In the past they were known as Tho, a division of the Thai group.

- The Thu Lao, a group with more than 1,000 people living around the border between Muong Khuong and Bac Ha districts in Lao Cai province. The name Thu Lao is used for this group by the Han, but it has also been known as the Pu Lao, the Cu Lao, the Tho Lao and the Day.[22]

- The Pa Di, with more than 1,000 people living in several of the communes of Muong Khuong district, towards the border with Kim Binh district of Yunnan, China.[23]

Today, the Tay are found in almost all provinces and cities throughout Vietnam. They are, however, concentrated in the northwestern region of Viet Bac, which includes the provinces of Cao Bang (247,841 people), Lang Son (219,496 people), Bac Thai (173,213 people), Tuyen Quang (136,036 people), Ha Giang (121,056 people), Yen Bai (99,348 people), and Lao Cai (61,034 people).

In Tay Nguyen and southeastern Vietnam, there are tens of thousands of Tay people. For example, there are 8,303 people living in Dong Nai province, 6,605 people living in Lam Dong province, 3,119

Table 34: The number of communes containing the Tay through three population censuses

YEAR	< 20%	21–40%	41–60%	61–80%	81–100%	TOTAL
1960	481	157	181	176	171	1,166
1979	1,231	226	212	176	77	1,922
1989	1,617	193	207	180	107	2,304

people living in Thuan Hai province, and 1,741 people living in Gia Lai province. The number of communes in which Tay are found is very large. Only the Kinh and Hoa are found more widely (see Table 34).

30. The Thai ethnic group call themselves Tay, which means "human". *Phu Tay*, for example, means Thai people. According to their own records, their ancestors arrived in Vietnam in the ninth century, either from Sipsong Pan Na (Yunnan, in China) or along the Mekong River from Thailand.

The Thai group which came from Sipsong Pan Na divided into two further groups; one travelled along the Red River to Lao Cai, Yen Bai, and then to Son La, and the other travelled along the Da River to settle in Phong Tho, Quynh Nhai and Muong Lay. The group which came via the Mekong River travelled to Moc Chau, Yen Chau, Dien Bien and along the Ma River to western Nghe An province.[24]

The Thai in Vietnam now form two main groups: the Thai Trang (White Thai) and the Thai Den (Black Thai). The Thai Trang can be further divided into two small sub-groups. The first lives in the northern part of Muong Lay, Muong Te, and Phong Tho districts, as well as in Tuan Giao, Quynh Nhai, Sin Ho, and Tua Chua in Lai Chau province. The second lives in the southern areas of Moc Chau and Phu Yen districts in Son La province, and also in Van Chan district in Yen Bai province. Thai Den are now found in the districts of Van Chan (mainly in the Muong Lo valley) and Than Uyen in Lao Cai province, in Muong La, Thuan Chau, Mai Son, Song Ma, Quynh Nhai in Son La province, and in Tuan Giao, Dien Bien, and part of Phong Tho and Sin Ho in Lai Chau province.[25] Some also contend that the Thai in Moc Chau (Son La), Mai Chau (Hoa Binh), Thanh Hoa and Nghe An actually constitute a separate sub-group.[26]

Today, the Thai in Vietnam are concentrated mainly in the provinces of Son La (376,037 people), Nghe An (213,604 people), Thanh Hoa (177,836 people), Lai Chau (156,532 people), Lao Cai (37,485 people), Yen Bai (34,564 people), and Hoa Binh (25,923

Table 35: The number of communes containing the Thai through three population censuses

YEAR	< 20%	21–40%	41–60%	61–80%	81–100%	TOTAL
1960	123	42	48	58	190	461
1979	426	67	82	119	136	830
1989	556	69	77	112	158	972

people). In the central highland provinces, there are several thousand Thai people living in Lam Dong (3,731 people) and Dac Lac (3,153 people). In the thirty years between 1960 and 1989, the Thai population doubled (see Table 35).

31. The Nung ethnic group. One group of Nung have lived in Vietnam for a very long time, most of them having merged into the Tay. But most of the present-day Nung migrated into Vietnam several centuries ago. Different arrivals at different periods of time, from different points of departure, have led to the existence of dozens of local sub-groups. Groups that arrived more recently generally settled in less fertile areas of land. The Nung may be divided into two main groups, according to their names.

a. The first group, which consists of several sub-groups, are distinguished according to their special style of dress: Nung Khen Lai (those with patched sleeves); Nung Hu Lai (those who wear indigo scarves with white dots); Nung Slu Tin (those who wear short shirts and blouses to the waist), and so on.

b. The second group are named according to their place of origin, and the names are often taken from different Chau (an administrative division) in China. Examples include Nung An (the Nung from An Ket Chau), Nung Inh (from Long Anh Chau), Nung Phan Slinh (from Van Thanh Chau), Nung Chao (from Long Chau), Nung Quy Rin (from Qui Thuan Chau), Nung Loi (from Ha Loi Chau), and Nung Slin (from Sung Thien Chau).

Besides these groups, there are also others whose origins have not yet been established, such as Nung Din, Nung Xuong, Nung Vien and Nung Chu.[27]

The Nung are found in most of the provinces and cities of Vietnam, with the exception of Ben Tre, Quang Tri, Thua Thien-Hue, Tien Giang, and Quang Ngai, where there are less than ten in each. In each province, the number of Nung ranges from a few dozen to several thousand, but they are concentrated mainly in the midland and mountainous regions of north Vietnam, from the Red River basin to the coastal province of Quang Ninh. Since the 1950s, and increasingly in recent years, the Nung have been migrating to Tay Nguyen (Central Highlands) and the surrounding provinces. The Nung population for Lang Son is 268,010, in Cao Bang it is 185,614, in Bac Thai it is 59,180, in Ha Bac it is 51,530, in Ha Giang it is 46,207, in Lao Cai it is 17,996, in Tuyen Quang it is 11,670, in Ben Yai it is 10,732, in Dac Lac it is 18,594, in Dong Nai it is 10,927, and in Lam Dong it is 8,491. Since the migration rate of the Nung is high, the number of communes in which they are found is also high (see Table 36).

Table 36: The number of communes containing the Nung through three population censuses

YEAR	< 20%	21–40%	41–60%	61–80%	81–100%	TOTAL
1960	381	136	101	95	57	770
1979	948	151	101	89	65	1,354
1989	1,196	150	1,117	70	74	1,607

32. The San Chay ethnic group is the name used by both Cao Lan and San Chi to refer to themselves (as discussed earlier). Before arriving in Vietnam, these groups settled in Kham Chou, Lien Chou, Linh Son, and Loi Chou in Guangdong province, and in Thuong Tu and Ninh Minh in Guangxi province (China). They migrated to Vietnam towards the end of the Ming Dynasty and in the early part of the Qing Dynasty. Initially, they crossed the China-Vietnam border at Mong Cai in Quang Ninh province and other places along the border to Lang Son, but they later moved south and west to Ha Bac (now Bac Ninh and Bac Giang provinces), Bac Thai, Vinh Phu (now Phu Tho and Vinh Phuc provinces), Tuyen Quang, and Yen Bai provinces.[28]

The Cao Lan group now has a population of over 69,000 people, who live mostly in Tuyen Quang province, in the districts of Son Duong, Yen Son, and Ham Yen, and in the Ha Bac province in the districts of Son Dong, Luc Ngan, Luc Nam, and Yen The. They are also found scattered throughout Vo Nhai and Dong Hy districts of Bac Thai province, in Lap Thach district in Vinh Phu province and in Huu Lung district of Lang Son province.

The San Chi group has a population of 45,000 who are widely scattered throughout the districts of Phu Luong, Dinh Hoa, and Dai Tu in Bac Thai province, in Bao Lac, Cao Bang (provincial capital of Cao Bang province), Luc Ngan, Son Dong, and Tan Yen in Ha Bac province, in Binh Lieu and Tien Yen in Quang Ninh province, and finally in Son Duong in Tuyen Quang province.

Generally speaking, the San Chay are now clustered in the provinces of Tuyen Quang (42,819 people), Bac Thai (24,096 people), Ha Bac (18,047 people), Quang Ninh (9,003 people), Yen Bai (6,000 people), Cao Bang (5,109 people), Lang Son (3,483 people), and Vinh Phu (2,925 people). The number of communes in which San Chay are found increased nearly three-fold in the thirty years between 1960 and 1989 (see Table 37).

Table 37: The number of communes containing the San Chay through three population censuses

YEAR	< 20%	21–40%	41–60%	61–80%	81–100%	TOTAL
1960	76	20	9	3	9	127
1979	222	32	18	8	2	282
1989	300	32	12	5	3	352

33. The Giay ethnic group is the name this group uses to refer to itself. The Giay were formerly known by names such as Nhang, Giang and Sa. They are scattered over a large area stretching from Ha Giang province to Muong Te district (Lai Chau province). According to the current classification, the Giay include the Pu Na group, who are also known as the Cui Chu (referring to their origin in Guizhou province, China). The group is concentrated mainly in Phong Tho district in Lai Chau province, with a few residing in Cao Bang province.

Today, the Giay live mainly in Lao Cai province (18,554 people), Bat Sat district (8,497 people), the provincial capital (3,363 people), as well as the following districts: Bao Thang (2,398 people), Muong Khuong (1,458 people) and Van Ban (1,265 people). They are also found in Ha Giang province (9,848 people), in the districts of Yen Minh (3,564 people) and Meo Vac (3,152 people), and in Ha Giang provincial capital (1,258 people). There are also 6,694 living in Phong Tho district in Lai Chau province and 2,071 Giay people living in Van Chan district in Yen Bai province. The number of communes in which Giay lived doubled in the thirty years between 1960 and 1989 (see Table 38).

Table 38: The number of communes containing the Giay through three population censuses

YEAR	< 20%	21–40%	41–60%	61–80%	81–100%	TOTAL
1960	40	16	11	3	2	72
1979	101	13	7	2	1	124
1989	134	13	5	4	0	156

34. The Lao ethnic group is, in many ways, more like the Thai than the Lao Thay in Laos. Although the group is relatively small, it is scattered from Than Uyen in Lao Cai province (1,189 people) to Phong Tho (1,958 people), and as far as Dien Bien (3,285 people). They have also crossed over to Song Ma in Son La province (2,357 people) and down to Ky Son in the central province of Nghe An (437 people). There are also some 200 Lao people in the Central Highlands province of Dac Lac. Nevertheless, the number of communes in which Lao people live is not high (see Table 39).

Table 39: The number of communes containing the Lao through three population censuses

YEAR	< 20%	21–40%	41–60%	61–80%	81–100%	TOTAL
1979	23	3	0	1	0	27
1989	33	3	0	0	1	37

35. The Lu ethnic group numbers more than 4,000 people in Vietnam. The group is also known by other names such as Thay U, Thay Sin and Thay Hung. Thay is the common name of the Lao Thay group in Laos, which includes the Lu ethnic group. Other names used for the Lu include place-names, which refer to their place of residence. In Vietnam, the Lu are found only in Lai Chau (3,668 people), mostly in the Sin Ho (1,895 people) and Phong Tho (1,768 people) districts, where they are found in five communes. They live there mixed with the Lao and the Thai.

36. The Bo Y ethnic group. According to the current system of classification, the Bo Y ethnic group consists of two groups of people which are similar in many respects: the Bo Y and the Tu Di. The Bo Y are also known to the Chinese as the Pau Y, Chung Cha or Trong Gia. They immigrated to Vietnam around the middle of the nineteenth century from Vong Mo and La Dien in Guizhou province, China. They first arrived in Quan Ba and Dong Van districts in Ha Giang province. Later, many merged with other local groups such as the Nung and Giay.

The name Tu Di refers to the place Do Van in Guizhou province, China, where the group originated. They migrated to Vietnam and settled in some of the communes bordering China, in Muong Khuong district, Lao Cai province, around one hundred years ago.

Today, the Bo Y are found mostly in Lao Cai (907 people), Ha Giang (451 people), Tuyen Quang (30 people), and Yen Bai (22 people). Although they are scattered widely, they are not found in many communes. In 1979, they were found in seventeen communes: ten in Lao Cai, four in Ha Giang, and three in Yen Bai province. In 1989 they were found in twenty communes: ten in Lao Cai, seven in Ha Giang, two in Tuyen Quang and one in Yen Bai province. The proportion of Bo Y relative to the total population of these communes was less than 20%.

37. The Gia Rai ethnic group has the largest population of any group living in Tay Nguyen. The Gia Rai occupy a large area which extends over several provinces, including Kon Tum, Gia Lai, and Dac Lac. They are neighbors to the Xo Dang and Ba Na to the north, the Kinh in the east, the E De in the south, and to the west they meet the Vietnam-Cambodia border. Gia Rai, or Gio Rai (in French Jarai or Jorai), the name they use for themselves, means waterfall. The ancestors of this group may have come from the Iadun and Ialy Rivers. Their local sub-groups include the Chor, the Hdrung, the Arap, the Mthur, and the Tbuan.

The Gia Rai live in the following districts: Chu Pa (51,179 people), A Dun Pa (48,561 people), Chu Se (40,301 people), Chu Pong (26,096 people), Krong Pa (26,967 people), the provincial capital, Pleiku (12,002 people), Mang Giang (11,772 people) in Gia Lai province, Sa Thay (6,667 people), the provincial capital Kon Tum (5,563 people), Eahleo (6,255 people), Ea Sup in Dac Lac province (1,769 people), Ham Thuan Bac and Tanh Linh in Binh Thuan province, each with more than five hundred people. In terms of population, the Gia Rai outnumber the E De by 48,000, but they are found in twenty-five fewer communes than the E De (see Table 40).

Table 40: The number of communes containing the Gia Rai through two population censuses

YEAR	< 20%	21–40%	41–60%	61–80%	81–100%	TOTAL
1979	66	10	5	9	42	132
1989	99	9	15	11	20	154

38. The E De (Ede) ethnic group also call themselves the Anak E De (meaning E De people). The name derives from the term *e te* or *e de*, meaning bamboo forest, or those who live in bamboo forests. In the past, the E De community was known as Ra De (in French Rhade), but this name has fallen out of use over the past thirty years.

The E De can also be subdivided into some local sub-groups, such as the Kpa, the Adtham, the Krung, the Mthur, the Ktul, the Dhie, the Rue, the Krung, the Bih, the Blo, the Kdrao, the Dong Kay, the Dong Mak, the Ening, the Arul and the Hwing.

The E De live over an area which falls within the boundaries of Dac Lac province (179,134 people). They are present in all seventeen districts and provincial towns of the province, but tend to be concentrated in the districts of Chum Gar (33,586 people), Krong Ana (24,671 people), Krong Buk (21,431 people), and Krong Pach (20,840 people). The number of communes containing E De is the highest of all the ethnic groups living in Tay Nguyen (Central Highlands) (see Table 41).

Table 41: The number of communes containing the E De through two population censuses

YEAR	< 20%	21–40%	41–60%	61–80%	81–100%	TOTAL
1979	47	11	9	10	18	95
1989	114	15	21	11	13	174

39. The Cham ethnic group is also known as the Chàm, the Chiem, the Chiem Thanh, and the Hoi, and includes several local sub-groups as well: the Hroi (or Aroi), who live in the southwestern part of the central province of Binh Dinh and the northwestern part of Phu Yen province. They have lived in close contact with other ethnic groups, such as the Ba Na, the Gia Rai and the E De. As a consequence of this intermingling, the Cham now reflect these local influences. There are, however, some notable differences between the Cham group which lives in south-central Vietnam in the provinces of Ninh Thuan, and Binh Thuan and those Cham living in the southern provinces, who are Muslims. There are also Cham in Phan Ri who consider themselves to belong to the Kinh. Intermarriage between Cham and Kinh has also given rise to the Kinh Cuu (the name used by Kinh) or the Duon Cham (the name used by Cham). Today their origin is confirmed as being both Kinh and Cham, though they tend to register themselves as Kinh.[29]

The Cham are spread over a vast area stretching from the south-central province of Binh Dinh to the southernmost province of Minh Hai. At present, they are clustered in various districts in the provinces of Binh Dinh (3,219 people), Phu Yen (12,490 people), Ninh Thuan (41,786 people), Binh Thuan (21,237 people), Dong Nai (1,622 people), Ho Chi Minh City (3,636 people), Tay Ninh (1,816 people), and An Giang (11,585 people).

Most of the provinces in the Mekong River Delta contain between a few dozen to several hundred Cham. The number of communes containing Cham has increased between 1979 and 1989 by 100, almost 43% (see Table 42).

Table 42: The number of communes containing the Cham people through two population censuses

YEAR	< 20%	21–40%	41–60%	61–80%	81–100%	TOTAL
1979	207	7	7	5	5	231
1989	310	5	8	4	3	330

40. The Raglai ethnic group, Raglai (or Ranglai), has long been the official name of this group. They are also known by other names which refer to various place locations, such as Rai (in Ham Tan, Binh Thuan province) and La Oang (in Di Linh, Lam Dong province). They live in the highlands, over an area stretching discontinuously from Khanh Hoa to Ninh Thuan, Binh Thuan, and Lam Dong. Districts in which greatest numbers of Raglai can be found include Khanh Son (9,049 people), Khanh Vinh (8,791 people), Cam Ranh (6,350 people), and Dien Khanh (1,193 people) in Khanh Hoa province; Ninh Son (19,518 people), Ninh Hai (13,882 people), and Ninh Phuoc (3,100 people) in Ninh Thuan province; Tanh Linh (2,608 people), Bac Binh (1,927 people), and Ham Thuan Nam (1,799 people) in Binh Thuan province; Di Linh (780 people) in Lam Dong province. The number of communes containing Raglai did not increase substantially over the ten years between 1979 and 1989 (see Table 43).

Table 43: The number of communes containing the Raglai through two population censuses

YEAR	< 20%	21–40%	41–60%	61–80%	81–100%	TOTAL
1979	66	5	2	2	22	97
1989	68	5	4	6	19	102

41. The Chu Ru ethnic group, also known as Cho Ru, whose name means literally "those who migrated to the new land," live mainly in two districts of Don Duong (5,939 people) and Duc Trong (4,426 people) in Lam Dong province. There are also some three hundred Chu Ru in Ninh Son in Ninh Thuan province. The number of communes containing Chu Ru is small, and increased by only two between 1979 and 1989, from eleven to thirteen.

42. The Hoa ethnic group (Vietnamese of Chinese origin) in Vietnam is known by various names, such as the Guangdong, the

Hainan, the Lien Chau, the Trieu Chau, the Fukien, the Sang Fang, the Sia Fong, the Sang Fang, the Thong Nham and the Minh Huong. According to Chinese and Vietnamese sources, the Hoa in countries other than China are named after the various Chinese feudal dynasties during which they arrived in Vietnam, or after the Chinese localities from which they originate.

The Hoa migrated to Vietnam from a number of places, along a variety of routes, and at different times. The bulk of their immigration to Vietnam took place during the first half of the twentieth century. Today, they are found in almost all of the provinces and cities of Vietnam. Thirty-three of Vietnam's more than fifty provinces and cities contain over one thousand Hoa people. Hoa are, however, concentrated mainly in the following provinces and cities: Ho Chi Minh City (433,551 people), Dong Nai (99,779 people), Soc Trang (77,316 people), Minh Hai (41,006 people), Kien Giang (35,236 people), Can Tho (21,589 people), An Giang (17,910 people), Song Be (17,456 people), and Ha Bac (14,049 people).

The number of communes containing Hoa is very large; there are more communes containing Hoa than there are containing any other ethnic group, with the exception of the Kinh, in Vietnam (see Table 44).

Table 44: The number of communes containing the Hoa through three population censuses

YEAR	< 20%	21–40%	41–60%	61–80%	81–100%	TOTAL
1960*	711	59	31	20	32	853
1979	2,900	41	49	17	4	3,011
1989	2,739	46	21	23	3	2,832

* Only in the North from Vinh Linh northwards.

As the table above shows, the total number of communes containing Hoa in 1989 had diminished by 179, when compared with the 1979 figures. This fact is due to the large numbers of Hoa who emigrated in the late 1970s and early 1980s. Furthermore, some of the Hoa who stayed now consider that they to belong to other groups.

43. The San Diu ethnic group has long been known as the San Deo Nhin (meaning San Diu people). They are also known as Trai Dat, Man Dat, Man Quan Coc, Slan Dao and Son Man.[30]

The San Diu groups first migrated from China to Vietnam some three hundred years ago, at the end of the Ming Dynasty and in the early part of the Qing Dynasty. They travelled mainly to Ha Loi and Tien Yen and onwards to the coastal province of Quang Ninh, as well as to Hai Hung, Ha Bac, Thai Nguyen, Vinh Phu, and Tuyen Quang provinces.

The San Diu live in the semi-mountainous area north of the midlands and south of the mountainous provinces of north Vietnam. At present, San Diu are found in the provinces of Bac Thai (28,471 people), Vinh Phu (23,544 people), Ha Bac (17,060 people), Quang Ninh (14,691 people), and Tuyen Quang (8,133 people). There are also 1,249 San Diu living in Chi Linh district, Hai Hung province.

The largest number of communes in which the San Diu live is in Quang Ninh province. As can be seen in Table 45 below, the number of communes in which they were found increased between 1960 and 1989.

Table 45: The number of communes containing the San Diu people through three population censuses

YEAR	< 20%	21–40%	41–60%	61–80%	81–100%	TOTAL
1960	69	12	10	2	6	99
1979	194	19	6	2	1	222
1989	258	16	5	2	1	282

44. The Ngai ethnic group is also known as Xin, Le, Dan, Xuyen, Hac Ca and Ngai Lau Man. The Ngai refer to themselves as the San Ngai, which means mountain people. They consider themselves to be locals, although in fact their community is made up of several groups which immigrated to Vietnam from China some three hundred years ago. These groups tended to congregate in valleys, along rivers and coastal areas, and on islands. During the Vietnam-China border war, 1979 to 1980, many migrated to other places. Some have now registered themselves as members of other ethnic groups. In 1979, Quang Ninh province contained the third largest population of Ngai after Cao Bang and Bac Thai. However, in 1989, only two Ngai remained in Quang Ninh province, while Bac Thai became the province with the largest number of Ngai (436 people). In those communes containing Ngai, the Ngai population accounts for just 20% of the total.

Table 46: The number of communes containing the Ngai through two population censuses

Year	Bac Thai	Quang Ninh	Cao Bang	Tuyen Quang	Ha Bac	Dong Nai	Lang Son
1979	25	23	8	0	0	0	0
1989	27	0	1	3	3	5	2

45. The Ha Nhi ethnic group has the largest population of any of the groups speaking Tibeto-Burman languages. The Ha Nhi live in hamlets along the Vietnam-China border, in the districts of Muong Te (6,613 people), Phong Tho (1,755 people), Sin Ho (1,691 people), all of which are in Lai Chau province, and Bat Sat (2,213 people) in Lao Cai province. They refer to themselves as Ha Nhi, while other ethnic groups call them Uni or Xa Uni.

Ha Nhi ethic group have some sub-groups such as Co Cho, Lam and Ha Nhi Den (Black Ha Nhi). Most of Ha Nhi in Vietnam now came from Kim Binh district, Yunnan province, China, about three hundred years ago.[31]

Table 47. The number of communes containing the Ha Nhi through three population censuses

YEAR	< 20%	21–40%	41–60%	61–80%	81–100%	TOTAL
1960	11	6	1	3	2	23
1979	20	4	4	1	5	34
1989	18	5	2	1	4	30

46. The Phu La ethnic group. Currently, the Phu La ethnic group lives mainly in the province of Lao Cai (5,320 people). They are found in almost all of the districts of the province, with concentrations in Bac Ha (1,159 people), Van Ban (1,117 people), Muong Khuong (763 people), Bao Thang (702 people), and Cam Duong provincial capital (632 people). They are also found in the districts of Van Yen in Yen Bai province (483 people), Bac Quang (206 people), and Xin Man (138 people) in Ha Giang province and in Tua Chua (61 people) in Lai Chau province.

The Phu La includes several local sub-groups: the Phu La Hoa in Bat Sat district, the Phu La Den in Sin Man district, the Phu La Han in Bac Ha, Muong Khuong, and the Xa Pho in Lao Cai and Lai Chau. The number of communes containing Phu La shows unusual variation over the thirty-year period of the censuses. This is due to the emigration patterns of, particularly, the Phu La Han group.

Table 48: The number of communes containing the Phu La through three population censuses

YEAR	< 20%	21–40%	41–60%	61–80%	81–100%	TOTAL
1960	27	5	1	1	0	34
1979	54	5	2	1	0	62
1989	58	3	0	0	0	61

47. The La Hu ethnic group was formerly known as the Xa Toong Luong (Xa La Vang), the Kha Quy (Xa Quy), the Xa Puoi (Xa without dresses) or the Khu Sung (the poor). La Hu is the name the group uses for themselves and it means tiger. The La Hu include several local groups: the La Hu Su (La Hu Vang or Yellow La Hu), the La Hu Na (La Hu Den or Black La Hu) and La Hu Phung (La Hu Trang or White La Hu).

The La Hu often live on inaccessible mountain slopes in hamlets consisting of only four or five houses. Today, the La Hu are only found in Muong Te district in Lai Chau province (5,279 people), in the communes of Pa Ve Su, Pa U, Ca Lang, Bun To and Nam Khao. The number of communes containing La Hu has shown abnormal fluctuations (see Table 49).

Table 49: The number of communes containing the La Hu through three population censuses

YEAR	< 20%	21–40%	41–60%	61–80%	81–100%	TOTAL
1960	3	2	0	0	2	7
1979	7	2	1	0	2	12
1989	5	1	1	1	2	10

48. The Lo Lo ethnic group live in hamlets mixed with Tay, Nung, Hmong, and Thai, along the Vietnam-China border, from Bao Lac (Cao Bang province) to Dong Van and Meo Vac (Ha Giang province), and to Phong Tho (Lai Chau province). Today they live in the four provinces of Cao Bang (1,565 people), Ha Giang (1,068 people), Lai Chau (441 people), and Tuyen Quang (22 people).

Lo Lo is the name these people use to refer to themselves, but they were formerly known by such names as O Man, La La, Qua La, Di Nhan, Di Gia and Lac To. In China, they were known as Di. Today in Vietnam, the Lo Lo consist of three main sub-groups: the Lo Lo Den (or Man Di No) who live mainly in Ha Giang, the Man Te, who live mainly in Cao Bang province, and the Lo Lo Hoa (or Man Di Qua or Man Di Pu), who live in Ha Giang province.

Table 50: The number of communes containing the Lo Lo through three population censuses

YEAR	< 20%	21–40%	41–60%	61–80%	81–100%	TOTAL
1960	14	2	2	0	0	18
1979	17	1	0	0	0	18
1989	19	1	0	0	2	20

49. The Cong ethnic group was previously found in Muong Te district, Lai Chau province. In the population census of 1979, Cong were also registered in Muong Lay district, but in the 1989 census they had spread to various other districts such as Muong Te (863), Muong Lay (185 people), Dien Bien (176 people), and Tuan Giao (11 people). The number of communes containing Cong, however, only totals eight.

The Cong are also known as the Xa, or the Xa Kong. They have also frequently been given place names by other ethnic groups, such as Cong Tac Nga, Cong Bo Kham, and Cong Bo Lek. These names refer to the residential areas of the group before they left China and migrated to Vietnam. The Cong refer to themselves as Xam Khong, which means iron mine. The name Cong may well originate from this.[32]

50. The Si La ethnic group members refer to themselves as Cu De Su. They were also formerly known as the Kha Pe (a name which distinguishes their mode of wearing skirts from that of the Thai). According to folklore, the Si La migrated to Vietnam from Laos, arriving first in Muong Tung in Lai Chau province, and then in Muong Lay and Muong Te.[33] At present, the Si La have a population of only 480 people living in Muong Te district. In 1979, they were present in five communes of this district, but in 1989 they were found in only three. There were a few Si La living in the Mekong River Delta in An Giang province.

51. The La Chi ethnic group, like many other groups, is also known by other names such as the Xa. They may also be the group, referred to as the Xa Tu, mentioned by Le Quy Don in his book *Kien Van Tieu Luc.*

The name La Chi appeared early in the twentieth century.[34] Today, the La Chi live mainly in Ha Giang province (7,542 people), in the districts of Xin Man (3,094 people), Hoang Xu Phi (2,274 people), and Bac Quang. In Bac Ha district in Lao Cai province, there are 168 La Chi. In 1979, the La Chi were found in twenty-five communes and in 1989, in forty-two (see Table 51).

Table 51: The number of communes containing the La Chi through two population censuses

YEAR	< 20%	21–40%	41–60%	61–80%	81–100%	TOTAL
1979	22	0	1	1	1	25
1989	39	0	0	2	1	42

52. The La Ha ethnic group also used to be known as Xa. Together with the Cong and the Khang, the La Ha were also called Xa Khao. neighboring ethnic groups referred to the La Ha by many different names; the Thai called them the Xa Cha, the Xa Uo, the Xa Khao, the Xa Tau Nha, and the Xa Poong, Xa Pung, while the Khang called them the Bu Ha, and the Kho Mu called them the Pua.

The La Ha have only two main sub-groups: the La Ha Ung (Water La Ha) and the La Ha Phlao or Rla Phlao (Dry La Ha). The La Ha have long been present in northwestern Vietnam and may well be responsible for clearing wet paddyfields in the mountain valleys of the region, prior to the arrival of the Thai.

According to the book, *Ethnic Groups of the Austro-Asiatic Language Family*, the La Ha are said to have been concentrated in the following communes of the northwestern region: Nam Gion, Chieng Dong, Pi Toong, Chieng Xang, Muong Bu in Muong La district; Chieng Xom, Noong Lay, Nam Et, Liep Te in Thuan Chau district; Nam Can, Ta Mit, and Pha Mu in Than Uyen District.[35] According to the 1989 census, however, the La Ha were found mainly in Thuan Chau district (1,263 people) in the communes of Chieng An, Noong Lay and Liep Te, while in Muong La district, 121 La Ha were found in Ngu Chien commune.

53. The Co Lao ethnic group comprises several local groups: the White Co Lao or Tu Du in the Co Lao language (meaning "people who wear white scarves in mourning"), the Blue Co Lao or Ho Ki (meaning "men who often wear long blue dresses"), and Red Co Lao or Voa Do (meaning "skirts woven with red thread").

The first Co Lao group migrated to Vietnam from China around two hundred years ago. Today, they live only in Ha Giang province (1,462 people), scattered throughout the districts of Hoang Su Phi (560 people), Dong Van (401 people), Yen Minh (237 people), and Vi Xuyen (96 people). The number of communes in which Co Lao were found increased slightly between 1979 and 1989 (see Table 52).

Table 52: The number of communes containing the Co Lao through two population censuses

YEAR	< 20%	21–40%	41–60%	61–80%	81–100%	TOTAL
1979	11	1	0	0	0	12
1989	17	0	0	0	0	17

54. The Pu Peo ethnic group. The Pu Peo is the name they are called by Tay-Nung ethnic groups. Formerly they called themselves the Ka Beo. The Pu Peo were also known by other names, such as the La Qua and the Pen Ti Lo Lo (indigenous Lo Lo). They migrated from China to Vietnam over a period from before the eighteenth century, while the last arrivals came in the early nineteenth century at the latest.

Today, the Pu Peo live mainly in Ha Giang province (319 people), scattered throughout the districts of Dong Van (165 people), Yen Minh (98 people), and Bac Me (46 people). There are also around seventy Pu Peo living in other places. The number of communes containing Pu Peo was ten for both 1979 and 1989, and the proportion of Pu Peo in each commune was less than 20%.

CHAPTER III

THE PROCESS OF MIGRATION AND POPULATION REDISTRIBUTION

T HROUGHOUT history, there has always been migration; it has played a part in the development of societies from primitive and tribal societies to modern ones. Research studies on migration, regardless of their time frame or area of focus, share the same objective, which can be held to explain and/or reform society. However, only a few large-scale studies of migration have actually been carried out.

The British demographer, E. Ravenstein, on the basis of his research on migration in several countries, draws the following conclusions:

1. The number of migrants decreases as distance increases. Migrants who travel long distances are generally those who end their journey in major commercial or industrial areas.

2. The process of migration often takes place in the following manner: a well-developed city attracts people from surrounding areas. The resulting void is filled by other migrants who move in from farther away. Thus, the number of migrants is inversely related to the distance between origin and destination, while it is directly related to the importance of the host center.

3. Each main migration has a reverse compensation.

4. Urban dwellers tend to migrate less frequently than do rural dwellers.

5. Women migrate in greater numbers than men, at least over short distances.

6. Increases in the number of migrants correspond to the development of industry, trade, and transport facilities.

7. Although many factors influence migration, economic factors are by far the most important.[1]

Although some controversy has arisen from statements such as these, which were made a century ago, the principal points remain valid today. While there is no intention to carry out any in-depth analysis here, some comments on the Vietnamese situation are in order.

I. AN OVERVIEW OF MIGRATION IN VIETNAM

IT is well known that the mainstay of Vietnamese agricultural production has always been the area of land lying between the mountains and the plains. However, with the passing of time, population pressure on this area became so great that it could no longer support those living there. In order to survive, therefore, the ancestors of today's Vietnamese were forced to expand their territories and move into neighbouring areas. First they moved eastwards, and later towards the south. Early migration was spontaneous, but later waves of migrants were the result of state policies implemented by various regimes.[2]

According to information retrieved from both documents and geological surveys, an average of more than one thousand hectares of land is reclaimed from the sea each year in the region from Thai Binh southwards. This is an area sufficient to feed some four to five thousand people.[3] Mangrove swamps may have enlarged by 80–100 m per year.[4] Vestiges of the sea may be seen in many places in the Red River delta area and in the north central delta. Than Phu, for example, which was once an estuary, now lies inland to Kim Son and Nga Son, some 10 km from the coast.[5] In the early part of the tenth century, Bo Hai Khau was a coastal area, whereas it is now the capital city of Thai Binh province, lying some 14 km from the coast. Phat Diem Cathedral, too, was originally built on the coast, but now, some 100 years later, it is to be found 10 km inland. Similarly, the Hong Duc Dike (in Yen Mo, Ninh Binh province) was constructed in 1427 to hold back sea water, but now it lies 20 km from the sea. Also, the hill which can now be seen in Quynh Luu district, Nghe An province, was once an island on the Cam River.[6]

Land clearance in the midland and mountainous regions began around the time of the Le-Tran dynasties. The cleared land was then used for the establishment of farms and villages, including Vinh Khang (Tuong Duong, Nghe An province) and Dang Chau (Quy Hoa, Vinh Phu province). The main labor force used in this work consisted of prisoners.

Up until the beginning of the Le Dynasty, a system known as the "army in the service of farming" was applied. During Le Thai To's reign from 1428 to 1433, the regular army, comprising some 100,000 men, was divided into five sections. While one was responsible for keeping guard, the other four were employed in farming. Under King Le Thanh Tong, the regular force was increased to 160,000 men but these were divided into only two sections which took turns at farming.[7]

Generally speaking, the policy of clearing land and establishing farms continued to develop under Le Thanh Tong and in some areas was implemented in the following way:

- Citizens who were allocated land by Le Thanh Tong recruited others to clear their land for them;

- The village inhabitants themselves organized land clearance;

- Land clearance was organized centrally by the state administration.[8]

Most of the forty-three plantations established in the period of 1470–80 were in the north, although a few were also being created in the south.

In the period of conflict between the two northern feudal chieftainships, the Trinh and the Nguyen, agricultural economy declined dramatically, particularly on the Thanh-Nghe plain which suffered severely. Fields were left fallow and people were forced to leave their homes and migrate to other areas. No measures were taken at this time by the feudal leaders to promote land reclamation or develop irrigation systems. Meanwhile, in the south, though it too was ravaged by war, economic development remained less affected. Many of the impoverished farmers of the north migrated southwards to clear land there, where they set up many new villages. Land clearance projects, then, transformed the area from a sparsely populated and backward region into a prosperous and populous one. At the beginning of the fifteenth century, Thuan Hoa had a population of only 5,662, with 7,100 *mau* or Vietnamese acres (10,000 sq m) of cultivable land. By 1776, however, the population had risen to 126,857, and there were 265,507 *mau* of cultivable land.[9] According to Nguyen Dinh Dau, the first clearance of land in Dong Nai-Gia Dinh probably took place at the end of the sixtenth century or in the early part of the seventeenth century. "The Vietnamese peasants themselves used their rough hands and dynamic minds to turn deserted land into fertile land. They went first and the State followed. Where settlement and farming were stable, the administrative authorities came to set up district headquarters to rule the region and collect taxes. It is true that the south was the sweat, tears, and blood of the Vietnamese people; the south was truly Vietnam."(Nguyen Dinh Dau, 1992)[10]

Nguyen Anh continued the policy of the "army supportive farming" until the beginning of the Nguyen dynasty. Two types of plantations were organized: one managed by soldiers, the other by employed peasants. In 1804, the first kind was expanded to all parts of Quang Ngai province in Central Vietnam, and by 1810 the second kind had spread to all six provinces in the south and had become militarized. Every plantation had to offer half of its population to local army service. This means that Gia Long (as Nguyen Anh was known after he became emperor) tried to develop the first type of plantation, while at the same time pursuing a policy of tax reduction and miltarization of the second type, with the aim of developing the economy, military capability, and political force.

During Minh Menh's rule, all the plantations of the second kind described above were transformed into the first kind. All 10,000 civilians were brought into military service. The plantations were named at this time according to municipality and they were also given military code-names.

During Thieu Tri's reign, little attention was paid to the system of military plantations. The state decreed that all plantations in the four provinces of Son Tay, Dinh Tuong, Khanh Hoa, and Bien Hoa be dissolved, and their land handed out to local villages as communal land.

Under Tu Duc, the question of military plantations was again raised, when the central government realized their importance in the defence of border areas.[11] Plantations were strongly promoted, especially after the appointment of Nguyen Tri Phuong as viceroy of the south in 1850. After six months in office, he outlined a proposal whose first aim was "to organize meetings with people to develop plantations to help them earn their living." Phan Thanh Gian, then deputy viceroy of southern Vietnam, reported to King Tu Duc that An Giang and Ha Tien were crucial areas. He therefore asked permission to recruit men from plantations along the Vinh Te River in order to form two brigades of fifty men each who would then work reclaiming land in these two provinces. Towards the end of the nineteenth century in the north, Do Ton Phat, who was in charge of land reclamation, directed the establishment of Que Hai canton and four Ly hamlets (in present day Hai Hau district, Nam Ha province). Eight thousand hectares of land were reclaimed and 2,600 people were settled there to engage in sedentary farming.[12]

During the Nguyen dynasty, since many areas in the south remained unpopulated, migration tended to be from the north southwards. Out of the twenty-five points listed for land reclamation for the period 1802–1855, sixteen of these concerned the south, while only two concerned the north. One was specific for the capital city of Kinh Ky, while six others were for nationwide application.[13]

So migration began, then, with people moving spontaneously from one area to another, looking for a place in which they might earn a living. Later, however, the State began to involve itself in the controlling and direction of migration, and various tensions arose. The State justified its policies with the idea that *"Phi doc bat anh hung"* (lack of monopoly organization is anti-heroic), and readily ostracized those who refused to comply. The State did not hesitate to force people to migrate. The forced migrations which took place under the Nguyen lords in the south are worthy of note in this respect: the army was used to conscript citizens from seven districts in present-day Ha Tinh province to go and clear land in the deserted Chau Thanh region in the south. People were also encouraged to migrate voluntarily. Nguyen Cong Tru organized many migrations, two of which earned him a place in history. The first of these was when he ordered the army to reclaim land, and once it was ready, invited landless peasants to settle in the new area, in the Quang Yen region of present day Quang Ninh province. The second was larger, and consisted of the establishment of two districts: Tien Hai (in 1828) and Kim Son (in 1829).[14] Nguyen Cong Tru also set up municipalities in Hai Hau and Giao Thuy districts, and within a relatively short period of time tens of thousands of landless people were able to settle there.

Other achievements include those of Nguyen Van Thoai, who was responsible for the digging of both the Sap Thoai Ha and the Vinh Te canals, and also directed the reclamation of land in Chau Doc. Truong Minh Giang set up twenty-five hamlets along the Vietnam-Cambodia border, and Nguyen Tri Phuong set up twenty-one plantations and one hundred and twenty-four hamlets in the six-province region of the south.[15]

During this period, the Nguyen dynasty adopted a policy for the movement of people according to the following six principles:

1. The State allocated land and seed as a loan to be repaid. Those who refused to engage in farming were fined three baskets of rice paddy and were forcibly conscripted into the army. Not surprisingly, these measures were unpopular.

2. The State recruited people, whom it paid with money, seed, and goods, and sent them to settle selected areas. This was applied mainly in the south. In the north it was used only once, by Nguyen Cong Tru, for land reclamation in the Minh Huyen region of Hai Duong province.

3. The State compensated those who volunteered to clear land in their own areas with money and goods. After the harvest, the farmers repaid an equivalent to what they had received from the State. This system was applied only in Quang Tri and Bien Hoa provinces.

4. The State hired men to clear land. Once the fields were ready, the men were allowed to farm them and taxes were only levied six years later.

5. The State encouraged individual citizens to recruit other men to clear land. Successful employers were then awarded mandarin status and allowed to hold administrative positions.

6. All citizens of the land were allowed to apply to clear land in the place of their choice. Three years after clearance, the first taxes were then levied upon the land.[16]

In order to promote land reclamation in Nam Dinh and Ninh Binh, Nguyen Cong Tru asked the court to grant permission to anyone able to recruit fifty men to set up a village. That person would then be appointed village headman. Similarly, he asked that anyone able to recruit thirty men be allowed to establish and head a hamlet. The organizational forms used by Nguyen Cong Tru included:

- A village of 50 men with 600 *mau* of land, 100 *quan* (the ligature, an old unit of money) to build houses, 300 *quan* to buy buffaloes and cows and 40 *quan* to buy agricultural tools.

- A hamlet of 30 people with 400 *mau* of land (60, 180 and 24 *quan*)

- A farm of 15 people with 200 *mau* of land (30, 90 and 12 *quan*)

- A sub-hamlet of ten people with 12 *mau* of land (20, 60 and 8 *quan*)

So, on average, a buffalo, a harrow, a plough, a spade, a hoe, and a sickle were allocated for every five persons.

In the south in 1853, Nguyen Tri Phuong and Phan Thanh Gian proposed that volunteers from anywhere in the country might recruit at least ten landless people to settle in an area of their choice in southern Vietnam, set up hamlets and farms, and receive a certificate. Those responsible for recruiting could be either regular citizens, or convicts living in the south.

If the organizer was a regular citizen and recruited at least thirty people to set up a hamlet, he was exempted from state taxes and forced labor. Those who recruited fifty or more were promoted to chief civilian village notable (mandarin eighth grade). Those who succeeded in recruiting two hundred or more were promoted to chief civilian village notable (mandarin ninth grade) and appointed governors. Additionally, recruits were exempted from taxes, including the poll tax, for ten years.

If the organizer was a convict who recruited more than fifty people, and his recruitment was certified by village officials and relatives, he was acquitted either temporarily or permanently, as long as the recruitment target was fulfilled.

One year after these measures had been introduced, 124 new hamlets had been established. In contrast with the situation in the north, those who recruited men to go southwards were awarded higher bonuses, but were not given money or other means of production by the State.

Thanks to these concrete policies, the Nguyen dynasty could expand its settlements and ensure agricultural development. This was, however, only a process of migration, albeit one on a nationwide scale. Although peasants moved from one region to another, the economic structure of the country was barely affected by it. People's living standards saw no significant improvement. The Nguyen dynasty did not limit the movement of people's drifting and wandering. This sometimes resulted in large populations inhabiting small areas, the most extreme example being that of the Red River Delta.

From the sixteenth century onwards, Vietnam's feudal regimes began to disintegrate, a process which finally ended in the nineteenth century. There were constant disputes among members of the ruling classes, and this had devastating effects on the already fragile economy. This paved the way for the occupation by the French.

After the French colonial regime was established, colonial entrepreneurs and administrators pursued harsh policies to repress, exploit, and effectively impoverish the people. Many social contradictions, which were already quite pronounced, became increasingly severe. The primary strategy was to monopolise the economy, a strategy which left half of the Vietnamese peasants landless.[17] Having already been subjected to exploitation by feudal landlords, the peasants were now further marginalised by the French; they lived in abject poverty and misery.

With regard to southern Vietnam, the French considered themselves the owners of the entire region, based on what they called their "legally conquered ownership." They issued a number of decrees expressing this ownership, including a decree signed on 11 April 1861 concerning the appropriation of 2,500 ha of land for the construction of Saigon, which was to be the new capital for the French colonists. A further decree (signed 5 November 1863) ordered the removal of people from Hiep Hoa village in the southern region. On 25 February 1864, a decision was made to allow the French capitalists to lease or sell the whole of the Dai Don land area for a twenty-five year period.

In northern and southern Vietnam, the French employed a policy, euphemistically termed "legal diplomacy," to appropriate the land of the citizens.[18] In 1888, the Indochinese governor issued a decree allowing the landowners and colonialists to set up plantations in those areas designated "land without owners." This was mainly fertile land from which peasants had been previously driven away. The land of the Can Vuong and Van Than insurrection armies and that of peasants who had been evacuated was thus considered "ownerless," as were the terraced fields of the ethnic minorities living in some of the northern provinces, along the Truong Son Range, and in the Central Highlands. Much of southeastern Vietnam too became "land without owners," and was consequently appropriated. Schemes such as these meant that by 1890, the French had appropriated 10,900 ha, by 1900 they had 301,000 ha, and by 1912, a total of 470,000 ha, throughout the whole country. Southern Vietnam accounted for 308,000 ha, central Vietnam for 26,000 ha, and northern Vietnam, 136,000 ha.[19]

During a ten-year period (1920 to 1930), the French appropriated a further 775,700 ha of land, including 104,000 ha in northern Vietnam, 168,400 ha in central Vietnam and 503,300 ha in southern Vietnam. According to the incomplete statistics that are available, by the end of 1930, a total of 1,245,424 ha of agricultural land had been taken over by the French colonialists for the establishment of plantations alone. This area is almost equal to that of the land cultivated by Kinh (ethnic Vietnamese) in southern Vietnam at the end of 1912 (1,530,000 ha).[20]

As a consequence of these policies, many farmers were driven into bankruptcy and the number of landless people increased dramatically. In the period 1936 to 1939, around half of the 1,933,000 adult men living in the Red River Delta were without land. Nationwide, almost two thirds of the farmers, some 13 million people, were without land.[21]

In desperation, people began migrating. Between 1802 and 1806, people from 372 municipalities and villages on the right bank of the Red River were forced to move away. In 1827, the people of 108 municipalities and villages in Hai Duong alone left their native areas, leaving 12,700 *mau* of land fallow.[22] To attract the "ranks of the unemployed" to work for dirt-cheap wages, the French made great efforts to develop the plantation economy. By 1890, the country had 116 plantations and hamlets owned by French, and by 1901 the number had increased to 717.[23]

By the final decades of the nineteenth century, the plantations comprised not only rice cultivation, but also coffee, tea, and rubber. Alongside plantations, the French also set up a mining industry in

Vietnam. Coal was first extracted from Phan Me mine, Thai Nguyen province, in 1910. Later came the Thanh Tuyen mine (1915), the Dong Trieu mine (1916), and the Trang Bach mine in Hai Dong province (1917). By 1916, a total of 17,000 people were employed in mining.

Other industries were established as well. The Ba Son Shipyard was founded in Saigon in 1864. This was only two years after the French had begun building the city, and the population was still small. By 1883, however, the population of Saigon-Cho Lon was over 100,000. By 1895, there were more than 200 rice-husking mills which prepared rice for export. By 1906, there were already a total of ninety factories in the country. By 1909, there were 55,000 people employed in industry, plantations, and trading. Nam Dinh Textile Mill alone employed some 7,000 workers, while Hai Phong Cement Plant employed another 1,500.

According to statistics gathered by the Indochinese Labor Inspection Department, there were 140,000 workers in 1929. Of these, 53,000 were miners, 86,000 were factory workers and traders, and 81,000 were employed in the plantations.[24]

Farmers were now also being forced away from their farms and into work in public services, such as road and fortification construction, and dike and canal digging. When these projects were completed, they attracted migrants from other parts of the country and new villages mushroomed. In 1881, the French began building the Saigon-My Tho railway and in 1890 the rails were laid for the Phu Lang Thuong to Lang Son railway and later the Phu Lang Thuong to Hanoi railway, which was completed in five years. Following this, the Hanoi to Yunnan (China) railway was constructed, using manpower forced from thousands of farms in northern Vietnam. It is estimated that some 200,000 farmers were forced from their native villages to participate in the completion of the Yen Bai to Yunnan section of the railway.[25]

Migration throughout the whole country increased rapidly during the nineteenth and twentieth centuries. Despite a certain amount of migration from the plains towards the mountains, the general migratory trend continued to be from the north to the south.[26] The delta provinces, due to their already high population densities, continued to build dikes and reclaim land from the sea.

The Red River Delta was the area which witnessed the greatest out-migration waves at this time. In the late nineteenth and early twentieth century, on average, the south received 4,000–5,000 migrants from the north, while the center received 1,000–2,000.[27] Over 170,000 plantation workers arrived in Saigon harbour from the northern and central regions between 1923 and 1931. Some were recruited on three-year contracts, but many moved spontaneously to seek work in the plantation or industrial sectors, or to settle in urban areas and set up small trading businesses.

The migrants came mainly from the provinces of Nam Dinh, Ha Dong, Thai Binh, Hai Duong, Hung Yen, Thanh Hoa, and Nghe An. Very few of those from the central or southern-central regions migrated, and of those who did, most settled in the Central Highlands. Exploitation of Kon Tum province began in 1851.

As for the Mekong Delta region, most of the migrants came from southeastern Vietnam, not from the northern or central regions. The intensity of migration at this time meant that the population of southern Vietnam increased rapidly from less than two million in 1861, to three million in 1901, to 4.6 million in 1936, and 5.6 million in 1943. This means that during this period, the population of southern Vietnam increased by 2.8 times, while the population of the north doubled, and that of the center rose by 50%.

In short, over a period of less than one hundred years, migration in Vietnam increased at a very high rate, primarily as a result of colonial policies aimed towards maximizing profits.[28] For this reason, the peoples' lives and Vietnamese society were full of inequality. For many, the growing class contradictions, injustice, and poverty meant that people's living standards could only be improved and ultimately solved through democratic revolution (involving the liberation of the nation), and socialist revolution.

After the August 1945 revolution, which freed the Vietnamese from colonial rule and established the first socialist state in Southeast Asia, the Vietnamese engaged in a protracted war of resistance against the French. People were evacuated from the cities and plains areas temporarily occupied by the enemy. They moved to the midlands and mountainous regions, known as the "free" or "liberated" zones, where they set up new towns and temporary settlements. This was the first step in a new stage of Vietnam's migration history. These moves were not only made for economic reasons, and did not follow traditional migration routes; they responded to the exigencies of revolution and war. The economic and demographic structures of the free zones were given a new impetus for development, and the agricultural, trade, handicraft, and industrial sectors all received a boost from the new situation.

With the Geneva Agreement in 1954, peace was restored in the north and the country was temporarily divided into two parts. This agreement sparked a massive migration movement. Party workers,

workers, civil servants, students, as well as ordinary people, returned to urban areas, towns, and villages in the plains from the resistance bases and liberated zones in the midlands and highlands. This flow reversed the migration patterns established during the first years of the war of resistance. In addition, hundreds of thousands of officers and soldiers and members of revolutionary families in the south regrouped and returned to the north. Hundreds of thousands of people working for the French colonial administration and army, as well as others, primarily Catholics, migrated south. This was one of the century's great migrations, both in terms of the number of people involved and for the short time in which it took place.

With the country now divided into two parts, migration patterns began to assume different characteristics. In the south, artificial patterns of urbanization occurred. After inciting and supporting the French landlords to seize land from farmers, which was allotted to them by the revolutionary administration during the war of resistance, Ngo Dinh Diem then forced French landlords to resell the land to him (according to Decision 57 on Agrarian Reform).[29]

Land loss, unbalanced economic development, and the consequences of the war caused by the American neo-colonialists and the regime in South Vietnam, caused many rural people to move to the towns and the cities to earn their living. In the three years 1965–1967, for example, more than two million people had to leave their home villages.[30] By 1972, some 4.8 million people in the south had to leave their home villages for urban areas to seek jobs. That meant that one-third of the population in South Vietnam migrated.

In the 1969–1972 period, the United States military levelled more than 3,000 populated areas, that is 26% of the residential areas, in order to concentrate people into "strategic hamlets" and "refugee camps," as well as cities and towns where they could be more easily controlled.[31] As a result, development in the south was very unbalanced. For example, in 1960, there were 191,630 workers in Saigon, but 48,890 of them worked for the processing industry. In the whole of South Vietnam, the number of workers was 54,000 in 1955; 59,300 in 1960; 120,000 in 1966; and 175,000 in 1968, but the number of plantation workers was 51,500 in 1958; 26,000 in 1968; and only 10,000 in 1975. In particular, the number of employees working for American-run establishments was 7,600 in 1964; 51,000 in 1965; 145,900 in 1968. However, the growing impact of the war on Saigon, especially the Tet offensive in 1968, lowered the number of Vietnamese employees at American-run establishments from 128,000 in 1970 to only 100,000 in 1971.[32]

The number of unemployed in southern urban areas increased daily. Their numbers were swelled by migrants from rural areas who lost their land due to the war. This phenomenon greatly complicated the social situation in urban areas and throughout South Vietnam as this time.

In the north, the war caused by the French had serious consequences, and after the French colonial army withdrew, 150,000 people were left unemployed, including 100,000 in the cities. In addition to the problem of the long-term unemployed, which could not be resolved very quickly, a further difficulty presented itself. This was the rather large number of people from upland and rural areas who now returned to the cities and towns, and also took time to find work and earn a stable living. Famine broke out at this time, further increasing the number of newly unemployed. In 1955, the number of jobless people in Hanoi was 20,753, Hai Phong 31,000, Nam Dinh 4,222, Hong Quang 2,385 people.

The success of land reform went some way towards solving the unemployment problem and had a positive impact on the redistribution of population in certain areas. One measure which helped deal with the problems of unemployment, unbalanced population, and labor distribution was the creation and expansion of new construction sites, state farms, enterprises, and factories, as well as the restoration of the existing ones built by the French. The state farms made a remarkable contribution to this issue. The number of state farms increased markedly from ten in 1955 to forty-one in 1959, and fifty-six in 1960. In 1955 alone, the number of workers drawn to the state economic sector included 40,000 for the railways, 40,000 for transport and irrigation work, and 15,000 for the Hong Quang mining region.

In 1958, the State employed thousands of workers and employees to work at the central and local levels. For this reason, the number of local enterprises also increased rapidly. By 1965, north Vietnam had 927 local enterprises.[33]

During the six-year period of economic rehabilitation and reconstruction, there were sizeable migration movements, in terms of both scope and intensity, in North Vietnam. If, during this period in the south, most of the rural farmers were forced to rural areas to earn a living, in the north, the reverse held true; a great number of people left urban areas to go to rural, mountainous, and industrial areas. A rationally constituted working class thus came into being. Over subsequent years, the number of workers further increased, particularly in the industrial sector. For example, the total number of workers in industry was 111,900 in 1960, rose to 220,900 in 1965, 285,000 in 1970, and 355,800 in 1975.

The resolution of the Third National Congress of the Communist Party (1960), as well as resolutions passed at the Party Central Committee's plenums, focused a great deal of attention on migration and the redistribution of labor. In particular, the Central Committee's resolution on agricultural development (at the fifth plenum in July 1961), which was part of its first five-year plan 1961–1965, stated, "Regarding the clearing of land by the people, it is necessary to make full use of fallow land and wastelands along rivers and sea coasts. The clearance of small and nearby plots of land should be combined with the organization of lowland people to clear land in the mountainous regions, relying on the organizational strength of agricultural cooperatives as well as the State's positive support and aid."

In February 1963, the Political Bureau of the Party Central Committee issued Resolution No. 71/NQ-TW. Two months later, the Party Central Committee issued Resolution No. 8 for the mobilization of people in the plains to participate in economic development in the mountainous regions, to expand the total land area under cultivation, and to build new economic zones. It set the target of reclaiming another 450,000 ha (including state farms) over five years. By 1965, the average land per capita in the country had increased by 180 %.

Upland provinces received and welcomed laborers coming from the plains, and also arranged appropriate population distribution patterns. To help accomplish this, the Political Bureau of the Party's Central Committee began implementing Resolution No. 71, and, particularly, Resolution No. 38 (1968), which was designed to encourage sedentary forms of farming. Although some lessons remain to be learned from this experience in order to produce better results, the implementation of this policy over a fifteen year period achieved some noteworthy successes.

According to a 1984 report from the Central Resettlement Committee, by 1982, 47,771 households (totalling 267,580 members and 103,176 working hands) had been made sedentary, and 114,443 ha of land had been cleared for cultivation, including 39,172 ha of wet rice fields and 75,321 ha of subsidiary crops.

During the twenty years of Vietnam's partition (1955–1975), traditional migrations were sometimes disrupted in the north. Attention was still paid to reclaiming land from the sea and dredging rivers, but the main trend of migration in this period was from south to north and east to west. From 1 March 1960 to 1 April 1974, the period between the two population censuses, some 380,000 people emigrated from the plains to the midland and mountainous regions to settle down or to work. However, the level of migration in each region and province varied. The Red River Delta an provides example in Table 53.

Table 53: Number of people moving from the lowland to the upland regions
(1960–1974)[34]

(unit: person)

Areas	Total number of migrants	Number of recruited or mobilized*	Settlers in new economic zones
The whole of northern Vietnam	384,000	188,000	164,000
Hanoi	14,000	9,000	4,000
Hai Phong	16,000	6,000	7,000
Ha Son Binh (former)	28,000	12,000	14,000
Hai Hung (former)	65,000	31,000	29,000
Thai Binh		31,000	28,000
Ha Nam Ninh (former)	85,000	35,000	43,000

* There were other reasons for migration besides mobilization or recruitment for the development of new economic zones in the mountainous regions.

In the period to the liberation of South Vietnam (1975), as discussed earlier, the trend of migration was mainly to the midlands and mountainous regions and the former Zone 4. The main aim was to carry out population redistribution and land clearance for agricultural production in local areas, over short distances, and on a small scale, under the guideline, "Relying mainly on agricultural cooperatives, with support from the State." Many localities launched campaigns "Twinning districts and communes in the mountainous regions with those in the plains," "Everyone contributes to property," "Communes build communes and cooperatives build cooperatives," etc.[35]

When the country was completely reunified, there was another major migration. Traditional patterns, interrupted for twenty years, now resumed. Tens of thousands of cadres, workers, and State employees, together with their family members, returned to live and work in the south. The withdrawal of the United States' military and the subsequent collapse of the government of South Vietnam created a very high number of unemployed, forcing the Vietnamese State to try to solve the problem. According to statistics of the population census of southern Vietnam conducted on 2 May 1976, there were approximately 283,000 unemployed people in southern urban areas. The largest number was in Saigon, next came Hau Giang (now Can

Tho), Quang Nam-Da Nang, Nghia Binh, Dong Nai, Song Be, and Tien Giang.[37] In addition to this, from 1976 to 1980, about 20,000 workers in light industry in southern Vietnam quit their jobs.[38] The social situation became more complicated as a consequence. To create jobs for all these people, the situation required policies which would redistribute the population and, in particular, the labor force across the entire country. In the south, the government proceeded to mobilize and move tens of thousands of people from urban areas to be resettled in rural villages and new economic zones.

By 1988, that is, twelve years later (1976–1988), 3.6 million people (nearly 1.5 million of them of working age) had gone to build new economic zones across the entire country. In other words, 280,000 people (and 110,000 workers) moved each year. Regions which witnessed major migrations included the Red River Delta (610,000 people) and the former Zone 4 (230,000 people). Regions which received large numbers of immigrants included Tay Nguyen (the Central Highlands–610,000 people), southeastern Vietnam (160,000 people), the Mekong River Delta (230,000 people), as well as the midlands and mountainous regions in north Vietnam (200,000 people). The scale of migration between regions was also large (see Table 54).

Table 54: Emigration scales between regions in the 1976–1980 period [38]

(unit: person)

No.	Regions	Intra-region migration	Inter-region	
			emigrants	immigrants
1	Northern midland and mountainous region	224,000	6,000	207,000
2	Red River Delta	95,000	610,000	
3	Former Zone 4	362,000	231,000	
4	Central coastal region	329,000	210,000	34,000
5	Central Highlands	231,000	400	616,400
6	Southeastern region	595,000	200,000	163,300
7	Mekong River Delta	507,000		237,000
	Total	2,343,000	1,257,400	1,257,400

In inter-regional migration, the Red River Delta and the former Zone 4 was an area of out-migration and received no new migrants. The Mekong River Delta on the contrary, was a zone of in-migration. Tay Nguyen was the region receiving the largest number of immigrants, accounting for 49.02% of the national total during that period of time.

The migration to destination regions met the requirements of the regions and their main economic sectors. It created a change for the better in the redistribution of labor and population between regions in the whole country. When we look at the organization of production and settlement, we can see that many new economic zones, four hundred state farms and forestry enterprises, and hundreds of cooperatives and production collectives were formed. Many new communes and districts were set up. Newly cleared land was mostly in the midland, mountainous, border regions and on islands, which were all seen as key strategic areas for national defence and security. The formation of a system of stable populated regions with newly cleared land has contributed to the solid defence of essential regions throughout the country. This is one of the fundamental successes of the resettlement policy during this period.

In the 1981–1988 period, the relocation of population was important in terms of its scale and intensity. Throughout the whole country, 900,000 people of working age and their families, a total of more than two million people, were mobilized to build new economic zones; this included 280,000 people of working age and their families, a total of 560,000 people, who moved between other provinces. The Red River Delta saw the largest number of out-migrants. In eight years, 154,000 people of working age and their families, a total of 301,000 people, migrated from this region. Out-migrants in this period, besides building new economic zones on the new lands to expand agricultural cultivation, also supplemented the labor force of some sectors, such as the rubber industry (175,000), coffee plantations (40,000), and forestry (13,000). A total of 23,000 demobilized soldiers also moved to build new economic zones. With this work force, 400,000 ha, including 200,000 ha for food production, were cleared and brought into production. In places of out-migration, 98,000 ha of gardens and cultivable land were left behind.[39]

In short, the government programs for redistributing the country's population, implemented over the fifteen year period since reunification, exhibited some special characteristics. Intra-regional relocation and relocation of population over short distances accounted for a large proportion of the total figures when compared with relocation outside the region and over long distances. If in the 1976–1980 period there was almost no disparity in these two forms of population relocation,[40] in the two following periods, this disparity became obvious.

In the 1981–1985 period, intra-regional migration accounted for 67%, in the 1986–1989 period, 83%. This was shown in each sub-region, as well as in provinces where the relocation of population was conducted. The frequency of migration tended to reduce, reaching about 2%–2.5% by the end of the period (see Table 55).

Table 55: Frequencies of emigration to build new economic zones[41]
(unit: %)

Year	Frequencies	Year	Frequencies
1976	7.1	1983	3.5
1977	6.9	1984	6.5
1978	9.1	1985	6.6
1979	4.9	1986	5.7
1980	1.6	1987	4.2
1981	2.2	1988	3.3
1982	2.7	1989	2.3

In short, in the thirty years since the start of the program to mobilize the population to build new economic zones, Vietnam relocated 4.82 million people to different parts of the country to clear and reclaim land. Many new communes, districts, and new economic zones were created as well. In the 1960–1974 period, 920,000 people migrated and in the 1976–1990 period, the figure was 3,880,000 (see Table 56).

Table 56: Number of migrants from 1976 to 1990[42]
(unit: 1,000 persons)

	1976–1980		1981–1985		1986–1990		Total 1976–1990	
	Qty	%	Qty	%	Qty	%	Qty	%
Total	1,520	100	1,260	100	1,100	100	3,880	100
Inter-region	852	54	840	66	930	84.5	2,595	67
Outside the region	695	46	420	34	170	15.5	1,285	33
South-south	294	-	83	-	33.6	-	410.6	-
North-south	206	-	323	-	126.1	-	654.1	-
North-north	195	-	14	-	1.7	-	210.7	-

However, this migration mostly involved rural farmers who moved from one place to another, and their production mode remained the same, creating no new commodity products for society.

II. MIGRATION OF ETHNIC GROUPS

WE touched earlier, in discussing the distribution of ethnic groups, on the migration of ethnic groups and gave an overview of migration throughout the country. Although we dealt with the general situation, we were mainly concerned with the migration of the majority Kinh people. The previous sections gave statistics on the population of the Kinh in mountainous regions. In this section we shall discuss the proportion of the Kinh in the two regions which were formerly considered the home of the ethnic minority groups (see Table 57).

Table 57: Proportion of the Kinh in the northern mountainous region
and Tay Nguyen
(unit: %)

No.	Provinces	1960	1979	1989
1	Ha Tuyen (former)	18.2	33.00	32.92
2	Cao Bang	3.4		4.20
3	Lang Son	10.0	15.63	15.26
4	Lai Chau	9.2		19.35
5	Hoang Lien Son (former)	27.8	45.96	45.07
6	Bac Thai (former)	58.9		68.27
7	Son La	12.0	20.25	18.04
8	Quang Ninh	63.9		89.23
9	Hoa Binh	13.7	32.37	30.97
10	Gia Lai-Kon Tum	36.93*		49.34
11	Dac Lac	51.42*	60.91	70.75
12	Lam Dong	66.55*		76.41

* 1976 statistics (Archive documents of the Institute of Ethnology).

It is clear from Table 57 that from 1960 to 1979 (or from 1976 to 1979 with regard to three provinces in Tay Nguyen Central Highlands), in both the northern mountainous region and Tay Nguyen, the Kinh population increased rapidly. But from 1979 to 1989, the Kinh population in the northern mountainous region was either constant or declined remarkably. However, in Tay Nguyen, the figures continued increasing at an unprecedented rate.

This is because by 1979, the northern mountainous provinces witnessed a border war with China, and many efforts were made in the region as part of the struggle for self-defence. As already noted, the traditional north-south pattern of migration was disrupted and as a result, the northern mountainous regions continued to attract more people. After the country was reunified, the north-south migration flow resumed and became the predominant direction of migration for

Kinh from the Red River Delta and midland provinces, the former Zone 4 and central coastal region. However, most of the population in Tay Nguyen did not originally come from the northern provinces, but from central and south-central provinces (see Table 58).

Table 58: Proportion of the Kinh who came to the Central Highlands from other provinces in 1975–1985 period[43]

(unit: %)

No.	Provinces	% compared with total	No.	Provinces	% compared with total
	TOTAL NUMBER OF PROVINCES	100.00			
			7	Ha Bac (former)	0.03
1	Thai Binh	9.58	8	Thanh Hoa	0.13
2	Ha Nam Ninh (former)	9.98	9	Nghe Tinh (former)	5.16
3	Hai Hung (former)	8.25	10	Binh Tri Thien (former)	15.53
4	Ha Son Binh (former)	3.95	11	Quang Nam-Da Nang (former)	21.55
5	Hanoi	4.58			
6	Vinh Phu (former)	0.07	12	Nghia Binh (former)	19.58

In the past, lowland Kinh people had a distinct viewpoint concerning the uplands: these were places of "terrifying ghosts and poisoned water," "fearful mountains and dangerous waters," places where "people go, but do not come back." In general, the Kinh were too frightened to travel to these places. But over the last half-century, due to a number of factors, such as war, demographic explosion, the requirements of economic and cultural development laid down by the State, and because of the progress made in the health, education, culture, and transport sectors, this outlook has changed. The uplands have now become an attractive place, and many Kinh move there from the plains to look for a better livelihood.

While, in the early years of the twentieth century, Kinh were rarely to be found in upland communes and districts, today Kinh households are scattered throughout the majority of the villages of the northern uplands and Tay Nguyen, where they live alongside members of other ethnic groups (see Table 59).

Certainly the migration of Kinh people to upland areas might have benefited from further discussion to improve its implementation. But the presence of Kinh there has helped diversify the distribution of population in the uplands; the situation of other ethnic groups regarding their settlement pattern throughout the country is now

Table 59: Number of communes having Kinh in northern mountainous regions and Tay Nguyen (1989)

No.	Province	Total number of communes	Communes where Kinh people are living	Per cent (%)
1	Ha Giang	172	96	55.81
2	Tuyen Quang	145	141	97.24
3	Cao Bang	223	128	57.40
4.	Lang Son	224	216	96.43
5	Son La	193	145	75.13
6	Lai Chau	151	124	82.20
7	Lao Cai	170	118	69.41
8	Yen Bai	174	166	95.40
9	Bac Thai (former)	254	253	99.61
10	Quang Ninh	176	176	100.00
11	Hoa Binh	207	196	94.68
12	Kon Tum	66	51	77.27
13	Gia Lai	143	110	76.92
14	Dac Lac	178	176	98.88
15	Lam Dong	118	113	95.76
	Total	2,594	2,209	85.15

better balanced. At the same time, it created favorable conditions for ethnic groups in Vietnam to further their mutual understanding and help each other to co-exist and develop.

Let us examine the situation of ethnic minority groups in the northern upland regions. Some of these groups have lived in Vietnam for a very long time. But the majority moved across the border from the north, as we have already seen, responding to different processes at different times in their history. Some were affected by war or were forced to flee; some were wanderers. Sometimes the region was very sparsely populated, and sometimes large numbers of in-migrants arrived, changing the ethnic composition of the area, creating disequilibrium in the population structure, and giving rise to social problems.

The Vietnam-China border is 1,463 km long (1,088 km on land and 383 km of rivers and streams) with 153 communes in thirty-one districts and the provincial towns of the six provinces: Quang Ninh, Lang Son, Cao Bang, Ha Giang, Lao Cai, and Lai Chau. These administrative divisions lie opposite more than 100 communes of fifteen districts of the two Chinese provinces of Quangxi and Yunnan In Vietnam there are 444 villages and hamlets lying along the border with hundreds of thousands of people from twenty-five ethnic groups: the largest are the Nung, Tay, Hmong, and Yao. In many areas close to the border, people of the same ethnic group live on both sides of the border. Some 60–80% of them have close relations, like family and clan members or close friends, on both sides. For example, in Y Ti and Ngai Thau communes (Bat Xat district, Lao Cai province), 489 households with about 3,188 people in fourteen villages have relatives on the other side of the border, and after 17 February 1979, 284 people left for the other side of the border.[44]

Over the ten or so years after the border war broke out (17 February 1979), there were some abnormal demographic movements in this region. Some headed northwards to China on the other side of the border, while others moved deeper into Vietnam, including many who moved down to southern Vietnam and Tay Nguyen. The migration occurred along the whole border, even where it had been peaceful for long periods, and was common to almost all ethnic groups. The constant changes meant, in fact, that no definite tendency or direction could be discerned from these movements. Most border districts saw high levels of migration both within the district and to other places. For example, many communes in Bac Me district (Ha Giang province) experienced population increases due to the arrival of a large number of migrants from border districts. Their arrival caused many difficulties for the local authorities and people. Forests and forest lands were destroyed and land grabbing occurred daily.

Moreover, there was "horizontal" migration (from east to west). Some of the Tay, Nung, Hmong, and Yao who had been living in the border provinces for many generations now moved westwards to Yen Bai, Son La, and Lai Chau provinces and, sometimes, even farther. This flow took place over time; it was not continuous, but was entirely spontaneous in character.[141]

However, if the "vertical" migration flow in the border region has returned to normal over the past few years and the people who left their native villages have come back to their old residential areas (except those spontaneous migrants from north to south who will be discussed later), the "horizontal" migration flow was not a continuous or mass movement. Its impacts can still be seen today; this means that such migration has recurred in some areas and at different periods.

Besides such sudden migrations just mentioned, many ethnic minority groups throughout Vietnam are migratory by nature. In the past, they migrated short distances, within a single commune, district or province. Recently, they have tended to migrate over longer distances. Statistics on migration for the five-year period (1 April 1984 to 1 April 1989) were released by the 1989 population census, and are reproduced in Table 60.

Table 60: Population over five years of age by sex and permanent residence on 1 April 1984

No.	Ethnic group	Total population > 5 years old	Per cent of population on 1 April 1984 compared with total of over 5 years of age					
			Same district Same province		Different district Same province		Different province	
			Total	Females	Total	Females	Total	Females
	TOTAL	54,247,000	95.41	53.00	1.79	51.48	2.63	42.78
1	Kinh	47,276,652	95.15	53.22	1.83	51.37	2.85	42.65
2	Tay	976,351	95.50	51.67	2.19	55.24	2.21	45.95
3	Thai	838,897	98.66	50.98	0.66	47.89	0.51	39.35
4	Hoa	803,920	96.41	50.08	2.18	53.37	1.33	48.18
5	Khmer	749,543	98.70	53.31	0.82	48.27	0.38	49.80
6	Muong	746,380	97.36	52.29	1.68	56.93	0.77	29.79
7	Nung	585,207	94.52	51.40	1.67	56.36	3.70	46.19
8	Hmong	437,543	96.86	50.52	2.36	50.56	0.61	50.33
9	Yao	382,740	97.15	50.22	1.83	51.58	0.90	49.45
10	Gia Rai	197,660	99.37	51.98	0.43	35.77	0.16	34.81
11	Ngai	892	94.17	46.78	2.02	44.44	3.70	57.57
12	E De	157,453	98.95	52.12	0.82	42.22	0.17	41.60
13	Ba Na	111,190	99.56	50.56	0.28	43.91	0.11	43.37
14	Xo Dang	76,891	98.61	50.85	1.23	45.04	0.10	52.56
15	San chay	92,449	97.81	50.97	0.75	55.65	1.36	43.22
16	Co Ho	75,088	98.12	52.26	1.41	42.45	0.33	35.77
17	Cham	81,140	98.22	51.60	0.91	38.40	0.83	40.98
18	San Diu	76,179	98.27	49.86	0.79	60.33	0.83	39.97
19	Hre	75,214	99.65	51.32	0.16	43.54	0.07	35.71
20	Mnong	54,282	98.75	52.40	0.97	44.57	0.22	42.97
21	Raglai	58,044	99.36	52.29	0.49	36.39	0.11	42.62
22	Stieng	40,988	99.39	52.98	0.41	47.30	0.16	49.25
23	Bru	32,534	96.83	49.95	2.51	49.02	0.46	48.34
24	Tho	41,120	98.39	51.17	0.72	65.87	0.69	37.89
25	Giay	30,967	92.07	50.48	7.44	50.84	0.40	51.61
26	Co Tu	29,130	98.78	49.47	0.76	36.37	0.13	38.46
27	Gie-Trieng	21,206	98.65	51.74	0.57	33.05	0.76	53.08
28	Ma	20,820	97.20	52.27	2.18	49.23	0.52	50.45
29	Kho Mu	33,916	98.56	49.89	1.16	45.29	0.15	37.25
30	Co	18,459	99.33	48.05	0.37	55.07	0.20	62.16
31	Ta Oi	20,832	97.77	49.60	1.59	50.75	0.17	30.55
32	Çho Ro	12,125	97.34	52.86	2.27	50.54	0.35	44.15
33	Khang	3,115	99.42	51.24	0.09	33.33	0.32	30.08
34	Xinh Mun	8,598	99.54	51.07	0.07	50.00	0.16	14.28

No.	Ethnic group	Total population > 5 years old	Per cent of population on 1 April 1984 compared with total of over 5 years of age					
			Same district Same province		Different district Same province		Different province	
			Total	Females	Total	Females	Total	Females
35	Ha Nhi	10,221	98.92	50.77	0.88	26.66	0.08	25.00
36	Chu Ru	8,605	80.81	52.94	18.90	53.47	0.13	18.18
37	Lao	7,571	98.24	49.78	0.41	32.26	0.42	43.75
38	La Chi	6,503	85.94	50.54	13.70	51.29	0.26	23.53
39	La Ha	1,131	99.64	49.87	0.35	50.00	-	-
40	Phu La	5,218	93.94	51.69	5.00	50.95	0.96	46.00
41	La Hu	4,485	99.64	52.39	0.06	-	-	-
42	Lu	2,974	99.29	46.85	0.57	35.29	-	-
43	Lo Lo	2,559	97.93	50.32	1.75	59.09	0.27	42.85
44	Chut	1,984	96.82	49.44	1.86	54.05	1.36	46.15
45	Mang	1,887	98.99	50.35	0.90	47.05	0.10	-
46	Pa Then	2,923	98.87	51.40	1.06	51.61	-	-
47	Co Lao	1,179	95.16	51.05	4.58	53.70	0.08	-
48	Cong	1,012	98.42	52.96	1.48	20.00	1.48	-
49	Bo Y	1,172	97.78	47.51	1.88	68.18	1.88	-
50	Si La	484	97.52	55.19	1.86	66.66	1.86	-
51	Pu Peo	307	85.01	-	14.33	54.55	14.33	-
52	Brau	185	98.92	58.24	0.54	-	0.54	-
53	O Du	25	100.00	48.40	-	-	-	-
54	Ro Mam	182	100.00	50.56	-	-	-	-

The table above does not show any of the traditional characteristics of ethnic minority groups in Vietnam, in particular, migration over short distances (within the commune or district). The striking nature of the current situation regarding the migration of ethnic minorities has many causes. Among these are the natural environment and eco-system, issues of social history, as well as cultural and economic factors. But the most important influence was the ethnic minorities' farming practices.

Some ethnic minority groups live a stable and sedentary life, and practise wet-rice agriculture. But as everyone knows, the majority of groups living in Vietnam's uplands practise shifting cultivation, or they live off forest products and forest land which they turn into terraced rice fields, which they then abandon when the land can no longer be used for farming. The Hmong and Yao people offer the best examples of this type of farming practice. A further type involves "slash and burn" clearance techniques on land which is then cultivated for two or three harvests, according to its fertility; a different place will then be chosen, and the farmers will return to the old place after five or ten years. This is known as semi-nomadic farming. Mon-Khmer ethnic groups commonly practise this type of agriculture.

The unscientific exploitation of the land has caused degradation of the natural environment, and forest resources have been exhausted. Forest loss leads to other losses: wild animals and plants become rarer; the soil is eroded and rapidly degraded. If the top 20–30 cm of soil is forest land, it will take an estimated 500,000 years for the layer to erode. If the land is only covered with grass, it will take 80,000 years. If the land is cleared and used for crops, the figure drops to forty years, while exposed and less fertile soils (currently classified in Vietnam as bare hills and wasteland), last less than twenty years. As productive topsoil is washed away, moisture levels drop, producing laterite and lumpy soils over time. Shifting cultivation results in very unstable yields and does not meet minimum daily needs for food, clothing, and housing. Therefore, the people have to have other occupations such as collecting and picking forest products, hunting, and fishing, etc. But due to forest destruction, such products have become increasingly scarce. It is worth noting that the rapid population growth (both natural and policy-driven) has increased pressures on the land and forced many to migrate. In other words, people were forced to replace their semi-nomadic farming practices with nomadic residential behavior. Moreover, due to a low level of comprehension of scientific and technical advances, natural calamities, crop failures, and epidemics are still considered to be caused by ghosts and evil spirits which force people, according to their traditional religious beliefs, to move to other places.

Due to such farming modes and ways of life, the ethnic minority groups living in the mountainous regions have always moved their place of residence. Sometimes, the whole hamlet or village moved. In many cases, whole clans or groups of families moved. According to reports of the Ministry of Forestry's Sedentarization Board, by the early 1980s, the number of people leading nomadic lives or performing semi-nomadic farming was more than two million. Most of the ethnic groups living in the mountainous regions, particularly in the highlands and remote areas, had some members who, at certain times, took part in such migrations. The ethnic groups with many people leading a nomadic life include the Hmong, the Kho Mu, and the La Hu in the northern mountainous region, and the Xo Dang, Gie-Trieng, and Gia Rai in Tay Nguyen.

Before the launch of the sedentarization program, the socio-economic situation of nomadic and semi-nomadic farmers was very low; their primary farming mode was shifting cultivation, which involved sowing seeds in holes, using very rudimentary farming tools to meet their own subsistence needs. Livestock were raised by simply letting the animals move around freely. For this reason, labor productivity was low. They did not have surplus products and always faced food shortages; they had low levels of education and high rates of morbidity. Food intake per capita in many places was only 70–100 kg.

To address this problem, the Political Bureau of the Party's Central Committee supplemented Resolution No. 71 in 1968 with Resolution No. 38 issued by the Council of Ministers. The latter resolution set out a national policy on sedentarization. This 1968 law was aimed at combining sedentarization with collectivization, resolving the problems of nomadic farming and forest destruction at the same time. The resolution had three clear objectives: to achieve stable livelihoods, stable mind-frames, and ethnic unity. By 1983, the necessary material foundations for this program were in place, in particular, the means of agricultural production (arable land) for the cultivation of cereals. The local people reclaimed 110,000 ha of land for both wet-rice cultivation and terraced fields, with an average of 300 to 550 sq m per person. New hamlets and villages were built, together with other public welfare projects. New houses were also built for 70,000 households (or about 420,000 people).

By 1990, after nearly 22 years of sedentarization, the Vietnamese Communist Party and State had devised many policies to improve the ethnic minority people's lives. In many places, sedentarization was implemented in combination with socio-economic development and the consolidation of national defence and security efforts. Some 133,000 ha of land was reclaimed and cleared for wet-rice cultivation and turned into terraced fields. Intensive farming was practised on 50,000 ha of land, and plantation crops such as tea, cinnamon and coffee were planted on nearly 45,000 ha. Reservoirs and irrigation projects numbering 2,700 were built, bringing the total land area under cultivation for food production to between 300 sq m and 800 sq m per capita. In 1993 alone, the State invested Dong 110 billion in the implementation of 445 projects, including 344 projects in hamlets and villages, 76 projects for farmers in forest enterprises, and 25 projects at forest enterprises. Sixty of those projects organized the clearing of 4,000 ha of land for agriculture, 12,000 ha of land for industrial crops and special crops, 160 small irrigation projects, 1,000 km of roads and the construction of 160 commune health centers, schools, and headquarters. About 1,000 households had been moved to new settlement areas where house gardens and farms were established (according to *Nhan Dan* newspaper on 17 February1994).

However, planning in many areas remained poor and was often carried out in isolation, focusing solely on food production. Some places just followed a model without taking into account the local natural and ethnic conditions. Some local authorities just paid attention to the quantity, not quality of their activities. For this reason, the achievements in the following years negated those of previous years. This meant legalizing the nomadic process. Many of those nomadic groups who were supposed to settle down to sedentary farming did not, and the percentage of nomads in some ethnic groups actually increased.

In the previous sections, we discussed the number of communes where ethnic groups live and their proportion of the total population of each commune. In this section, we will give examples of two provinces which are home to many ethnic minority groups: Lao Cai (in the northern mountainous region) and Dac Lac (in the Central Highlands).

Although Lao Cai province does not have the largest number of ethnic groups, it has seen many changes in residential and migration patterns, since it lies between the northeastern and northwestern regions (see Table 61).

Table 61. Number of communes where ethnic minorities live in Lao Cai through the three population censuses (unit: communes)

No.	Ethnic group	1960	1979	1989
1	Tay	47	75	101
2	Thai	14	31	33
3	Hmong	79	109	117
4	Yao	72	110	114
5	Nung	41	52	53
6	Muong	0	11	29
7	Hoa	75	23	19
8	San Chay	0	0	3
9	Giay	34	44	53
10	La Chi	1	2	2
11	Bo Y	-	10	10
12	Phu La	24	48	43
13	Ha Nhi	7	7	6
14	Lao	-	1	2

Several ethnic minority groups show a remarkable increase in the total number of communes in which they can be found. They are the Tay, Hmong, Muong, Thai, and Giay. Other ethnic minority groups are now found in fewer communes. They are the Hoa, Phu La, and Ha Nhi. Migration is the primary reason for these changes. Some people spontaneously left the province for other provinces. Many others crossed to hamlets or villages located on the other side of the border.

Dac Lac, a province in the center of Central Highlands has also witnessed many changes as a result of the migration process (see Table 62).

Table 62. Number of communes where ethnic minorities live through the two population censuses in Dac Lac

(unit: communes)

No	Ethnic group	1979	1989
1	2	3	4
1	E De	74	104
2	Mnong	44	65
3	Co Ho	2	6
4	Ma	1	6
5	Raglai	0	6
6	Kho Me	15	13
7	Cham	0	7
8	Gia Rai	3	4
9	Bru	1	1
10	Ta Oi	0	1
11	Gie - Trieng	1	1
12	Xo Dang	3	7
13	Hre	2	7
14	Tay	16	89
15	Thai	23	39
16	Yao	4	7
17	Nung	20	79
18	Muong	30	45
19	Hoa	35	36
20	Tho	5	9
21	Lao	3	5

The table above shows that the ethnic groups (also called local subgroups) who have long lived in Dac Lac, as well as in Tay Nguyen, have migrated a great deal within the region. Tay Nguyen was the area which attracted many ethnic minority people.

Two characteristics of ethnic minority migration remain the short distance moves and the practise of shifting cultivation. However, a large proportion of people have settled down to sedentary farming and life in line with the policies of the Communist Party and State. The population of the ethnic minority groups which either lived in or moved to urban areas varies over time in terms of proportion. This population, in general, was not very numerous (see Tables 63 and 64).

Table 63. Population of some ethnic groups living in cities in northern Vietnam through the three population censuses

Ethnic group	Year	Hanoi*	Viet Tri	Thai Nguyen	Hai Phong**	Nam Dinh***	Total
Tay	1960	2,309	-	1,208	-	-	3,517
	1979	4,265	488	5,684	1,472	246	12,155
	1989	4,088	216	7,726	258	67	12,355
Nung	1960	-	-	430	-	-	430
	1979	1,817	138	1,666	635	47	4,303
	1989	1,037	54	3,768	97	5	4,961
Muong	1960	322	17	-	-	-	339
	1979	608	137	231	1,062	23	2,061
	1989	675	130	632	67	25	1,529
Thai	1960	-	-	-	-	-	-
	1979	670	223	143	518	317	1,871
	1989	495	52	216	16	25	804
Yao	1960	-	-	-	-	-	-
	1979	24	16	253	100	139	532
	1989	77	30	270	11	1	389

* Excluding districts which have been separated and merged with Ha Tay and Vinh Phu province.
** According to statistics of the 1960 population census, 39 people registered as "other ethnic groups."
*** According to statistics of the 1960 population census, 206 people registered as "other ethnic groups."

Table 64. Ethnic groups living in Buon Ma Thuot provincial capital and Dalat City through two population censuses

No.	Location	E De		Mnong		Co Ho		Ma	
		1979	1989	1979	1989	1979	1989	1979	1989
1	Buon Ma Thuot	31,986	31,148	1,707	175	14	27	-	2
2	Da Lat	7	7	3	18	904	1,404	10	13
	TOTAL	31,993	31,155	1,710	193	918	1,431	10	15

Table 63 shows that in 1979, there was an increase in the population of the five ethnic groups listed here in the five cities (the Tay increased by 245.6%, the Nung 900.7%, the Muong 507.9%, the Thai from zero to 1,871 people, and the Yao from zero to 532 people). Thai Nguyen City may be a special case, being a city where two ethnic minority groups of Tay and Nung have lived for a long time, but other cities have received ethnic minority peoples who came to work at government offices and enterprises. During the 1979–1989 period, except in Thai Nguyen City, the number of ethnic minority peoples (as mentioned above) decreased. This was mostly because they returned to their native villages to work or retire. We may conclude from this that cities and towns in the mountainous regions do not attract ethnic minority workers and laborers.

E De, Mnong, Co Ho, and Ma are local ethnic groups in the two cities shown in Table 64, and one would expect their numbers to grow at a rate corresponding to the natural growth of the population. The table shows, however, that not only did they not increase, or increased only slightly, but in some cases the numbers actually fell. We may once again conclude that urban areas, even when built in the traditional regions where they have lived for generations, are not attractive to such groups.

A recent feature of some ethnic group behavior, evident over the last three to five years, has been spontaneous, or so-called "free" migration. This means migration which does not follow any State plan and creates many problems for government departments, ministries, and local authorities. In the past, ethnic groups followed their semi-nomadic traditions and practised intra-regional migration. But now, even those minorities which have long lived a sedentary life are starting to migrate over very great distances.

In three Central Highland provinces and Song Be province alone, by 1991, 19,000 households including some 85,000 people of different ethnic groups arrived, migrants from other provinces. In 1990 and the first half of 1991 alone the figure was 8,250 households with 34,065 people.[46] The State issued plans for the implementation of planned migration through Communiqué No. 68/TB dated 13 April 1991, and Communiqué No. 39/TB dated 9 May 1992. However, the ministries and local authorities responsible for their implementation failed to coordinate their activities or take specific and suitable measures.

Many incidents took place without timely settlement. For this reason, by 1993, 30,000 households (nearly 200,000 people) migrated freely from the northern mountainous provinces to the south. In 1992, in Dac Lac province alone, 10,000 free migrants from different ethnic minority groups arrived from the northern provinces of Cao Bang, Lang Son, Quang Ninh, and Ha Bac without reference to any State plan. From 1990 to 1993, at least 96,355 people migrated to Lam Dong province from all parts of the country.[143]

Most of the ethnic minority free migrants sought places to settle with old forests and watershed forests, including remote and out-of-the-way areas. In their experience, the soil is suitable in those places for shifting cultivation. Moreover, those areas are still forested and can be exploited for raw materials to build houses and collect firewood for cooking and for heating during winter. Complete statistics on the loss of forests and other natural resources due to such migration are not yet available. In Song Be province alone, by the middle of 1991, more than 5,000 ha of forests, including protected and reserved forests, were destroyed.

There are many causes behind spontaneous and unplanned migration. But the main reasons are population pressure, the limited amount of arable land per capita for high rotation rates of crops (particularly under the traditional system of shifting cultivation), and the failure to take measures to protect the soil from being eroded, with its consequent losses in fertility.

In the rocky mountain regions such as Dong Van and Meo Vac in Ha Giang province, the local people had to grow crops in stone holes for subsistence and now cannot feed their growing population. In some eastern mountainous regions such as Bac Ha and Si Ma Cai in Lao Cai province, and Tram Tau and Mu Cang Chai in Yen Bai province, the local people cannot grow any crops since the soil surface has been eroded, leaving only the rocky layer.[48] In addition, the natural resources, including water sources, have become impoverished and exhausted. In some places, the Hmong and Kho Mu people have to travel several kilometers, a whole morning's journey, to fetch water for daily use. In addition to the socio-economic situation described above, the provinces of Cao Bang, Lang Son, and Quang Ninh have also suffered from the negative impacts of the border war during the late 1970s and early 1980s of this century.

Over the past half-century, the two wars of resistance (against France and then the United States) and the twenty years of Socialist construction since reunification have given all the ethnic groups, in the lowlands and the mountains, in the north, center, and south, the opportunity for increased contact and mutual understanding.

Children of the ethnic minority groups from the northern mountainous provinces had opportunities to live, work, and fight in the war of resistance in the southern provinces, particularly in the

Truong Son-Tay Nguyen region, the central coastal region, and southeastern Vietnam. After demobilization, they returned to their native villages and then because of economic difficulties, as mentioned above, took their families south to places they knew from the past to earn their living. The local people, who knew them from the past, welcomed and accepted them. At first, this would be a single family, but gradually other families, from their clan in their village of origin would follow.

At present, some "special services" are being provided for the unplanned migrants. Every day, privately owned trucks make their way into out-of-the-way parts of the northern uplands, to pick up people and families there and take them south (mainly to the Central Highlands and the southeast). This form of migration has had serious consequences, as the owners of those trucks often transport migrants to remote and watershed forest regions to clear land. By the time the local people and authorities discover their arrival, it is too late to stop them. The newcomers come up against great difficulties at first in terms of food and shelter, health care, and education for their children.

It is clear now that spontaneous migration is taking place with growing intensity. The challenge is to carry out research and surveys with a view to taking effective measures to deal with the problem. It is obviously not enough to treat the issue with administrative measures in a hurried and voluntarist manner, or to seek solutions in punitive measures which are not in accordance with the policies of the Communist Party and State.

CHAPTER IV

POPULATION STRUCTURE AND POPULATION GROWTH

I. POPULATION STRUCTURE

VIETNAM is a country small in areawith a large population, but its demographic distribution is unbalanced. First of all, there is the inappropriate population distribution between urban and rural areas, as well as between the agricultural and non-agricultural sectors. Prior to the French occupation, the Vietnamese were mostly farmers. During the colonial period, most of the population remained farmers, but the urban population increased somewhat as a result of the development of cities, provincial towns and district towns (see Table 65).

Table 65. Population by urban and rural areas in the three regions[1]

Region	Year	Total population (1,000 persons)	Urban population as % of the total population (%)
North	1931	7,000	4.6
Center	1936	5,644	3.5
South	1936	4,613	14.0

Natural, social, and economic factors explain the disparities in population growth between urban and rural areas. These disparities can only be reduced by harmonizing developments in industry, agriculture, trade, and so on. The State has formulated plans to regulate and redistribute population between areas and regions in the whole country, as well as in each locality.

By 1975 in the northern, midland, and highland regions, some industrial zones, cities and towns had been built, attracting farmers from the plains and the mountainous regions. From 1960 to 1974, the proportion of urban dwellers to the total population of the two midland provinces of Vinh Phu and Ha Bac increased from 4.54% to 7.34% and from 4.83% to 5.79%, respectively. In the mountainous region, the urban population increased rapidly in proportion, particularly in the mining province of Quang Ninh, the Thai Nguyen iron and steel complex and Tay Bac (northwestern) region (see Table 66).

Table 66. Proportion of urban population in some northern mountainous provinces through the two population censuses

Provinces	Proportion of urban population of the total population	
	1960	1974
Hoang Lien Son	8.92	13.53
Ha Tuyen	4.63	7.35
Bac Thai	11.25	17.66
Cao Lang	7.73	8.37
Quang Ninh	25.04	32.63
Son La-Lai Chau	3.20	12.90

It is clear that there were some changes in northern Vietnam's population structure during that period. Each city and provincial town grew remarkably in numbers of inhabitants. In 1960, the largest city, Hanoi, had a population of 640,000, Hai Phong had 370,000 people, and Nam Dinh, 86,000. By 1979, nine cities and towns had a population of over 100,000 each.

In 1960, only eleven cities and provincial towns in north Vietnam had a population of more than 20,000 people. Their combined population was 1,337,455 people. In 1979, the figure was twenty-six cities, and in 1989, thirty-four cities and provincial towns had some 20,000 people each, with a combined population of 6,940,988. The population of six cities alone, Thai Nguyen, Viet Tri, Hanoi, Hai Phong, Nam Dinh and Vinh, was 5,186,350 people (see Table 67).

Of course, after nearly thirty years, the population of those cities and provincial capitals and towns increased due to natural population growth, as well as administrative changes by which urban areas expanded to include suburban populations previously counted as belonging to other districts and provinces.

Table 67. Cities and provincial capitals in north Vietnam with a population of more than 20,000 people each in 1960 and 1989

1960		
No.	Cities and Provincial capitals	Population (persons)
1	Hanoi City	643,576
2	Hai Phong	369,248
3	Nam Dinh	86,123
4	Vinh provincial capital	44,921
5	Hon Gai	35,412
6	Cam Pha	32,228
7	Thanh Hoa	31,860
8	Ha Dong	25,001
9	Hai Duong	24,752
10	Bac Ninh	22,520
11	Thai Nguyen	21,805
	TOTAL	1,337,455
1989		
No.	Cities and Provincial capitals	Population (persons)
1	Hanoi City	3,056,146
2	Hai Phong	1,447,523
3	Nam Dinh	219,615
4	Vinh	175,167
5	Thai Nguyen	171,815
6	Viet Tri	116,084
7	Hon Gai provincial capital	139,394
8	Cam Pha	127,408
9	Thanh Hoa	126,942
10	Thai Binh	121,037
11	Hai Duong	110,846
12	Son Tay	90,888
13	Hoa Binh	87,873
14	Bac Giang	84,106
15	Uong Bi	79,005
16	Ha Dong	74,462
17	Yen Bai	70,400
18	Dong Hoi	65,864
19	Bac Ninh	64,150
20	Lang Son	52,181
21	Son La	50,013
22	Tuyen Quang	47,982
23	Sam Son	45,004
24	Bim Son	44,313
25	Tam Diep	41,317
26	Ninh Binh	38,864
27	Lao Cai	36,909
28	Phu Tho	36,362
29	Cao Bang	35,081
30	Hung Yen	34,876
31	Song Cong	32,225

1989		
No.	Cities and Provincial capitals	Population (persons)
32	Vinh Yen	31,072
33	Ha Nam	30,395
34	Do Son	25,679
35	Ha Giang	25,390
36	Lai Chau	21,257
	TOTAL	7,057,645

In the south, meanwhile, war exacerbated the disequilibrium in the population structure. During the war period, southern urban areas witnessed two typical problems rapid development of a number of cities and an abnormally rapid urbanization process. Population growth of some major cities from 1960 to 1971 was the highest ever seen. For example: the population growth rate increased by 214% in Can Tho, 237% in Cam Ranh, 308% in Nha Trang, 321% in Da Nang and 509% in Quy Nhon.

It is also generally appreciated that most of the important cities in the former colonies were not industrial centers established to meet the requirements for economic development of the country, but the products of colonial policies. Cities served as administrative centers, hubs for the export of the colony's natural resources, and entry points to receive and market unsold products. This led to the unbalanced development and expansion of some cities through artificial prosperity, and urbanization without corresponding economic and industrial development. The United States military's campaigns in the countryside, combined with the government of South Vietnam's policy to force rural people into cities and provincial towns to isolate rural areas in order to destroy the revolutionary forces, made this process worse. The proportion of the total population in South Vietnam living in cities increased dramatically over fifteen years, from 20.7% in 1959 to 43% in 1974.

Since the liberation of South Vietnam in 1975, the policies of the Vietnamese Communist Party and State concerning the redistribution of the population and labor force have normalized the urban/rural population structure there. In particular, the population of some major cities was redistributed (see Table 68)

The urban population of Vietnam has increased to a certain extent over the years. Over the sixty year period 1931–1990, the urban population rose 3.7 times, against 2.9 times in the thirty years prior to 1951. However, over the last twenty years, the urban population only increased by 25,000 people. In some years, its numbers, as a proportion of

Table 68. Population of some cities in south Vietnam in selected years
(unit: persons)

No.	Cities and provincial capitals	1960	1974	1979	1989
1	Ho Chi Minh City	2,296,000	3,600,000*	3,419,978	3,924,435
2	Da Nang	104,000	492,000	318,653	369,734
3	Hue	103,000	207,000	210,953	260,489
4	Nha Trang	49,000	216,000	212,483	263,093
5	Da Lat	49,000	105,000	96,978	115,959
6	Bien Hoa	38,000	332,000	345,753	313,816
7	Qui Nhon	31,000	213,500	165,540	201,972
	TOTAL	2,670,000	5,165,500	4,770,338	5,449,498

*Statistics released in 1972.

Table 69. Average population by urban and rural areas in selected years

Year	Population (in thousands)	Structure (%)	
		Urban areas	Rural areas
1931*	17,702	7.5	92.5
1936*	18,972	7.9	92.1
1939*	19,600	8.7	91.3
1943*	22,159	9.2	90.8
1951*	23,061	10.0	90.0
1955*	25,074	11.0	89.0
1960*	30,172	15.0	85.0
1965*	34,929	17.2	82.8
1970*	41,063	20.7	79.3
1975*	47,638	21.5	78.5
1976**	49,160	20.6	79.4
1977**	50,413	20.1	79.9
1978**	51,421	19.7	80.3
1979**	52,462	19.2	80.8
1980**	53,722	19.1	80.9
1981**	54,927	18.6	81.4
1982**	56,170	19.2	80.8
1983**	57,373	19.1	80.9
1984**	58,770	19.1	80.9
1985***	59,872	18.1	81.9
1986***	61,109	19.3	80.7
1987***	62,452	19.6	80.4
1988***	63,727	19.9	80.1
1989***	64,412	19.8	80.2
1990****	66,233	20.0	80.0

*General Statistic Office. 1990. *Vietnam Facts and Figures (1945–1989)*. Su That Publishing House. Hanoi.

**General Statistic Office. 1985. *Statistical Data 1930–1984*. Statistics Publishing House, p. 17.

***Nguyen Viet Cuong, Pham Son, 1992. Impacts of increasing population growth on socio-economic development. *Ethnological Review*, No. 4, p. 23.

****Statistical Yearbook 1990, Statistics Publishing House, Hanoi 1992, p. 7.

the whole population, actually fell. There remains a major imbalance in population structure between urban and rural areas (see Table 69).

At present, there is a disparity in the proportion of urban population between different regions in the country. Vietnam is divided into seven regions and according to State legal documents. Southeastern Vietnam has the highest proportion of urban population (49.39%), next come the central coastal provinces (24.30%), Tay Nguyen (22.79%), the Red River Delta (17.58%), the Mekong River Delta (16.34%), the northern midland and mountainous region (13.76%), and the provinces in the former Zone 4 (10.12%).

Analysed by ethnic group, only the Kinh and the Hoa have a large proportion of their total population living in urban areas. The urban populations of other ethnic groups are very low. For example, in the northern mountainous region, according to the 1989 statistics, the proportion of urban population of each ethnic group is as follows (see Table 70).

Table 70. Urban population of ethnic groups in eleven northern mountainous provinces (including those who live in district towns, provincial towns and cities)

No.	Ethnic group	Total population (persons)	Urban population (persons)	% of population of ethnic group in the region
	TOTAL	6,856,302	1,353,881	19.74
1	Kinh	2,760,827	1,073,770	38.89
2	Tay	1,109,462	107,472	9.68
3	Thai	631,137	49,588	7.85
4	Nung	600,035	48,711	8.12
5	Hmong	534,815	4,404	0.82
6	Muong	466,399	23,191	4.97
7	Yao	450,051	10,897	2.47
8	San Chay	90,743	1,064	1.17
9	San Diu	51,418	8,849	17.21
10	Giay	37,554	5,317	14.16
11	Hoa	26,972	5,886	21.82
12	Kho Mu	22,961	458	1.99
13	Ha Nhi	12,387	48	0.39
14	Xinh Mun	10,856	47	0.43
15	Lao	8,843	129	1.46
16	La Chi	7,816	51	0.65
17	Phu La	6,273	732	11.67
18	Khang	3,566	27	0.75
19	Lo Lo	3,110	23	0.74
20	Bo Y	1,412	44	3.12
21	Tho	831	32	3.85

It is clear that a high proportion of Kinh people in this mountainous region live in urban areas (38.89%), followed by the Hoa (21.82%), San Diu (17.21%), and Giay (14.16%).

There are large proportions of Hoa and Kinh live in urban areas (see Table 71) in the Tay Nguyen (Central Highlands) region.

Ethnic minority groups in urban areas (including district and provincial towns and cities) often reside in the suburban areas, living mostly on shifting cultivation. Apart from the Hoa, few ethnic minority households engaging in commerce, handicraft production, or small industrial businesses.

Table 71. Urban population of some ethnic groups in four Central Highland provinces (1989)

No.	Ethnic group	Total population (persons)	Urban population (persons)	% of population of ethnic group in the region
1	2	3	4	5
	TOTAL	2,490,078	799,995	32.13
1	Kinh	1,607,555	647,002	40.24
2	Gia Rai	240,264	25,599	10.65
3	E De	179,297	44,207	24.65
4	Ba Na	120,728	26,096	21.61
5	Co Ho	83,072	7,994	9.62
6	Xo Dang	66,660	8,038	12.06
7	Mnong	50,303	3,234	6.43
8	Ma	24,078	2,702	11.22
9	Gie-Trieng	20,807	486	2.33
10	Hoa	14,583	9,712	66.60
11	Chu Ru	10,402	202	1.94
12	Raglai	988	13	1.32

Regarding the question of population structure by age, in southern provinces, prior to 1975, due to a high birth rate and the consequences of twenty years of war, the population structure became abnormal and seriously imbalanced. This is expressed in the great disparity between age groups. According to the statistics concerning age (1962, 1967, 1970, and 1971 figures), some cities and rural areas in South Vietnam had a population structure where 48% of the population was in the 0–14 age group, while 60% was in the under-twenty age group. The proportion of the population of working age (15–60) only accounted for 45% of the total population. So each working person had to support 1.2 dependants. Moreover, due to the large number of war casualties, the number of males in the 20–25 age group was half that in the 15–19 age group. In particular, in the rural areas, the number of people in the 20–25 age group was just one third of that in the 15–19 age group.[2]

In the north, census data show that children under fifteen constituted 42.8% of the population in 1960, which is high compared with other countries of the world. One year after reunification, the proportion of children of that age in the entire country was even higher. This meant that people under working age accounted for nearly half of the total population. The reasons for this include the influence of structural disequilibrium inherited from the previous system in the south, the high birth rate, and the high proportion of dependents. The implementation of family planning policies over the years after reunification brought the proportion of children in the population down from 42.5% in 1979 to 39.8% in 1989.

Population statistics for the whole country over the past twenty years show that Vietnamese population remains very young. This is clearly expressed in the age pyramid: the base is large, the two base angles are sharp, and the top of the pyramid is also sharp. This shows that the birth rate remains high, the number of children is high, while the number of the elderly is low. It also suggests low performance of population policies and programs (see Table 72).

Table 72. Population structure by age in the whole country in selected years
(unit: 1,000 persons)

Age Group	1976*		1979**		1989***	
	Population	%	Population	%	Population	%
TOTAL	48,060	100.00	52,742	100.00	64,375	100.00
0–14	21,681	45.11	22,442	42.55	25,222	39.18
15–60	22,939	47.74	26,572	50.38	34,553	53.67
61 +	3,440	7.15	3,728	7.07	4,600	7.15

* *Population of the Socialist Republic of Vietnam. 1976.* General Statistic Office. Hanoi, 1 p. 17.
** *Population of Vietnam October 1, 1979.* Hanoi. 1983. p. 34.
*** General Population Census 1989.1991. *Results of the comprehensive surveys, Volume 1.* Hanoi, p. 16.

The table shows that the number of people under working age compared with the total population tended to decline over time. There were also some remarkable changes in the spatial composition of the age pyramid. Statistics from 1979, the year of the first population census conducted throughout the country, show this trend very clearly (see Table 73).

Table 73. Population in the 0–14 age group by region (1979)[3]

No.	Location	Total population (persons)	Population aged 0–14 (persons)	(%)
	WHOLE COUNTRY	52,741,776	22,403,156	42.5
1	Northern Mountainous Provinces	4,900,180	2,097,542	42.8
	- Ha Tuyen	782,453	349,817	44.7
	- Cao Bang	479,823	201,553	42.0
	- Lang Son	484,657	204,32	42.1
	- Lai Chau	322,077	148,154	46.0
	- Hoang Lien Son	778,217	346,266	44.5
	- Bac Thai	815,105	358,147	43.9
	- Son La	487,793	224,349	46.0
	- Quang Ninh	750,055	264,924	35.3
2	Midlands	3,151,019	1,285,623	40.8
3	Red River Delta	11,820,468	4,456,910	37.7
4	Former Zone 4	7,545,963	3,064,458	40.6
5	Central Highlands	1,482,761	651,436	43.9
	- Gia Lai-Kon Tum	595,906	251,436	42.2
	- Dac Lac	490,198	223,688	45.6
	- Lam Dong	396,657	175,855	44.3
6	Central Coast	5,843,376	2,677,777	45.8
7	Southeastern Vietnam	2,640,898	1,200,082	45.4
8	Mekong River Delta	15,350,101	7,008,815	45.6

The table shows that the proportion of children in southern provinces is higher than in northern provinces. In the south, the proportion of children in the plains is higher than in the mountainous regions, while in the north it is the reverse. There is also a disparity even among mountainous provinces. While the proportion in Quang Ninh is only 35.3%, it is 46.0% in Lai Chau. In Tay Nguyen, the proportion in Gia Lai-Kon Tum is 42.2% while that in Dac Lac is 45.6%. Disparities become even clearer when comparisons are made between ethnic groups (see Table 74).

Table 74. Proportion of population in two age groups: 0–4 and 0–14 of the total population of each ethnic group[4]

No.	Ethnic group	0–4 age group (%)	0–14 age group (%)
	IN THE WHOLE COUNTRY	14.34	39.82
1	Kinh	13.90	39.27
2	Tay	16.47	41.60
3	Thai	18.78	46.07
4	Hoa	10.64	32.80
5	Khmer	16.19	43.48
6	Muong	17.40	42.40

No.	Ethnic group	0–4 age group (%)	0–14 age group (%)
7	Nung	16.33	41.72
8	Hmong	21.44	49.99
9	Yao	19.27	46.38
10	Gia Rai	18.27	45.88
11	E De	18.98	46.25
12	Ba Na	18.66	46.03
13	Xo Dang	20.34	48.01
14	San Chay	18.27	46.49
15	Co Ho	18.40	44.79
16	Cham	17.97	46.46
17	San Diu	18.84	48.87
18	Hre	19.91	48.84
19	Mnong	19.05	46.40
20	Raglai	18.95	45.26
21	Stieng	18.22	45.11
22	Bru	18.79	48.21
23	Tho	18.52	44.26
24	Giay	18.11	44.92
25	Co Tu	20.97	53.29
26	Gie-Trieng	20.76	48.05
27	Ma	17.73	42.89
28	Kho Mu	20.58	49.07
29	Co	18.24	47.49
30	Ta Oi	19.70	53.38
31	Cho Ro	19.23	45.83
32	Khang	20.47	48.73
33	Xinh Mun	20.87	50.28
34	Ha Nhi	17.55	46.11
35	Chu Ru	19.73	47.50
36	Lao	20.83	50.04
37	La Chi	16.87	41.97
38	La Hu	15.58	46.52
39	Lu	18.96	48.50
40	Lo Lo	17.90	43.59
41	Pa Then	20.26	47.43
42	Co Lao	19.63	43.69
43	Cong	18.91	50.08
44	Bo Y	17.17	43.03
45	Si La	15.08	43.50
46	Pu Peo	17.47	43.01
47	Brau	19.21	44.54
48	Ro Mam	18.75	47.32
49	Ngai	12.72	38.65
50	La Ha	18.86	48.78
51	Phu La	18.08	46.21
52	Chut	17.94	49.21
53	Mang	15.70	41.16
54	O Du*	14.36	41.49

* Statistics of the surveys conducted in 1992.

The number of people in the 0–4 and 0–14 age groups, as a proportion of the total population, varies widely between ethnic groups. These age groups account for only 10.64% and 32.80% of the total number of Hoa people, for example. For the Kinh, the figures are slightly higher: 13.90% and 39.27% respectively. But for other ethnic groups, they represent very large sections of the population: Hmong (21.44% and 49.99%), Co Tu (20.97% and 53.29%), Xinh Mun (20.87% and 50.28%), and Lao (20.83% and 50.04%).

These proportions may also be compared between linguistic groups. They are low for groups in the Hoa linguistic family: Hoa (as mentioned above), Ngai (12.72% and 38.65%), San Diu (18.84% and 48.87%). Slightly higher, again, are the figures for the Viet-Muong family: Kinh, Muong (17.40% and 42.40%), Tho (18.52% and 44.26%) and Chut (17.94% and 49.21%). The highest proportions are found in the Mon-Khmer linguistic group: Co Tu, Gie-Trieng (20.76% and 48.05%), Kho Mu (20.58% and 49.07%), Khang (20.47% and 48.73%). The percentages are slightly lower in the Hmong-Yao linguistic groups: Hmong, Yao (19.27% and 46.38%) and Pa Then (20.26% and 47.43%).

Within the same ethnic group, the proportion varies between local groups and from one region to another. For example, while the proportion of Yao people in the 0–14 age group given by the above table is 46.38%, fieldwork conducted among local groups in 1989, 1990, and 1991 gives different results. The results showed that in the Yao Ao Dai (long shirts or blouses) group in the Tan Trinh commune, Bac Quang district, Ha Giang province, the figure was 41.77%; in the Yao Tien group in the Minh Huong commune, Ham Yen district, Tuyen Quang province, the figure is 42.50%; in the Yao Thanh Y group in the Chiem Yen commune, Yen Son district, Tuyen Quang province it is 45.31%, and in the Yao Quang Chet group in the Yen Huong commune, Ham Yen district, Tuyen Quang province, it is 45.63%. Meanwhile there was a very low proportion of young people recorded among the Yao group in Cong Son Commune, Cao Loc district, Lang Son province, at just over 30%.

In other instances, two local sub-groups of the same ethnic group have different proportions. For example, the proportion of the Nung Phan Sinh sub-group in different communes in Cao Loc district varies greatly: in Tan Thanh commune, the proportion is 39.16%, while in Hai Yen commune it is 46.36%.[5]

The results of socio-economic surveys conducted in eleven mountainous provinces in northern Vietnam by the Institutes of Economics, Ethnology, Sociology, the Center for Women Studies, and the Center for Economic Geography under the National Center of Social Sciences and Humanities in 1992, are shown in the Table below (see Table 75).

Table 75. Population in the 0–14 age group in selected ethnic groups in northern mountainous provinces

No	Ethnic group	Total surveyed population (persons)	Population in 0–14 age group (persons)	(%)
1	Kinh	7,644	2,500	32.70
2	Tay	4,583	1,758	38.56
3	Nung	3,464	1,264	36.49
4	Thai	5,262	2,103	39.96
5	Muong	3,194	1,261	45.31
6	Hmong	3,103	1,422	45.82
7	Yao	2,746	1,171	42.64
8	Hoa	137	38	27.73
9	San Chay	574	196	34.15
10	San Diu	143	16	32.16
11	Giay	205	87	42.44
12	Pa Then	477	209	43.82
13	Phu La	189	87	46.03
14	Lo Lo	197	73	37.06
15	Ngai	87	44	50.57
16	Kho Mu	84	42	50.80

Data in this table allows us to conclude that the population in the 0–14 age group is decreasing. Compared with Table 73, which showed statistics from the 1989 census, the above table shows that the proportion of population in the 0–14 age group has decreased considerably. However, the proportion in some ethnic groups such as the Phu La, has dropped very little, from 46.21% to 46.03%. In other instances, the proportion in some ethnic groups increased slightly, as in the Kho Mu (from 49.07% to 50.80%).

In tables 74 and 75, comparison between the absolute and general figures (Table 74) and regional data with statistics from selected sites (Table 75) suggests that there might be some discrepancies in the data. But these figures are valuable for the insights they offer into the general tendency by which Vietnam's population is developing, as well as for improving our understanding of the demographic development of the individual ethnic groups.

Comparison between regions, as we might expect, shows that in remote, highland, and border areas (along the borders with Laos and

China), the proportion of the young population (0–14) is higher than in lowland areas; likewise, the proportion is higher in rural areas than in the towns and cities.

The number of people of working age in Vietnam represents a small proportion of the total population. This is partly because the average life expectancy is low. In 1960, in North Vietnam, the proportion of people aged 60 and above accounted for 5.73% of the total population. In subsequent years, the proportion increased a little, fluctuating around 7%. For example, in 1976, the proportion in the whole country was 7.13%. In 1979, it was 7.07%, and in 1989, 7.14%. Meanwhile, the number of those who live to be one hundred declined. In 1960, that proportion was 0.04% when compared with the total population of North Vietnam. In 1976, the figure was 0.13%, and in 1979, 0.01%, when compared with the total population.

In 1979, people living in the upland provinces accounted for a high proportion of the total number who reached the age of one hundred. A total of 3,118 lived to one hundred that year, of whom 456 lived in Son La, 253 in Lai Chau, 185 in Hoang Lien Son, 101 in Gai Lai-Kon Tum, and 40 in Lam Dong. Comparison of regional variations in the proportion of people aged over 85 offers the results shown in Table 76.

Table 76. Proportion of people aged 85 and over in the two population censuses of 1979 and 1989 in some provinces (unit: %)

No.	Localities	Proportion of population aged 85 and over in 1979*	Proportion of population aged 85 and over in 1989**
	WHOLE COUNTRY	0.25	0.24
1	Hanoi	0.20	0.24
2	Thai Binh	0.19	0.24
3	Ho Chi Minh	0.18	0.21
4	Ben Tre	0.22	0.27
5	Ha Tuyen	0.23	0.21
6	Cao Bang	0.22	0.23
7	Lang Son	0.15	0.15
8	Lai Chau	0.58	0.39
9	Son La	0.45	0.39
10	Hoang Lien Son	0.23	0.22
11	Bac Thai	0.14	0.16
12	Quang Ninh	0.12	0.20
13	Gia Lai-Kon Tum	0.20	0.18
14	Dac Lac	0.17	0.15
15	Lam Dong	0.27	0.22

* Vietnam Population Oct. 1, 1979. (already cited), pp. 34–74
** Result of the General Population Census in Vietnam in 1989. Volume 1 (already cited), pp. 16–57.

The proportion of the elderly in urban and lowland areas over ten years (1979–1989) increased slightly. No discernable pattern emerged in upland areas. Provinces such as Cao Bang, Bac Thai, and Quang Ninh saw an increase. There was no change in Lang Son, while other provinces saw a decrease, particularly in the northwestern region and Central Highlands.

Comparison between ethnic groups in 1989 shows that the proportion of the elderly (aged sixty and over) within each ethnic group is highest among the Ro Mam, next come the Ma, the Brau, the Hoa, the Kinh, and so on. The same proportion is found among the Hre (see Table 77).

Table 77. Number of people aged 60 and among the ethnic groups
(in order of decreasing population) [6]

No.	Ethnic group	People aged 60+ (%)	% of the total aged people in the whole country	% of the population of that ethnic group
	TOTAL	4,595,765	100.00	7.26
1	Kinh	4,064,112	88.39	7.40
2	Tay	77,971	1.69	6.67
3	Hoa	74,868	1.63	8.32
4	Thai	65,576	1.43	6.64
5	Muong	60,068	1.31	6.64
6	Khmer	54,504	1.18	6.09
7	Nung	44,666	0.97	6.38
8	Hmong	27,158	0.59	4.87
9	Yao	25,667	0.56	5.43
10	E De	13,833	0.30	7.11
11	Gia Rai	13,062	0.28	5.40
12	Ba Na	7,197	0.16	5.26
13	San Chay	6,417	0.14	5.67
14	Co Ho	5,979	0.13	6.49
15	Cham	5,639	0.12	5.70
16	Xo Dang	5,486	0.11	5.68
17	Hre	4,878	0.11	5.19
18	San Diu	4,538	0.10	4.83
19	Mnong	4,445	0.10	6.62
20	Tho	3,306	0.07	6.55
21	Raglai	3,130	0.07	4.37
22	Stieng	3,005	0.07	5.99
23	Bru	2,385	0.05	5.95
24	Kho Mu	2,381	0.05	5.57
25	Ma	2,243	0.05	8.86
26	Giay	1,992	0.05	5.26
27	Co Tu	1,709	0.04	4.63
28	Co	1,507	0.03	6.67

No.	Ethnic group	People aged 60+ (%)	% of the total aged people in the whole country	% of the population of that ethnic group
29	Gie - Trieng	1,216	0.03	4.54
30	Ta Oi	1,193	0.03	4.59
31	Cho Ro	777	0.02	5.17
32	Xinh Mun	675	0.01	6.21
33	Lao	591	0.01	6.18
34	Ha Nhi	544	0.01	4.39
35	La Chi	472	0.01	6.03
36	Chu Ru	467	0.01	4.35
37	Phu La	306	0.01	4.80
38	Khang	275	0.01	7.02
39	Lu	249	0.01	6.78
40	Mang	190	0.01	8.50
41	Lo Lo	181	-	5.80
42	La Hu	166	-	3.12
43	Pa Then	145	-	3.95
44	Chut	109	-	4.13
45	La Ha	89	-	6.38
46	Co Lao	80	-	5.45
47	Bo Y	79	-	5.58
48	Ngai	75	-	7.34
49	Cong	67	-	5.36
50	Si La	34	-	5.96
51	Brau	20	-	8.73
52	Ro Mam	20	-	8.92
53	Pu Peo	14	-	3.76
54	O Du*	9	-	4.78

* Statistics of the surveys conducted by ethnological researchers in 1992.

Table 77 shows that elderly Kinh people make up 88.39% of the country's elderly population as a whole, while the Kinh make up only 86.83% of the population of all age groups. Indeed, comparison of columns 4 and 5 of the table leads to similar conclusions for other ethnic groups. There are clear differences between the proportion of elderly people in the whole country (column 4) and the proportion within each ethnic group (column 5). For example, in column 4, the Kinh are at the top with 88.39% and the O Du come last, while in column 5, the Ro Mam are at the top and the La Hu last (with 3.12%).

The proportion of the elderly of the population of each ethnic group is clearly different. There are, in fact, about six levels of difference by natural numbers:

Table 78. Proportion of elderly people of selected ethnic groups of in certain localities*

(unit: %)

No.	Ethnic group	Location	% of the elderly people of the total population	Proportion of females (%)
1	Tay	- Mai Son, Luc Yen in Yen Bai	5.96	56.8
2	Tay	- Hung Dao, Binh Gia in Lang Son	9.02	61.5
3	Nung Phan Slinh	- Xuat Le, Cao Loc in Lang Son	5.90	70.0
4	Nung Phan Slinh	- Hai Yen, Cao Loc in Lang Son	6.42	65.2
5	Nung Phan Slinh	- Tan Thanh, Cao Loc in Lang Son	6.11	54.5
6	Nung Chao	- Doi Can, Trang Dinh in Lang Son	7.41	60.0
7	Nung An	- Linh Ho, Vi Xuyen in Ha Giang	4.31	67.3
8	Nung	- Po Lo, Hoang Xu Phi in Ha Giang	5.00	60.1
9	Thai	- Kim Da, Tuong Duong in Nghe An	4.10	48.1
10	Thai	- Phu Nhan, Van Chan in Yen Bai	7.00	58.1
11	Hmong	- Ta Phinh, Tua Chua in Lai Chau	8.86	61.1
12	Hmong	- Pa Co, Mai Chau in Hoa Binh	3.60	54.2
13	Yao	- Cong Son, Cao Loc in Lang Son	4.71	50.0
14	Yao	- Chieu Yen, Yen Son in Tuyen Quang	5.21	51.0
15	Yao	- Tan Trinh, Bac Quang in Ha Giang	6.33	60.2
16	Yao	- Yen Huong, Ham Yen in Tuyen Quang	4.91	46.7
17	Yao	- Minh Huong, Ham Yen in Tuyen Quang	4.17	60.0
18	Kho Mu	- Nghia Son, Van Chan in Yen Bai	6.85	52.3
19	Kho Mu	- Xa Luong, Tuong Duong in Nge An	4.12	50.0
20	Mang	- Nam Ban, Sin Ho in Lai Chau	4.26	32.1
21	La Hu	- Pa Ve Su, Muong Te in Lai Chau	5.28	62.1
22	La Ha	- Nong Lay, Thuan Chau in Son La	4.32	46.1
23	Phu La	- Lung Phin, Bac Ha in Lao Cai	6.91	56.5
24	E De	- Chu Pong, Krong Buk in Dac Lac	7.13	54.1
25	Gia Rai	- La Rbon, Ajun Pa in Gia Lai	6.2	56.2
26	Ba Na	- Dak Tre, Krong Plong in Kon Tum	5.60	58.2
27	Xo Dang	- Dak Tore, Krong Plong in Kon Tum	5.82	60.0

* Statistics of the surveys conducted by ethnological researchers in 1990s.

From 8% up	:	5 ethnic groups
7–8%	:	4 ethnic groups
6–7%	:	14 ethnic groups
5–6%	:	17 ethnic groups
4–5%	:	11 ethnic groups
3–4%	:	3 ethnic groups

Moreover, within ethnic groups, the proportion differs over time and space. Table 78 below shows the proportion of population aged over 60 compared with the population of each ethnic group, in different locations, according to data collected in ethnological studies.

Table 79. Proportion of the elderly people in selected ethnic groups in the mountainous region of northern Vietnam

(unit: %)

No.	Ethnic group	% of aged people in the total surveyed population	% Proportion of females
1	Kinh	7.87	51.16
2	Tay	7.79	51.82
3	Nung	6.84	54.85
4	Thai	8.53	54.12
5	Muong	7.39	55.08
6	Hmong	6.41	61.81
7	Yao	6.41	54.54
8	Hoa	6.57	55.55
9	San Chay	7.32	54.76
10	Pa Then	4.82	54.78
11	Phu La	7.94	53.33
12	Lo Lo	7.61	40.00
13	Ngai	10.34	55.55
14	Kho Mu	5.92	40.00

Although the sites surveyed are not large and the number of respondents is small, the statistics of Table 78 compared with Table 77 show that the proportion of the elderly of the ethnic groups has in the past few years tended to increase. To have a clearer understanding, see Table 79 above, showing statistics extracted from the socio-economic surveys in northern mountainous provinces conducted by the Institutes of Economics, Ethnology and Sociology in 1992.

Table 80. Proportion of females in the population of some ethnic groups
(unit: %)

No.	Ethnic group	1974	1979	1989
1	Kinh	53.7	51.1	51.6
2	Khmer	52.9*	52.7	52.6
3	Stieng	53.7*	52.9	52.4
4	Chu Ru	53.1	53.2	52.4
5	Ro Mam	-	56.6	56.4
6	Bru	49.7	49.7	49.7
7	Co Tu	49.3*	49.3	49.1
8	Ta Oi	51.2*	49.1	49.6
9	Kho Mu	50.7	50.2	49.1
10	Co	48.6*	47.1	48.3

* 1976 Statistics

In-depth comparative analyses of regional and national statistics (Table 77) may be misleading, and conclusions should be restricted to the observation that, among all ethnic groups, the proportion of elderly people is on the increase. Among the many reasons for this are improved health care and general living conditions.

The results of the last two population censuses (1979 and 1989) in Vietnam nonetheless show that the Vietnamese population is very young. The average age was 18 in 1979 and rose to over 20 in 1989. In 1990 the average age was 21).[7]

The proportion of the elderly over 65 years was 4.8% of the total population in 1979 and 4.7% in 1989. The proportion of children under 15 years of age dropped from 42.5% in 1979 to 39.2% in 1989. The proportion of elderly people (aged 65 and above) compared with children (in the 0–14 age group) in 1979 was 11.2% and in 1989 was 12%. The proportion of dependants in 1979 was 89.8% and in 1989 was 78.2%. The proportion of elderly people aged 64 and above compared with people aged between 15–65 was 9.1% in 1979 and 8.4% in 1989. The proportion of children aged 0–14 compared with people aged 15–64 was 80.8% in 1979 and 69.8% in 1989. So the Vietnamese population is ageing: the rate of growth of the elderly population is higher than that of children under fifteen. Although this ageing tendency is not strong, it reflects the fact that the birthrate is lower and the mortality rate of the elderly is falling.[8]

Let us turn now to the population structure by gender. Gender disparities between regions are affected by local conditions such as geography, the socio-economic situation, diet, the availability of health-care services, the type of work and professions practised, the organization of work, as well as ethnic characteristics. Respective proportions of men and women in the population are also a function of migration, past and present. In Vietnam, major changes in the residence patterns of the population have taken place in order to promote economic development, national defence and security, and in the implementation of plans for the redistribution of the population and labor force. These migrations have taken place between different regions throughout the country. In the northern border region, for example, at the time when the border war broke out, the proportion of males in the area was high, owing to the conflict. Similarly, in areas of heavy industry, there are more men than women. An example of the latter case would by the city of Thai Nguyen, with its large iron and steel works, where men comprised 54% of the population during the 1970s. At the Tinh Tuc tin mine in Cao Bang, men made up 60% of the population, and in the Hon Gai coal mining region, the percentage of women dropped to only 42% and in Cam Pha to about 38%. On the contrary, in the regions where there are many state farms and light industries, the proportion of females is much higher. For example in Moc Chau district in 1979, the proportion of females was 53.40 % and in Ha Son Binh province 53.36%.

Comparing mountainous regions with lowland regions, there is a higher proportion of males in the mountainous regions. But these proportions have varied at different historical periods. For example, in 1960 in the north, the proportion of females was 51.7% compared to the total population and in 1974, it was 53.37%. This reflects the impact of the war of resistance against the United States.

Comparison of different ethnic groups shows that the proportion of females within the Kinh population is rather high. The Khmer, Stieng, Chu Ru, and Ro Mam also have a high proportion of females. Meanwhile, in other ethnic groups of the Mon-Khmer linguistic family along the Vietnam-Lao border, the proportion of females is very low (see Table 80).

Regrettably, the statistical data of the censuses in Vietnam lack some indicators regarding ethnic groups. Therefore it is difficult to explain this phenomenon. But one interesting pattern may be discerned from the comparison of the age structures of almost all ethnic groups. The proportion of females among newborn babies is lower than that of males; by the age of 16–17, there are roughly equal numbers of both sexes; after that age, the proportion of females grows steadily (see Table 81).

Table 81. Proportion of females to males in selected age groups in the whole country in 1989

(unit: %)

Age group	General	Urban	Rural
Under 1 year	93	93	93
1 year old	94	93	95
2 years old	95	94	95
3 years old	95	94	95
4 years old	95	94	95
5–9	96	94	96
10–14	95	95	95
15–19	102	103	106
30–34	109	112	115
45–49	122	113	128
60–64	121	113	123
65–69	135	132	136
70–74	146	154	145
75–79	165	181	162
80–84	198	224	195
from 85 and over	215	269	223

Comparison between urban and rural areas shows that in both areas, the number of females less than one year of age is about 93% of the number of males of the same age. The proportion of women in the age group 1–60 years is slightly higher in the countryside. But from the age of 70, the proportion of women in urban areas increases sharply. In the countryside, the number of women over 85 is about 223% the number of similarly aged men in the city, 269%.

II. POPULATION GROWTH

POPULATION growth depends on two factors: natural growth (the difference between births and mortality) and the movement of people. In the previous section the migration issue was discussed and this section will focus on the question of natural growth factors.

a. The birth rate: The birth rate and the fertility rate are expressed through two measures: the crude birth rate (CBR) and the total fertility rate (TFR).

In 1931, according to surveys conducted by Guru, the CBR in the north was 47.8 per thousand. In 1936 it was 48 per thousand; and in 1960 it declined to 46 per thousand. In the south, the figure in 1967 was about 44 per thousand and in 1969, 43 per thousand. Table 82 presents CBR data for selected years since 1960.

Table 82. Crude birth rate (CBR) for selected years

Year	%	Year	%	Year	%
1960*	46.0	1974*	34.4	1982**	30.4
1965*	37.8	1975*	31.3	1983**	30.1
1967*	32.9	1976**	39.5	1984**	29.4
1969*	37.5	1977***	36.0	1985****	28.4
1970*	34.6	1978***	31.4	1986****	27.8
1971*	35.7	1979***	32.5	1987*****	27.4
1972*	36.0	1980**	31.7	1988******	26.6
1973*	33.8	1981**	30.0		

* In North Vietnam only. According to the *Statistical Year Book 1979*, p. 77.
** According to *Statistical Year Book 1985*, p. 13.
*** According to *Statistical Year Book 1980*, p. 408.
**** According to *Statistical Year Book 1986*, p. 12.
***** According to *Statistical Year Book 1987*, p. 12.
****** According to *Statistical Year Book 1988*, p. 7.

The above figures are subject to some controversy, and many researchers hold that they are still lower than reality. The CBR in Vietnam has fallen from about 40 per thousand (from 1936–1960) to 30 per thousand (1965–1983). In 1984, the figure had dropped to approximately 20 per thousand.[9] So it is clear that the family planning movement has achieved some measurable successes. The CBR differs, however, from region to region (see Table 83).

Table 83. Crude birth rate (CBR) by geographical region by some years
1979–1988

(unit: %)

Year	Northern Midland mountain region	Red River Delta	Former Zone 4	Central Coastal region	Central High-lands	South-eastern Vietnam	Mekong River Delta
1979 *	34.3	29.2	31.1	33.8	38.3	29.1	35.5
1984**	31.2	27.9	29.9	28.2	35.0	26.2	30.9
1985***	30.2	25.2	29.9	26.8	35.8	25.6	30.7
1986****	30.0	24.2	29.8	25.6	35.7	24.9	30.1
1987*****	29.8	23.3	29.2	25.7	35.5	24.9	30.6
1988******	28.9	22.5	28.3	25.2	34.5	23.8	28.8

* According to *Statistical Book 1980*, p. 404
** According to *Statistical Year Book 1984*, pp. 17, 18
*** According to *Statistical Year Book 1985*, p. 13.
**** According to *Statistical Year Book 1986*, p. 12.
***** According to *Statistical Year Book 1987*, p. 12.
****** According to *Statistical Year Book 1988*, pp. 7–8.

The statistics of Table 83 prove the above assessment, that is, the crude birth rate in Vietnam has been falling throughout the whole country as well as in each region. In the northern mountainous and midland regions, the crude birth rate dropped from 34.3 per thousand in 1979 to 28.9 per thousand in 1988; this means that over a ten year period, the rate fell by 5.4 per thousand. In the Red River Delta, over the same period, the CBR fell by 6.7 per thousand, in the former Zone 4 by 2.8 per thousand, in the central coast by 8.6 per thousand, in Central Highlands by 3.8 per thousand, in the southeastern region by 5.3 per thousand, and in the Mekong River Delta by 6.7 per thousand.

Comparing the seven regions above, it will be noted that in the central coastal region, the drop in CBR was the highest, while the former Zone 4 recorded the smallest change. However, the regions with the highest birth rate are the Central Highlands, the Mekong River Delta, and the northern mountainous and midland regions, while the regions having the lowest birth rate are the Red River Delta and the southeastern region.

Comparison of urban and rural areas shows that the birth rate in rural areas is always higher. This is the general situation throughout the country as well as in each region. Taking Ha Tuyen, a province in the center of the northern mountainous region, as an example, while the birth rate in the urban areas is more than 20 per thousand, it was more than 30 per thousand in rural areas (see Table 84)

Table 84. Crude birth rate of Ha Tuyen province in selected years[10]
(unit: %)

Year	General	Urban	Rural
1976	32.9	30.8	33.1
1981	33.3	27.3	33.8
1982	30.7	28.4	31.2
1983	32.8	25.5	33.4
1984	30.8	29.3	30.9

Following the number of children born in the last two or three decades, it is clearly seen that the highest number of children were born to women in the 25–29 age group, in both urban and rural areas (see Table 85).

If the first birth correlated is with the total number of births in each region, it can be seen clearly that the proportion of first births is higher in urban areas than in rural areas. In northern Vietnam, the proportion is higher than in the south. If we make the same correlation for the fourth birth, however, the proportion in rural areas is higher than in urban areas, and also higher in the south than in the

Table 85. Live births by age group and number of births of mothers in 1986
(in 10,000 live births)

Age group	Total	Number of births			
		First	Second	Third	Fourth +
(1)	(2)	(3)	(4)	(5)	(6)
The whole country[11]					
TOTAL	10,000	2,862	2,685	1,700	2,753
15–19	246	213	28	5	-
20–24	2,936	1,738	922	216	60
25–29	3,448	730	1,338	848	532
30–34	1,912	137	315	472	988
35–39	969	35	67	131	736
40–44	358	7	13	22	316
45–49	131	2	2	6	121
Urban areas					
TOTAL	10,000	3,809	2,661	1,457	2,073
15–19	307	263	34	10	-
20–24	2,911	1,976	697	188	50
25–29	3,563	1,201	1,341	613	408
30–34	1,969	293	453	454	769
35–39	866	63	116	162	525
40–44	288	11	19	24	234
45–49	96	2	1	6	87
Rural areas					
TOTAL	10,000	2,729	2,689	1,734	2,848
15–19	237	206	27	4	-
20–24	2,937	1,704	953	220	60
25–29	3,432	664	1,338	881	549
30–34	1,905	115	296	475	1,019
35–39	984	31	60	126	767
40–44	368	7	12	22	327
45–49	137	2	3	6	126
Structure according to the number of births[12]					
Whole country	100.0	29.0	27.7	18.8	21.5
Urban areas	100.0	39.5	30.3	15.1	15.1
Rural areas	100.0	27.8	27.4	19.2	25.6
North	100.0	30.3	29.8	19.4	20.5
South	100.0	26.0	22.4	17.2	34.4

north. By 1987, the family planning policy had been under way for more than twenty years. But mothers having four births or more still accounted for a high proportion of the total.

Turning now to the crude births of ethnic minority groups, the average crude birth rate of the majority Kinh in the urban and lowland provinces has been around 30 per thousand over the last few years, but much higher in mountainous provinces. For example, in Chu Pong commune, Krong Buk district, Dac Lac province, the crude birth rate of the Kinh was 35 per thousand in 1991 and 34 per thousand in 1992. In Iar Bol commune, Iajun Pa district, Gia Lai province, the figure was 32 per thousand in 1991 and 31 per thousand in 1992, while the figure in Huyen Tung commune in Bach Thong district, Bac Thai province was 40 per thousand in 1991 and 39 per thousand in 1992. Worthy of note is that in Nay Lua commune, Muong Lay district, Lai Chau province, the figure was 51 per thousand in 1991 and 49 per thousand in 1992. These examples allow us to conclude that family planning policies have not yet had a great

Table 86. Crude birth rate (CBR) in some ethnic groups
(unit %)

Ethnic group	Location	Year	Crude birth rate %	Birth rate in the 15–49 age group %
Tay	- Mai Son, Luc Yen in Yen Bai	1986	37.1	182.0
Tay	- Tan Tien, Trang Dinh in Lang Son	1988	40.0	192.1
Tay (Tho)	- Trung Thanh, Da Bac in Hoa Binh	1988	43.8	189.3
Nung	- Xuat Le, Cao Loc in Lang Son	1986	36.0	178.2
Nung	- Linh Ho, Vi Xuyen in Ha Giang	1988	34.8	182.1
Nung	- Po Lo, Hoang Xu Phi in Ha Giang	1988	43.4	198.7
Thai	- Muong So, Phong Tho in Lai Chau	1992	41.2	192.3
Thai	- Na Phon, Mai Chau in Hoa Binh	1988	38.8	187.3
Thai	- Kim Da, Tuong Duong in Nghe An	1991	37.5	198.5
Muong	- Ngoi Hoa, Tan Lac in Hoa Binh	1988	43.8	189.3
Muong	- Muong Tuong in Da Bac in Hoa Binh	1988	47.0	213.3
Hmong	- Ta Phinh, Tua Chua in Lai Chau	1986	50.9	219.2
Hmong	- Muong Bu, Muong La in Son La	1992	38.4	187.3
Hmong	- Nay Lua, Muong Lay in Lai Chau	1992	43.0	194.1
Hmong	- Pa Co, Mai Chau in Hoa Binh	1989	49.0	231.0
Yao	- Huyen Tung, Bach Thong in Bac Thai	1991	40.0	231.0
Yao	- Cong San, Cao Loc in Lang Son	1988	38.2	193.9
Yao	- Yen Huong, Ham Yen in Tuyen Quang	1988	44.8	199.3
Kho Mu	- Nghia Son, Van Chan in Yen Bai	1986	34.2	171.4
Kho Mu	- Xa Luong, Tuong Duong in Nghe An	1991	44.2	198.5
Phu La	- Lung Phin, Bac Ha in Lao Cai	1991	48.0	182.5
La Hu	- Pa Ve Su, Muong Te in Lai Chau	1992	48.1	207.2
La Ha	- Noong Lay, Thuan Chau in Son La	1992	52.5	232.5
Mang	- Nam Ban, Sin Ho in Lai Chau	1992	35.9	194.4
Giay	- Yen Minh, Yen Minh in Tuyen Quang	1989	56.0	199.8
San Chay	- Doc Binh, Yen Son in Tuyen Quang	1988	38.2	181.5
O Du	- Kim Da, Tuong Duong in Nghe An	1991	45.0	180.8
E De	- Chu Pong, Krong Buk in Dac Lac	1991	38.0	179.9
Gia Rai	- Iarbon, Iajun Pa in Gia Lai	1992	59.1	221.2
Brau	- Bo Y, Ngoc Hoi in Kon Tum	1991	57.0	205.8

impact on the Kinh living in the mountainous regions. With regard to ethnic minorities, it is clear that the crude birth rate is very high. However, the rate varies between each ethnic minority group and region. The results of our surveys of some ethnic groups since 1986 are shown in Table 86.

As a result of socio-economic baseline surveys conducted by the Institutes of Economics, Ethnology and Sociology in eleven northern mountainous provinces in 1992, statistics are available of the crude birth rate of certain ethnic minority groups in selected regions as follows:

Tay	34.2 per thousand
Muong	34.4 per thousand
Phu La	37.0 per thousand
Yao	38.2 per thousand
Giay	39.0 per thousand
Thai	40.4 per thousand
Pa Then	41.9 per thousand
Ngai	46.0 per thousand
San Diu	48.9 per thousand, and
Muong	55.1 per thousand.

In Tay Nguyen, the crude birth rate of local ethnic groups in the 1980s is as follows:

Gia Rai	43.07 per thousand
E De	44.15 per thousand
Ba Na	43.68 per thousand
Xo Dang	45.26 per thousand
Gie-Trieng	44.83 per thousand
Co Ho	47.07 per thousand
Mnong	49.24 per thousand and
Ma	50.31 per thousand.[13]

Assessing the situation throughout the country, it is noticeable that the crude birth rate has decreased each decade at a rate of approximately four per thousand.

The total fertility rate (TFR), on the other hand, is the average number of children of a woman of child-bearing age. The TFR rate in Vietnam dropped from 6.4 in the 1960–1964 period, to 5.9 in the 1970–1974 period, 4.7 in the 1980–1984 period, and 4.1 in the 1985–1989 period. Although in each decade the fall in crude births varied (from 8 to 13%), over the past three decades the total fertility rate dropped an average of 12% each decade. This means that in the 1960s, a Vietnamese woman had, on average, more than six children. In the 1970s, she had five or six children, and in the 1980s, only four or five[14] (see Table 87).

Table 87. Crude birth rate and total fertility rate by period

Period	Crude birth rate (%)	Total fertility rate	Change %
1960–1964	44.0	6.4	-
1965–1969	42.0	5.9	8
1970–1974	38.3	5.9 (5.5)*	-
1975–1979	34.6	5.2 (4.8)*	12
1980–1984	33.5	4.7 (4.6)*	10
1985–1989	31.0	4.1 (4.0)*	13

* The figure in parenthesis is the minimum

Table 88. Number of births (TFR) of ethnic groups and change over a five year period[15]

No.	Ethnic group	Number of births 1985–1989	% of change 1980–1984
1	Hoa	2.92	- 19.33
2	Kinh	3.84	- 13.51
3	Tay	5.00	+ 16.82
4	Si La	5.10	- 7.77
5	Khmer	5.14	- 7.72
6	Nung	5.20	+ 3.58
7	Muong	5.40	+ 7.78
8	Bo Y	5.60	+ 2.19
9	La Chi	5.70	- 3.63
10	La Hu	5.70	- 28.40
11	Tho	5.95	+ 7.01
12	Cham	6.10	- 7.30
13	Lo Lo	6.10	+ 12.96
14	Pu Peo	6.20	+ 12.72
15	Co Ho	6.20	+ 0.16
16	Ma	6.30	+ 3.28
17	San Chay	6.30	- 1.56
18	Giay	6.30	+ 3.62
19	Brau	6.40	+ 14.70
20	Thai	6.50	+ 1.41
21	Stieng	6.50	- 2.04
22	Ha Nhi	6.50	+ 4.41
23	Raglai	6.60	+ 7.66
24	Gia Rai	6.60	- 4.21
25	Chu Ru	6.60	+ 5.09
26	San Diu	6.65	- 10.37
27	Mnong	6.70	+ 5.84
28	E De	6.80	-13.48
29	Ba Na	6.80	-2.57
30	Ro Mam	6.90	- 13.83
31	Yao	7.00	+ 3.09
32	Cho Ro	7.10	+ 6.76
33	Cong	7.10	- 3.92
34	Co Lao	7.30	+ 24.57
35	Co	7.30	- 7.95

No.	Ethnic group	Number of births 1985–1989	% of change 1980–1984
36	Bru	7.40	- 3.64
37	Hre	7.50	+ 1.21
38	Lu	7.50	- 10.40
39	Gie-Trieng	7.50	+ 9.97
40	Xo Dang	7.56	+ 4.42
41	Pa Then	7.60	+ 8.72
42	Kho Mu	7.95	+ 3.25
43	Ta Oi	8.10	- 5.15
44	Khang	8.10	+ 1.63
45	Lao	8.20	+ 3.27
46	Xinh Mun	8.40	0.00
47	Co Tu	8.70	- 3.65
48	Hmong	8.80	+ 4.51

Comparing the total fertility rate of different geographical regions, the lowest rate is in the southeast region (2.9 children), next comes the Red River Delta (3 children), the Mekong River Delta (3.9 children), the northern mountainous and midland region (4.2 children), former Zone 4 (4.3 children), and the central coastal region (4.6 children). The highest rate is in the Central Highlands (six children). Comparing provinces and cities, three cities: Hanoi, Hai Phong, and Ho Chi Minh City, with the Vung Tau-Con Dao special zone, have the lowest total fertility rate.[16] Based on the results from the 1989 census and applying the Rele method, Dang Thu calculated the total fertility rate of each ethnic group (see Table 88).

According to these calculations, it is clear that the Hoa have the lowest number of children, then come the Kinh, Tay, Si La, Khmer, and so on. The ethnic groups having the highest number of children include the Hmong, Co Tu, Xinh Mun, and Lao. There is considerable difference between the ethnic group with the highest number of children (the Hmong) and that with the lowest number (the Hoa), about three times.

b. Mortality: In demography, some terminology is used to indicate the mortality rate, such as crude mortality rate (also called common mortality rate), mortality rate by age, and so on. The crude mortality rate is calculated as follows: the number of deaths over a certain period of time (often a year) divided by the average population in that period. But the crude mortality rate does not reflect fully and precisely mortality among the population. In those countries with a young population, the crude mortality rate is much lower than in those countries with an old population. This measure cannot, then, be used to conclude that the socio-economic situation in the former countries

127

(whose population is young) is superior to the latter countries (whose population is old). For this reason, people use other methods to calculate the mortality rate, such as mortality by age, mortality by cause, etc. Despite this, the crude mortality rate is still a widely-used measure. When Vietnam was under the domination of the French, the crude mortality rate was very high. According to Gourou, in 1939, the crude mortality rate in north Vietnam was 15.5 per thousand. Nguyen Thieu Lau, while collecting the resident registration books of the households in thirteen central coastal provinces (between 1935 and 1937), and particularly in Quang Binh province, found that the average mortality rate in those years was 15.1 per thousand. But he held that this figure was much lower in reality, since many people died without having their names ever registered in the local administration's records.[17] Meanwhile, in south Vietnam, the crude mortality rate in 1925 was 20.5 per thousand, in 1927, 23 per thousand, and in 1936, 24.2 per thousand. However, some people argued that the crude mortality rate in Vietnam in 1936 was 26 per thousand[18] and even 30 per thousand in the period prior to the August 1945 Revolution.[19]

During the 1950s, the crude mortality rate fell rapidly to only 12 per thousand; and in the first years of the 1960s, the rate fluctuated around 6 to 8 per thousand in 1970s. Over the past thirty years, the crude mortality rate has been fairly stable. Sample surveys of 10% of the total population in North Vietnam conducted in 1957, 1959, and 1960 (in almost all provinces and cities except Vinh Linh in 1957 and Vinh Phu in 1959) produced the statistics below (see Table 89).

Table 89. Crude mortality rate in different regions in North Vietnam in two years
1957 and 1960[20]

(unit: %)

Region	1957	1960	1957 compared to 1960
WHOLE NORTHERN REGION	12.2	12.0	- 0.2
Urban	7.0	5.2	- 1.8
Plains (lowland)	3.7		
Midlands	5.8		
Mountains	4.9		
Rural	12.3	12.7	- 0.4
Coastal	11.7	9.7	- 1.4
Plains	11.8	12.3	0.5
Midlands	13.3	12.4	- 0.9
Mountains	17.3	14.2	- 3.1
Uplands	23.3	20.4	- 2.9

The figures in this table show that the mortality rate in rural areas was higher than in urban areas; in the mountainous areas, particularly highland regions, it was higher than the lowlands and coastal regions. The mortality rate for the whole of northern Vietnam is falling (further explanation can be found in the next section). Compared with the period before the domination of the French (if it is accepted that the average annual mortality rate was 15 per thousand), then deaths were reduced by 3 per thousand, or 20.5%.

If regional figures for the years 1957 and 1960 are compared, for every 1,000 people there were reductions of:
- 1.8 deaths in urban areas
- 2.0 deaths in the coastal region
- 0.9 deaths in the midland region
- 3.1 deaths in the mountainous region
- 2.9 deaths in the uplands

The infant mortality rate (of children under fifteen) was high compared with the total number of deaths. If we take 1,000 as our base number, the proportion of people of different age groups at the time of death varied as shown in Table 90.[21]

Table 90. Infant mortality rate through 1957–1960

(unit: %)

Age group	1957	1959	1960
0–15 years of age	627	563.4	553.4
In which			
- Before one year	318	244.3	277.2
- 1–6 years	274	279.4	242.2
- 7–15 years	35	39.7	34.0

The younger the age group, the higher the mortality rate. Of 1,000 children who died in 1959, 507 were under one year old, 437 were from one to six years old, and 56 were aged seven to fifteen. Similarly, the rates for 1960 are 500, 440, and 60. For children aged less than one year, a month-by-month breakdown is provided in Table 91.

Table 91. Infant mortality rate by months

Month old	1959	1960	Compared 1960/1959
- Before one month	431	350	-81
- 1–3 months	315	358	43
- 4–6 months	141	157	16
- 7–11 months	113	135	22

129

In 1960, 63 of every 1,000 newborn babies in north Vietnam died before their first birthday. In Hanoi, there were 23 such deaths in all, in Hung Yen 115, Ha Dong 92, Thanh Hoa 53, in the Thai-Meo Autonomous Zone 70, and in other highland and border regions, a total of 236 deaths. The mortality rate of people aged 56 and above only accounted for one quarter of total deaths; (in 1959 it was 24.55%, in 1960, 26.00%). This was because of the low proportion of elderly people in the population. To give a clearer view of the mortality in different age groups in urban and rural areas, we reproduce the statistics released in 1963, the first year mortality rates stabilized, as an example (see Table 92).

Table 92. Mortality rate in different age groups in north Vietnam in 1963[22]
(unit: %)

Age group	General		Urban Areas		Rural Areas	
	Compared with the population of the age group	Compared with total population	Compared with the population of the age group	Compared with total population	Compared with population of the age group	Compared with total population
(1)	(2)	(3)	(4)	(5)	(6)	(7)
General	7.10	7.10	4.10	4.10	7.40	7.40
< 1 year	21.00	0.91	14.20	0.59	21.00	0.92
1–4	8.10	1.25	3.70	0.57	8.80	1.35
5–9	2.70	0.35	0.80	0.11	3.00	0.40
10–14	1.10	0.11	0.70	0.07	1.20	0.11
15–19	1.00	0.08	0.80	0.06	1.00	0.08
20–24	1.10	0.09	0.50	0.04	1.20	0.09
25–29	1.70	0.13	1.30	0.10	1.80	0.13
30–34	2.40	0.15	1.80	0.12	2.40	0.15
35–59	3.40	0.19	1.90	0.11	3.50	0.20
40–44	4.70	0.20	3.80	0.15	4.80	0.18
45–49	3.90	0.17	2.40	0.10	4.10	0.17
50–54	9.10	0.31	6.10	0.21	9.20	0.31
55–59	10.00	0.33	7.20	0.23	10.00	0.30
60 +	44.70	2.83	25.90	1.64	46.80	2.99

The infant mortality rate (under one year) remained rather high (21 per thousand), three times the general mortality rate. Comparing different age groups, the mortality rate in the 10–20 age group (compared with the population of this age group) is lowest. Comparing rural and urban areas, the infant mortality rate in rural areas is 1.5 times higher than that in urban areas. Comparing different periods from 1963 to the present, as noted above, the mortality rate throughout the century has seen no major changes (see Table 93).

130

Table 93. Crude mortality rate in north Vietnam and in the whole country
in different years[23]
(unit: %)

Year	Mortality rate	Year	Mortality rate	Year	Mortality rate
(1)	(2)	(3)	(4)	(5)	(6)
1960	12.0	1973	7.0	1981	7.0
1963	7.1	1974	7.2	1982	7.4
1965	6.7	1975	5.6	1983	7.2
1967	7.9	1976	7.5	1984	7.0
1969	7.0	1977	7.0	1985	6.9
1970	6.6	1978	7.1	1986	6.9
1971	6.7	1979	6.2	1987	6.7
1972	8.0	1980	7.0	1988	6.3

In the seven regions of Vietnam, the crude mortality rate in the Central Highlands is highest, followed by the northern mountainous and midland region and the Mekong Delta. The rate is lowest in the Red River Delta (see Table 94).

Table 94. Crude mortality rate by geographical regions in several years[24]
(unit: %)

Year	Northern midland and mountain region	Red River Delta	Former Zone 4	Central coastal region	Tay Nguyen	South-east Vietnam	Mekong River Delta
1979	6.1	6.6	6.6	6.4	6.1	5.5	6.4
1984	7.3	6.6	6.6	7.1	9.2	6.2	7.7
1985	7.5	6.2	6.7	6.8	9.2	6.3	7.4
1986	7.6	6.2	7.0	6.5	9.5	6.5	7.2
1987	7.1	6.0	6.9	6.4	9.4	6.3	6.8
1988	6.6	5.7	6.6	6.1	8.0	5.9	6.5

Comparison between provinces shows that the mortality rate in mountainous areas is rather high; in cities it is quite low. For example, the average mortality rate in Gia Lai-Kontum is 17 per thousand, while that in Hai Phong City is 5.3 per thousand. So the highest mortality rate is three times the lowest mortality rate.[25] This would indicate that the geographical factor remains an important determinant of the mortality rate (other important influences will be analysed in later sections).

The 1989 census statistics are taken as a basis to calculate the proportion of infant mortality rate of different regions (see Table 95). This led Le Van Duy to contend that, by contrast with developed

Table 95. Infant mortality rate in different regions[26]
(unit: %)

Region, Province	Mortality rate	Region, Province	Mortality rate
1. Northern midland & mountain region		4. Central Coastal region	
- Cao Bang	61.6	- Quang Nam-Da Nang	47.0
- Ha Tuyen	52.8	- Nghia Binh	51.5
- Lang Son	56.5	- Phu Khanh	44.8
- Lai Chau	66.1	- Thuan Hai	43.9
- Hoang Lien Son	59.3	5. Central Highlands	
- Son La	50.2	- Gia Lai-Kon Tum	78.8
- Bac Thai	42.2	- Dac Lac	44.9
- Quang Ninh	35.1	- Lam Dong	43.8
- Vinh Phu	33.1	6. Southeast Vietnam	
- Ha Bac	36.3	- Song Be	45.8
2. Red River Delta		- Tay Ninh	39.1
- Hanoi	39.8	- Dong Nai	33.8
- Hai Phong	26.1	- Ho Chi Minh City	30.1
- Ha Son Binh	48.0	7. Mekong River Delta	
- Hai Hung	38.0	- Dong Thap	49.0
- Thai Binh	31.6	- Long An	42.3
- Ha Nam Ninh	34.9	- An Giang	49.6
3. North-Central region (former Zone 4)		- Tien Giang	33.0
- Thanh Hoa	36.2	- Ben Tre	41.1
- Nghe Tinh	53.4	- Cuu Long	40.5
- Binh Tri Thien	49.9	- Hau Giang	45.4
		- Kien Giang	53.8
		- Minh Hai	44.4

countries where the geographical factor does not affect the mortality rate, in Vietnam, geographical conditions still have a strong impact on the mortality rate of the population.

Dang Nghia Phan also based his conclusions on the 1989 census data and argued that the crude mortality rate in Vietnam in 1989 was between 8 and 9 per thousand. According to him, in countries with an age pyramid similar to that of Vietnam, the infant mortality rate is more or less equal to the crude mortality rate. But data collected from the household registration books show that the infant mortality rate is about 7 per thousand. Data from sample surveys gave an even lower infant mortality rate. Infant mortality rates, by age group of the mother, are shown below.

Age group of mothers	Infant mortality rate (%)
20–24	49.9
25–29	52.0
30–34	57.6

35–39	64.4
40–44	78.8
45–49	92.9

The figures above differ from those given by the population census. They spell out a clear trend, however, that the greater the mother's age, the higher the infant mortality, particularly in the 45–49 age group.[27]

Turning now to the mortality rate by ethnic group, as discussed above, the mortality rate in the mountainous provinces, particularly in the highlands, differs greatly from that in the lowlands. Comparing different ethnic groups, the mortality rate in the ethnic minority groups is higher than the general mortality rate throughout the country; the mortality rate of ethnic minority groups living in the highlands, particularly those in remote and border regions, is higher than that of those living in the lowlands.

As everyone knows, the mortality rate depends on many different factors, such as socio-economic development, the availability of preventive and health-care services, environmental conditions, individual reproductive practices, etc. For this reason, prior to the August 1945 Revolution, the mortality rate of the ethnic minorities living in mountainous regions was very high. If in the lowlands the people suffered from flooding and famine, those in the mountainous region suffered from rampant diarrhoea, dysentery, and malaria. The people's health was poor, and hospitals were rarer than prisons. Under the French, there was on average one hospital bed for every 650 people, and a doctor or assistant physician for every 100,000 people in Vietnam. A further negative influence was the practice of child marriage, which was widespread, and affected both the birth rate and the health of children. Moreover, many ethnic minorities maintained backward customs. Pregnant mothers had to abstain from nutritious food, for fear of a hard delivery. If they had a hard delivery, they were denied medicine. They were not allowed to give birth inside their house. No proper care was given to the newborn baby, and when it fell ill it was not given medical treatment. The disease would be treated with prayer and other rituals. All these practices raised infant mortality in particular and mortality in general. The rate was, on average, about 60–70%.

At present, although the socio-economic conditions in the mountainous region where ethnic minorities are living have improved and many backward customs and habits have been dropped, mortality rates remains high. In 1984–1985, Dr. Le Huu Tinh and Dr

Vu Duc Vong conducted surveys on births among 1,190 women of the E De, Mnong, Gia Rai, Ba Na, and Xo Dang ethnic groups in the Central Highlands and produced the following data:

• For women over 45 years of age, the mortality rate of their children under five years of age was 45%. The figure for the Ba Na ethnic group was 56.7%, for the E De and Gia Rai was 35%.

• Of the 432 women over 45 years of age, 91.4 % had children who died before reaching the age of five.

• Of 1,171 women of all ages, the total number of deaths among their children was 2,292; that is, on average, each mother lost two children.

The Institute of Nutrition under the Ministry of Health conducted a survey on diet and health among the Ba Na people in Gia Lai-Kon Tum province in 1980–1981, which showed that about 50 % of children die under six years of age.

Data from a survey conducted by a research team headed by Dang Thu among the Gia Rai and Kinh in Chu Se district, Gia Lai-Kon Tum province and some other sites during the 1980s, concluded that children of women who gave birth prior to 1940 could expect to live to 36 years of age (among the Kinh), 34 (Gia Rai), and 30 (Ba Na). If they were born in 1941–1945, their life expectancy would be 40.5, 35.5, and 32, respectively. If born in the period 1946-1950, their lives would be slightly longer: 44, 40, and 37.7, respectively.[28]

Table 96. Mortality rate of ethnic groups in Tay Nguyen[29]

Ethnic group	Number of people surveyed (persons)	Mortality rate (%)	Ethnic group	Number of people surveyed (persons)	Mortality rate (%)
Kinh	9,234	7.46	Gie-Trieng	2,677	15.65
Gia Rai	4,808	13.32	Co Ho	1,735	12.72
E De	3,546	11.81	Mnong	1,020	12.44
Ba Na	2,965	15.04	Ma	3,879	14.33
Xo Dang	3,757	14.29			

Surveys conducted among ethnic groups in Tay Nguyen in 1991 and 1992, show a sharp fall in the mortality rate. Among the Gia Rai in Iajunpa district, Gia Lai province, the crude mortality rate in 1991 was 39 per thousand. A year later, it had dropped to 26 per thousand. For the Ba Na living in Kon Plong district, Kon Tum province, the rate was slightly higher: 55.6 per thousand in 1991, but only 36 per thousand in 1992. For the Xo Dang in the same district, the rate fell from 77.9 per thousand in 1991 to 23.2 per thousand in 1992.

The reason for this was that in the early 1990s, a serious malaria epidemic occurred in the mountainous region, particularly in the northwestern region, central border areas and Tay Nguyen. In some places such as western Nghe An province, the epidemic claimed thousands of lives.

Among the ethnic groups living in northern mountainous provinces, the crude mortality rate during the 1980s was higher than in the plains, though only slightly so. For example, the crude mortality rate among the Tay in Hung Dao commune, Binh Gia district, Lang Son province, in 1985 was 10.4 per thousand, among the Nung in Xuat Le commune, Cao Loc district, Lang Son province, in 1986, the rate was 8.9 per thousand, among the Nung in Linh Ho commune, Vi Xuyen district, Ha Giang province, it was 10.4 per thousand (45.5% died of malnutrition at an early age). However, in the early 1990s, the crude mortality rate among ethnic groups in the region increased suddenly, particularly in the northwest. For example, the crude mortality rate of the Hmong in Ta Phinh commune, Tua Chua district, Lai Chau province, was 110.3 per thousand of which 60.8% were people under the working age who died of malaria; the rate among the Hmong in Muong Bu commune, Muong La district, Son La province, was 44.0 per thousand in 1992; among the Mang in Nam Ban commune, Sin Ho district, Lai Chau province, it was 25.8 per thousand (of which 64.7% died of malaria); among the La Hu in Pa Ve Su commune, Muong Te district, Lai Chau province, it was 30.2 per thousand in 1992 and 13.6 per thousand in 1993 (of which 25% were newly born, 25% died of malaria, 11% died from delivery complications, 16.6% of diarrhoea and 22.2% of other causes). Evidently the mortality rate varies by ethnic group, by region, and over time.

Our analysis of the mortality situation in Vietnam over the last few decades shows that in general the mortality rate has fallen remarkably, from 20 per thousand prior to the August 1945 Revolution to between 6 and 8 per thousand in 1962 and 1963. This figure has remained unchanged up to now. Over the last thirty years, the average national mortality has been quite stable. With regard to ethnic groups living in the mountainous region, the mortality rate remains higher than the average. If there had not been a malaria epidemic in the 1990–1992 period, the mortality rate would have been stable. Compared with the period prior to the August 1945 Revolution, the mortality rate among the ethnic minorities, particularly those who live in highland and remote areas, has been reduced a great deal. However, a disparity remains, and the Vietnamese Party, State and authorities at all levels face a challenge to work out policies and concrete measures to overcome this.

c. Population growth: Vietnam has a large population, more than 70 million, ranking thirteenth in the world, seventh in Asia and second in Southeast Asia (after Indonesia). Population growth was slow until the first half of the twentieth century. But from the second half of this century on, its population growth rate has increased rapidly, particularly from the late 1950s to the early 1970s.

It has been said that Vietnam's population under the reign of King Hung Vuong some two thousand years ago, was one million; by the reign of King Tu Duc (1847–1883), it was seven million.[30] This means that after thousand years, the population only increased seven times. Since then, in just over a century, Vietnam's population has increased ten fold. However, the population growth rate differed according to the period (see Table 97).

Table 97. Vietnam's population growth rate, 1921–1965
(unit: %):

Period	Annual population growth rate	Period	Annual population growth rate
1921–1931	1.4	1965–1970	3.3
1931–1936	1.4	1970–1975	3.0
1936–1939	1.2	1975–1976	3.2
1939–1943	3.0	1976–1978	2.4
1943–1951	0.5	1978–1980	2.3
1951–1955	2.1	1980–989	2.2
1955–1960	3.8	1989–1992	2.1
1960–1965	2.9	–	–

Only in the 1939–1943 period was the rate of population growth 3%. At other times, before the Revolution, it was half that figure, just over 1%. But after the Revolution, war and famine reduced the rate of growth to a mere 0.5%. From the 1950s up to now, four periods recorded high population growth at more than 3%, and in other periods the rate was just over 2%. Although in recent years, the family planning movement has been very intensive, particularly in government offices, enterprises, cities, and towns, and the population growth rate has remained at 2%. However, in rural and mountainous areas, the natural population growth rate was much higher than in cities and lowland provinces.

The population growth rate varies over time and between ethnic groups. For example, statistics from the two population censuses in North Vietnam (1960 and 1974) show the population growth rate for some ethnic groups (see Table 98).

Table 98. Population growth rate for some ethnic groups in North Vietnam
(1960–1974)

No. in the order of population size in 1974	Ethnic group	(%)	No. in the order of population growth rate
(1)	(2)	(3)	(4)
	General	41.75	
1	Kinh	39.63	16
2	Tay	47.70	13
3	Thai	64.01	8
4	Muong	43.43	15
5	Nung	50.59	12
6	Hmong (Meo)	58.86	9
7	Yao	56.28	11
8	Hoa	46.89	14
9	San Diu	69.37	5
10	Cao Lan	85.91	2
11	San Chi	78.51	3
12	Giay	56.76	10
13	Ha Nhi	69.17	6
14	Xinh Mun	68.94	7
15	Van Kieu	31.75	17
16	La Hu	69.72	4
17	Lu	94.76	1

Over the fourteen year period, the population of the Lu ethnic minority group increased by 94.76%, the Cao Lan by 85.91%, and the San Chi by 78.51%. The lowest increase was among the Van Kieu group at only 31.72%, the Kinh at 39.63%, and the Muong at 43.43%. Over this fourteen year period, the population of the Lo Lo decreased. In 1974, its population was only 38.19% of that in 1960. Regrettably, the result of the 1974 census did not cover some important indicators relating to population and the distribution of the ethnic groups, and no explanation can be found for the above figures. We should note, however, that a population increase or decrease also depends on the classification of ethnic groups which may change over time. To get an overview on ethnic groups' increase or decrease, let us examine data from the two censuses conducted in 1979 and 1989 (see Table 99).

Table 99. Population and population increase/decrease of ethnic groups in Vietnam through two population censuses[31]

No.	Ethnic Group	Population 10/04/1979 (persons)	Population 10/04/1989 (persons)	Population growth/ decrease 10/04/1979– 10/04/1989 (persons)	Average growth/ decrease (-) annually (%)
(1)	(2)	(3)	(4)	(5)	(6)
	TOTAL	52,471,766	64,375,762	11,633,996	2.1
1	Kinh	46,065,384	55,900,224	9,834,840	2.0
2	Tay	901,802	1,190,342	288,540	2.9
3	Thai	766,720	1,040,549	273,829	3.2
4	Hoa	935,074	900,185	34,889	-0.4
5	Khmer	717,291	895,299	178,008	2.3
6	Muong	686,082	914,596	228,514	3.0
7	Nung	559,702	705,709	146,007	2.4
8	Hmong	411,074	558,053	146,979	3.2
9	Yao	346,785	473,945	127,160	3.3
10	Gia Rai	184,507	242,291	57,784	2.9
11	Ngai	1,318	1,154	-164	-1.4
12	E De	140,884	194,710	53,826	3.4
13	Ba Na	109,063	136,859	27,796	2.4
14	Xo Dang	73,092	96,766	23,674	3.0
15	San Chay	77,104	114,012	36,908	4.1
16	Co Ho	70,407	92,190	21,720	2.8
17	Cham	77,012	98,971	21,959	2.6
18	San Diu	65,808	94,630	28,822	3.8
19	Hre	66,884	94,259	27,375	3.6
20	Mnong	45,954	67,340	21,386	4.0
21	Raglai	57,984	71,696	13,712	2.2
22	Stieng	40,763	50,194	9,431	2.2
23	Bru-Van	33,090	40,132	7,042	2.0
24	Kieu	24,839	51,274	26,435	7.6
25	Tho	27,913	37,964	10,051	3.2
26	Giay	26,993	36,967	9,974	3.3
27	Co Tu	16,824	26,924	10,100	5.0
28	Gie-Trieng	20,264	25,436	5,172	2.4
29	Ma	32,136	42,853	10,717	3.0
30	Kho Mu	16,828	22,649	5,821	3.1
31	Co	20,517	26,044	5,527	2.5
32	Ta Oi	7,090	15,022	7,932	7.9
33	Cho Ro	2,327	3,921	1,594	5.5
34	Khang	8,986	10,890	1,904	2.0
35	Xinh Mun	9,444	12,489	3,045	2.9
36	Ha Nhi	7,738	10,746	3,008	3.5
37	Chu Ru	6,781	9,614	2,833	3.7
38	Lao	5,855	7,863	2,008	3.1
39	La Chi	3,174	1,396	-1,778	-8.6
40	La Ha	6,872	6,424	-448	-0.7
41	Phu La	4,270	5,319	1,044	2.3

(1)	(2)	(3)	(4)	(5)	(6)
42	Lu	2,952	3,684	732	2.3
43	Lo Lo	2,371	3,134	763	2.9
44	Chut	2,984	2,427	-557	-2.2
45	Mang	2,434	2,247	-187	-0.8
46	Pa Then	2,181	3,680	1,499	5.5
47	Co Lao	1,185	1,473	288	2.3
48	Cong	843	1,261	418	4.2
49	Bo Y	1,342	1,420	78	0.6
50	Si La	404	594	190	4.1
51	Pu Peo	264	382	118	3.9
52	Brau	95	231	136	9.4
53	O Du	137	32	-105	-15.3
54	Ro Mam	143	227	84	4.9
55	Unidentified	8,830	21,320	12,490	...
56	Foreigners	32,903	5,749	-27,154	...

The above table shows that some ethnic groups experienced abnormal population increases (4% or higher) and decreases (1%). Some of these are examined in greater detail below.

- The Hoa: according to the above table, the average population decrease was 0.4% per year. This was due to the very tense relations between Vietnam and China which culminated in the border war in February 1979. Before and after the war, some ethnic Hoa people left Vietnam for China and other countries. Some who stayed on, out of fear, registered themselves as members of other ethnic groups in the population census in 1989.

- The Bo Y: As discussed in the section on ethnic classification, this ethnic group comprises the Bo Y and Tu Di groups belonging to two different linguistic families; in the 1989 population census some of them registered as members of other ethnic groups.

With regard to six ethnic groups: the Ngai, La Ha, Phu La, Chut, Mang, and O Du, because their population fell over the ten year inter-censal period, their statistics were not announced in the results of the 1989 census. Some viewpoints on these ethnic groups follow.

- The Ngai: their fate was similar to that of the Hoa. This ethnic group comprises several sub-groups such as the Xin, the Le, the Dan, and the Hac Ca who were concentrated on the mainland and on some islands of the province of Quang Ninh. In 1978 and 1979, due to tension along the border, many of them returned to China. In October 1979, there were 531 Ngai people in Cao Bang province, but by April 1989, only 203 remained. Over this period, only two Ngai persons remained in Quang Ninh province.

139

- The La Ha: In the past the La Ha belonged to the Xa ethnic group. According to researchers, in 1972, the La Ha population was 2,000 people, living mostly in Son La province and concentrated in the districts of Muong La, Thuan Chau, and Than Uyen.[32] In the statistics released in the 1979 population census, the population of the La Ha in Son La province was 3,172 people living mostly in the district of Song Ma, and Muong La. There might be a mistake here, made during the census or in the processing of data. In the 1989 census, the La Ha population in Son La was recorded as 1,386 people concentrated mainly in Thuan Chau district, with more than 100 people living in Muong La district. Than Uyen was not mentioned in either population census. In our opinion, the La Ha people may have merged into the Thai. Therefore the statistics from the 1989 census are more reliable than those from 1979. In fact, the population of this ethnic group did not decrease by 8.6% each year.

- The Phu La: According to the 1979 census, the Phu La population in Hoang Lien Son was 6,430. In 1989, there were only 5,844 people. The reason for the annual 0.7% population loss among the Phu La in general and in Hoang Lien Son province in particular was migration, in particular, the cross-border emigration of the Phu La Han group (the Phu La who speak Han Chinese). Even recently, some Phu La returned to the other side of the border and married those of the same ethnic group there.

- The Chut: As mentioned in the section on the distribution of ethnic groups, the Chut are concentrated in Quang Binh province, with a few in Ha Tinh province. According to the result of the 1979 population census, there were 1,243 Chut people living in Dong Nai province. This is a regrettable mistake. If the group living in Dong Nai is excluded from the Chut, in 1979, the Chut population was only 1,700 people. In our opinion, this figure is acceptable.[33] In 1989, the figure was 2,427 people. So after ten years, the Chut population grew by 700 people, representing an annual growth rate of 4%, not a loss of 2.2% as the statistics in Table 99 suggest.

- The Mang: This group in the past belonged to the Xa ethnic group. Therefore, like the La Ha, sometimes they declared themselves as Mang and sometimes as Xa; it is difficult to come to a conclusion whether they were in danger of population loss.

- The O Du: When studying the O Du, researchers observed that they were only found in Tuong Duong district, Nghe An province. But according to the result of the 1979 population census, the O Du population totalled 137, scattered across districts such as Que Phong, Nghia Dan, Quynh Luu, Do Luong, Dien Chau, Nam Dan, Duc Tho,

Huong Khe, and the Ha Tinh provincial capital. In our opinion this is also a mistake. According to the result of the 1989 population census, the O Du population was only 32 people, 30 of them in Nghe Tinh province. This figure, although it is quite different from the current real figure of the O Du population, in our opinion was correct at that time.

In surveys conducted in November 1992, it was noticed that the O Du now mostly live in Kim Da commune, Tuong Duong district, Nghe An province, alongside the Kho Mu and the Thai. Many of them no longer acknowledge themselves to be O Du, but call themselves Kho Mu or Thai. For a long time, the O Du have not used their own language for daily communication, and now only one or two of them can remember some terms for counting. It is also hard to identify the ethnic characteristics of the O Du expressed in terms of both material or spiritual culture.

In recent years, the availability of state investment for ethnic groups with very small populations, and the experiences of some O Du people who have had multiple contacts with other ethnic groups and have visited different places around the country, have prompted some O Du people to return to an awareness of their ethnicity. In November 1992, the number of registered O Du people was 200.[34]

There has been no reduction of the O Du population. According to surveys, the O Du crude birth rate is rather high (over 40 per thousand) and the crude mortality rate is nearly 10 per thousand. The 1991 malaria epidemic pushed the crude mortality rate up to nearly 20 per thousand. This means that the natural growth of the O Du population has not been affected. The O Du population growth chart shows a fluctuating curve, due to the process of emerging self-consciousness and ethnic consciousness among the O Du people.

With regard to two ethnic minority groups with small populations living in northern Tay Nguyen, the Brau and the Ro Mam, the statistics in the table above show that their population growth rate is rather high (the Ro Mam 4.9% and the Brau 9.4%). However, since the middle of 1992, the mass media has covered these ethnic minority groups, offering frequent warnings about what they call "the danger of extinction," and the customs of "blood marriage" and "endogamy" which have been occurring.

A survey was conducted in October 1992 by Vu Dinh Loi of the Institute of Ethnology in Dac Me village, Bo Y commune, Ngoc Hoi district, Kon Tum province where most of Vietnam's Brau people live. This research revealed the situation in Dac Me village at the time.[35] After a village fire in April 1991, the local administration assisted the people to build a new village along the district road leading to border gate No. 19. But in fact, the local families lived mainly in their tents on forest farms. At the end of 1991 and in early 1992, many of them suffered from malaria and goitre (in 1992, about 60% of the population of Ngoc Hoi district suffered from malaria and 20% suffered from goitre).

By October 1992, Dac Me village had 43 Brau households with 192 people. Commune figures, however, recorded 44 households and 208 people. The district statistics counted 214 Brau people. The reason for these discrepencies was that local authorities' reports did not account for mixed marriages between ethnic groups. In some cases, people from other ethnic groups who married Brau and came to live in the village acknowledged themselves to be Brau. By October 1992, the crude birth rate of the village was 57 per thousand, but due to malaria epidemics, the crude mortality rate reached 67 per thousand, of whom 71.4% died under five years of age. So in reality, there was a population reduction, but it was inappropriate to generalize it as a trend. This is because the malaria epidemics in Vietnam during the 1990–1992 period were abnormal and occurred among ethnic minority groups whose population was very small; their mortality rate was consequently high. If they had occurred among ethnic minority groups with populations counted in tens of thousands, the mortality rate would have been lower. Of course, much effort should be made by the Vietnamese State in general and the Ministry of Health in particular to prevent such epidemics. As for the opinion that "blood marriage" and "intra-ethnic marriage" led to these high levels of mortality, Vu Dinh Loi rejected it as untrue and contrary to our ethnological knowledge about these two ethnic groups.

- With regard to ethnic groups with rapid population growth rates, such as the San Chay (with an annual rate of 4.1%), we do not know the real reason for this. But we can say that during the 1960-1974 period, the population growth rate of the Cao Lan and San Chi of the San Chay ethnic group was also very high. Moreover, some local Yao groups, such as those living in Cao Bang province, were included in the San Chay ethnic group.

- The 7% annual population growth rate of the Tho is due to the fact that more and more people of other ethnic groups registered as Tho. For example, 17,000 people in Nghia Dan district, Nghe An province, who had in the past registered as other ethnic groups, in 1989 acknowledged themselves to be Tho (as discussed earlier).

- With regard to the Mnong ethnic group, as already discussed, more than 1,000 people living in Quang Nam-Da Nang called Pnong, Ba Noong, etc., did not belong to the Mnong ethnic group.

142

Other ethnic groups such as the Gie-Trieng, the Cho Ro, the Khang, the Pa Then, the Cong, the Si La, etc., might have had very high fertility rates, but we also cannot rule out ethnic factors (the process of ethnic consciousness as discussed earlier).

III. RELATINSHIP BETWEEN POPULATION AND SOCIO-ECONOMIC DEVELOPMENT

THERE has been a dialectical relationship between population and socio-economic development. If the population did not rise or fall under certain conditions, then society would stagnate. Population growth is needed to boost production. It allows better labor distribution and the specialization of the labor force. It allows the development of a consumer market, stimulates commodity production, thus improving the quality of products and reducing their costs. Moreover, population growth makes for a younger labor force, improving its dynamism and creativity, and promoting the development of science and technology.

But if the population grows too fast, out of step with socio-economic development, it can become a negative force preventing and hindering social development. For this reason, there is a real need to practice population control to bring it into line with socio-economic development.

While the current average world population growth rate is 1.7% per annum, the rate in developed countries is 0.65% while that in developing countries is 2.03%. Vietnam is a developing country and has an annual population growth rate of 2.2%, higher than the average rate for developing countries. Due to very rapid population growth, it faces a major challenge if it is to achieve the socio-economic development targets.

We turn now to examine some consequences for Vietnam of the imbalance between population growth and socio-economic development.

1. PRESSURE ON FOOD

Vietnam is an agricultural country, with 80% of its population living in rural areas. The failure of food production to grow in step with the increase in population has, for many years, led to a reduction in the per capita food share.

It is estimated that if the population grows by 100%, food production has to grow by 200 or 300%. Besides feeding humans, food is also used for raising livestock. To obtain a kilogram of meat, 6-8 kilograms of food are required. But from 1940 to 1980, that is over forty years, the food output in Vietnam only increased by 2.5 times while the population growth increased by 2.7 times. For this reason, the average food share per capita dropped from 295 kg to 268 kg.[36] The rice share per capita fell by 34%. In the past decade, food output increased remarkably; the per capita food share also increased but did not stabilize, and in some years it even fell by comparison with the previous year (see Table 100.)

Table 100: Food output and per capita food share[37]

	1980	1985	1986	1987	1988	1989	1990
- Food output (1,000 tons)	14,406	18,200	18,379	17,529	19,560	21,516	21,540
- Per capita food share (kg)	268	304	301	281	307	334	325

One of the reasons for Vietnam's unstable per capita food share in the past is that food output increase has not corresponded to the population growth. Obviously, rapid population growth affects the standards of living of the people, particularly in rural and mountainous regions. If positive measures are not taken, all plans and policies, including such programs as the national Poverty Reduction scheme currently being implemented, will bring about negligible results.

2. IMPACT ON THE QUANTITY AND QUALITY OF EDUCATION AND HEALTH CARE

Rapid population growth, primarily due to the increase in the number of children, changes the population structure. In Vietnam, over the past three or four decades, the population growth was very high, particularly in the 1955–1977 period. During these twenty-two years, the population doubled, from 25 million to 50 million people. For this reason, there was a large number of children under the working age. In 1960, the proportion of children aged from zero to fourteen was 42.8% in North Vietnam. In the years from 1974 to 1976, the figure in the whole country was 45.1%. Then the country applied birth control by launching a family planning campaign which resulted in the reduction of the proportion of children (down to 42.5% in 1979, and 39.8% in 1989). However, the proportion of children among ethnic minority groups remained very high. For example, 53.29% for the Co

Tu; 49.99% for the Hmong; 49.07% for the Kho Mu; 48.87% for the San Diu, 48.84 % for the Hre, etc. (1989 data).

To summarize, in Vietnam, there were 25.2 million children aged from zero to fourteen in 1989, which was equal to the total population of the country in 1955. This begs the question of how enough money can be found to invest in this young population, providing it with food, clothing, schooling, and health care.

According to World Health Organization surveys, the average food ration calculated for Asian people is 2,350 calories per day. In Vietnam, it is only 1,940 calories per day. In the areas often hit by natural calamities, resulting in food shortages, a ration of only 1,800 calories per day is recorded. Six percent of Vietnamese people get less than 1,500 calories per day. In rural Vietnam, 70% of pregnant mothers suffer from anaemia, and thus they and their children's foetuses are malnourished. The proportion of newborn babies suffering from high levels of malnutrition (weighing less than 2,500 grams) is 21.7%. The proportion of children in the 0–5 age group suffering from malnutrition is 51.5%. Of the children aged between six and fourteen who have been given health checks, only 32% have good health, 59% have average health, and 9% have poor health.[38] Moreover, due to multiple pregnancies and births, the health and lives of mothers have been affected. (According to Nafis Sadik;[39] at least 500,000 women in the world die of pregnancy and births every year). Health networks have not yet developed in step with population growth (see Table 101).

Table 101: Health network in the whole country over several years[40]

Year	Population (in 1,000 persons)	Health centers and hospitals	Hospital beds
1980	53,722	11,072	108,800
1984	58,770	11,316	211,400
1988	63,727	12,133	223,041
1990	66,322	12,105	205,136

The figures in the above table show that during the 1980s, the number of health centers and hospitals increased very little, and even decreased in some years while the population continued to grow rapidly (by some 13 million people). The number of hospital beds per capita fell noticeably. For example, the number of hospital beds per 10,000 people was 37.0 in 1980, 35.9 in 1984, 34.9 in 1988 and 30.9 in 1990.

An analysis of the educational system shows that in the 1990–1991 school year, there were more than 12 million students (including those in general education, vocational schools, colleges and universities), accounting for 18% of the total population. So one in every five people is a student. However, compared with the previous school years, the per capita enrollment in this school year was much lower (see Table 102).

Table 102. School enrollment in the whole country[41]

(unit: 1,000 persons)

YEAR	1986–1987	1987–1988	1988–1989	1989–1990	1990–1991
TOTAL ENROLLMENT:	13,270.0	13,305.1	12,820.2	12,183.7	...
• General education	12,482.9	12,623.1	12,203.8	11,710.1	11,882.5
• Complementary education	504.5	442.1	349.5	209.1	...
• Secondary vocational schools	156.0	147.0	138.6	138.5	135.4
• Universities and colleges	126.6	112.9	128.0	126.0	129.6

Table 102 shows the situation for the country as a whole. But the level of school enrollment in mountainous areas was lower than the average. For example, the data on school enrollment in Ha Tuyen province is shown in Table 103.

Table 103. Average number of general education students per 10,000 people in Ha Tuyen province:[42]

1980	1981	1982	1983	1984	1985	1986	1987	1988
208	206	189	180	175	171	167	183	167

According to results of a survey conducted by the Central Institute of Statistical Science and the Statistics Office of Lang Son province in 1992, only 84% of Nung and 35% of the Yao people of school age in the province know how to read and write. The number of people attending school is only 20% of the five years and more age group; the school drop-out rate is 60%; 19% of people have never been to school. Only 56.02% of children in the 5–9 age-group were attending school, which means that fully 43.05% of children have never attended school.[43]

The above analysis only deals with education in terms of quantity. But at all levels of the system and throughout the country, the quality of education has also been falling dramatically, and this trend has affected the children of ethnic minorities most seriously. Nghe An province Statistics Office reports that the performance of students in the province is becoming steadily poorer, especially in secondary schools. Thirty-five hamlets and villages in the province have no classes. In the 1991–1992 school year, the proportion of excellent graduates from primary school was 4.8%; the proportion of lower secondary schools was 0.2% and from upper secondary schools was 0.05%. In primary schools, the number of graduates was only 45.5% of the total number of first-grade pupils. For secondary schools, the rate of graduation was 18.2%.

According to Tran Si Nguyen and Dinh Xuan Ha, education of the ethnic minority groups, particularly those living in the highlands and remote areas, has met with many difficulties. The number of children between six and fourteen going to school is very low (15–40%). In particular, the number of female students is very small. In some communes, no girls were able to go to school. In some places, in both lower and upper secondary schools, all the students in the final grade did not achieve high enough marks to enter the next educational level.[44] With regard to the Hmong, by 1981, only 12.3% could read and write, 10.6% of them were at primary level, 0.8% at lower secondary level and 0.08% at upper secondary level.[45]

Population growth has created great pressure on the State, forcing it to spend a large portion of the budget on building cr?ches, schools, hospitals, and housing. But because of the rapid increase in the population, investment cannot fully meet requirements. This trend has a negative impact on people's health and quality of education as well as on the general knowledge of the young generation.

3. UNEMPLOYMENT

Population growth, sustained over a period of 15–18 years, leads to an increase in the size of the labor force. It is calculated that to maintain the living standards of the people, when the population grows by 1% national income has to increase by at least 8–9%. However, in reality Vietnam's national income only increased by 3.5%, less than half the amount required.[46] Moreover, if income does not increase and the labor force grows, the average income per capita will fall. Evidently, it is better to increase revenue and limit increases in the labor force. But this is no easy task. At present, on average, Vietnam has to provide jobs for more than one million people who join the work force each year. This does not include existing unemployed workers and those who will be made redundant in the future due to the restructuring of State-owned enterprises. Policy measures also have to be taken to ensure a living for elderly people and pensioners. There were 400,529 elderly people and pensioners in Vietnam in 1985, and 21,076 of them were over seventy years of age. Of these, 731 people lived alone and had no means of support.

Vietnam's labor force is also underemployed. Vietnam is an agricultural country with 80% of its population living in rural areas. Rural people account for more than 60% of the total labor force. But this labor force does not use all its working time, and this labor wastage is equivalent to the unemployment of nine million people. Cities and provincial/district towns have a proportion of the population which is unemployed or cannot find a stable job. But additionally, people from the countryside come to these urban areas looking for work, even very basic manual work. Work is hard to find, and these people swell the ranks of the unemployed. Job creation in urban areas is very difficult, as the cities lack resources, raw materials, and investment capital.

Increasing unemployment is a heavy burden on the shoulders of the laboring people themselves and affects the country's social and economic situation. For instance, unemployment means that scientific advances and new technologies cannot be applied, resulting in low labor productivity, limited savings and investment, and the development of social evils such as burglary, prostitution, gambling, drug addiction, and so on. To solve these problems, administrative measures are not enough. We have to take into consideration the relationship between population growth, labor force expansion, and socio-economic development if we are to take appropriate measures.

4. IMPACT ON THE LAND, FORESTS, AND NATURAL ENVIRONMENT

Rapid population growth rate has a great impact on natural resources, and primarily land. Land is becoming increasingly scarce, and the forests and natural environment are being degraded. As most people know, every year 26 billion tonnes of fertile surface soil are washed away and about 21 million ha of land become wasted. Vietnam has more than 33 million ha of land. With rapid population growth, land per capita, particularly agricultural land, has been falling (see Table 104).

Although land has been cleared and reclaimed in many localities and the cultivable land area has expanded, the average per capita agricultural land area has been reduced by half since 1940 because of rapid population growth. The cultivable land area is being narrowed because land requirements for construction of dwellings and public projects is growing due to population growth. Soil erosion has also be-

Table 104: Agricultural land use, 1940–1990

Year	Population (1,000,000 persons)	Food production (1,000,000 tonnes)	Agricultural land per capita (ha)
1940	20.2	6.0	0.26
1955	25.1	6.1	0.19
1975	47.6	11.6	0.12
1980	53.7	14.4	0.13
1984	58.7	17.9	0.13
1988	63.7	19.6	0.12
1990	66.2	21.5	0.12

Table 105. State of forests, land and population in selected regions in Vietnam (1990)

Region	Natural land area (1,000 ha)	Forest land (1,000 ha)	% of coverage	Population (in 1,000 persons)	Labor force (in 1,000 persons)
Total	33,054	19,065	28.18	22,242	14,361
Northwest	3,726	2,781	11.35	1,860	1,268
Northeast	3,368	2,141	23.40	2,877	2,323
Center	3,316	2,245	19.60	3,290	1,523
Tay Nguyen	5,613	4,037	59.30	1,906	963
Southeast	2,117	853	27.20	2,496	1,122

come more serious due to forest destruction and the inappropriate use of forest land. Three quarters of Vietnam's land is mountains and hills and the forest coverage should be 50% for ecological balance. But over the last fifty years, half of the forest area has been lost, and coverage is now only 28%. More than 20 million people (4 million households, from fifty ethnic groups) live on the 19 million hectares of forest land. Two million people from ethnic minority groups still practice semi-nomadism. Over the past few years, wanton exploitation, particularly by state farms and forestry enterprises, massive land clearance, as well as shifting cultivation, have combined to produce a dramatic reduction in Vietnam's forest areas (see Table 105).

Vietnam's forest coverage fell from 14.3 million ha, or 43.8% of the total land area in 1943 to 9.3 million ha fifty years later. Rich forests make up only 3.6 million ha of this total; young and poor forests, 5.7 million. Loss of forests and natural resources is a major danger for the country. It is estimated that if there is no reduction in the rate of forest loss, Vietnam will have no forest at all in ten or twenty years' time. Forest resources, such as wildlife, will be lost as a result. Rapid population growth and inappropriate exploitation of forests have been seriously degrading forests resources and even marine resources: the marine environment is polluted by petroleum exploitation and rain water which carries wastes and pollutants from the mainland to the sea.

Water and mineral resources as well as ecological systems have been exhausted. Land shortage and forest loss have led to migration, particularly free migration, which causes many complicated problems to society (as discussed earlier).

Vietnam's current population growth is clearly a hindrance to socio-economic development. To a certain extent, the population is a natural resource. At the same time, it is also the greatest threat to the environment. Population grows while forests, forest land and natural resources become more scarce and degraded. For this reason, it is urgent to adopt policies of investment in population limitation, especially in family planning, to stabilize the situation at a level where natural resources may be exploited in most efficient ways for development.

We have discussed the impact of population growth on socio-economic development. Let us now turn to the impact of socio-economic development on population growth. As mentioned above, population growth in developed countries is slow or stagnant, while in poor countries with under-developed economies, it is high. Factors affecting population growth include marriage age (the most important of all), labor practices, the mortality rate, cultural and educational levels, and the role of women. Let us examine each of these in turn.

A definition of the age of marriage is the age of first marriage among women. Normally, women's reproductive life lasts between thirty and thirty-five years (from 15 or 16 to 49 years of age). So the later the woman marries, the shorter the duration of her reproductive period and the fewer children she will have. On the contrary, the earlier she is married, the more children she might have if no contraceptives are used. In Vietnam, due to an under-developed economy and many backward cultural practices, the idea remains strong that the more children a couple has, the more hands to work they will have, and the greater their wealth and prosperity. For this reason, child marriage remains widespread in the countryside, especially in mountainous areas. Particularly over the last few years, children have been marrying at 15 or 16, in defiance of the law and without registering with the local authorities. The persistence of ancient customs such as *sororat* (marriage to one's wife's sisters) also encourages the marriage of children among some ethnic groups. This practice implies that if the elder sister dies, the younger sister or a daughter from the generation below that of the deceased must marry the widower. Marriage between cousins is also highly favoured by some ethnic groups of the

Mon-Khmer linguistic family. According to these groups' customs, cousins become husband and wife immediately after birth. The E De custom of family inheritance also follows this general pattern. This involves the marriage of very young women to the husband of the deceased wife, even if he belongs to the generation of the new wife's parents or grandparents.

In 1981, a total of 2.3% of Vietnamese women had given birth before the age of 19. Of these, 209 women had already experienced four deliveries. A total of 545,700 women of all ages had had more than four deliveries, and this figure represents no less than 33.2% of the women who had borne children. Some 14,000 women had given birth at least ten times, and 142,300 had given birth when they were over 40, and 7,306 when they were over 50.[47]

According to statistics from fieldwork, the proportion of women with three births or more during the 1980s and 1990s was high and the average number of children per woman was also high. Statistics from Hai Phong, Ha Bac, Hanoi, and Ho Chi Minh City show that of the 16,475 women giving birth, 1,456 of them had experienced three or more births. In Hanoi alone, women having more than three births accounted for 30% in the past. By 1985, the figure dropped to 10%.[48] According to the results of a survey conducted by the Institute of Sociology in the Red River Delta, a woman of child-bearing age had an average of 7.1 children. Of the interviewees, 52.6% said that a happy family should have many children. Of the 271 families selected in the survey, 199 of them (73.43%) had more than three children. Furthermore the desire for more children was strong: 78.6% said they wanted more than three children.[49]

Surveys conducted by Vi Van An and Mai Thanh Son (Institute of Ethnology) in late 1993 among the Mang ethnic group in Nam Ban commune, Sin Ho district, Lai Chau province, and the La Ha ethnic group in Noong Lay Commune, Thuan Chau district, Son La province, provided the following figures:

- 34% of the Mang women and 22% of the La Ha women married before the age of eighteen.

- 37% of the Mang women and 35% of the La Ha women gave birth one year after marriage.

- 34% of the Mang women and 30.3 % of the La Ha women (of those who had children) had their first birth under the age of eighteen.

- 46.8% of Mang women had more than four children (8.5% had more than ten children). Figures for the La Ha are 50.56% and 4.1 % respectively.

We can be in no doubt of the difference between uplands and

plains, and between the Kinh and other ethnic groups, when we examine the age of marriage, the age of first births, and the number of children each woman bears.

According to the 1989 census, women who married before the age stipulated by the Law on Marriage and Family accounted for 2.71% of legally marriageable age (see Table 106).

Table 106. Marital status of women belonging to selected ethnic groups in 1989 [50]

No.	Ethnic groups	Women in 13–17 age group	Number of married women (persons)	Compared with the total number in the age group (%)
(1)	(2)	(3)	(4)	(5)
	WHOLE COUNTRY	3,535,935	95,991	2.71
1	Hmong	30,757	6,563	21.33
2	Co Tu	1,546	319	20.63
3	Hre	3,418	666	19.48
4	Khang	203	39	19.21
5	Lu	231	43	18.61
6	Xinh Mun	543	97	17.86
7	Lao	540	93	17.22
8	Lo Lo	180	26	14.44
9	Gie-Trieng	1,091	148	13.56
10	Kho Mu	2,219	289	13.02
11	Cong	68	8	11.76
12	Dao	26,611	2,967	11.15
13	Co Lao	87	9	10.34
14	Ta Oi	1,394	145	10.04
15	Hoa	49,919	789	1.58
16	Kinh	3,081,557	64,076	2.08
17	Tho	2,867	930	3.24
18	Co	796	26	3.27
19	Muong	47,780	1,792	3.75
20	San Chay	6,508	263	4.04
21	Tay	63,836	2,636	4.13
22	San Diu	5,500	236	4.29
23	Ha Nhi	724	36	4.97

Nearly thirty years after the introduction of the Law on Marriage and Family, there remained some 96,000 women who married between at the age of 13 and 17. Besides the three ethnic groups, the Pu Peo, Brau and Ro Mam, whose population is very small, the remaining fifty ethnic groups all have women getting married before the legally eligible age. For the Hoa and the Kinh, the proportion of married women is only 1.58% and 2.08% respectively, of the total number in that same age group. This is lower than the average proportion for the whole country. But some ethnic groups, such as the Hmong and the Co Tu, record figures of 21.33% and 20.63%, respectively. The proportion of under-age brides in these ethnic groups is double the national average.

According to results of research conducted by the National Committee for Population and Family Planning in 1988, the average age of a woman's first marriage in Vietnam is 23.4, 22.5 in the north and 24.6 in the south.[51]

Initial calculations show that every year some 500,000 couples get married. In Hanoi alone, during the 1975–1980 period, some 7,000 wedding parties were organized annually and now the figure is more than 10,000. Some 80% of newly-weds do not have their own apartment or house and about 80% of them have children right after marriage.[52]

Poverty and an under-developed economy cause rapid population growth.

From 1980 to 1985, the world's average birth rate was 27 per thousand. In developed countries, it was 15.5 per thousand; in developing countries, 31 per thousand. Population growth rates are much higher in today's poor (developing or under-developed) countries, than they were in Western countries at the starting point of their development process.

Poverty and hunger are often found alongside large families with many children and, at any given moment in time, a large number of dependents. In an agricultural country like Vietnam, where production levels are low and 80% of the population lives off the land, where the agricultural labor force makes up 60% of the whole, where most work is simple manual labor easily performed by women and children, where dependents contribute to the family's labor force, people still want to have many children. The idea that "the more children you have, the more wealth you will possess" influenced many previous generations and still affects farmers' thinking today, especially in upland areas. Moreover, poverty ensures that investment in children's upbringing and education is low, thus inexpensive, and one or two extra children present very little extra burden to the parents (by contrast with urban families). Other old-fashioned ways of thinking remain powerful, evidenced in proverbs such as "heaven creates the elephant, so it will also provide the grass," and "this crab looks out for this crab's life, that crab looks out for that crab" (meaning that each cares only for his own fate). This outlook prevents people in rural and upland areas from doing anything to stop the increase in population.

One survey among people of the Mang ethnic group showed that 85.4% of the respondents thought it was best for every couple to have at least five children. Of the La Ha respondents, 60% answered this question in the same way.

High mortality rates are another factor leading to a high birth rate. A high mortality rate, whatever its cause (war, epidemics, or stillborn babies) generally forces people to have more births to compensate for the loss and risk. As is generally known, after each war, the population often grows very rapidly to compensate for the number of deaths. The killing caused by a war will linger on the minds of mothers, not only for one generation, but for many generations after. Vietnam's history has been dominated over the past few decades by the struggle against foreign invaders, and its people have undergone terrible wars of resistance. War claimed the lives of millions of people, particularly the young. This has affected the psychology of Vietnamese mothers. Such psychology cannot be overcome overnight.

Besides deaths due to natural disasters and epidemics, infant deaths greatly affect the birth rate among the population. According to a report by the Ministry of Health, the mortality rate of children under one year old in Vietnam was 46 per thousand, and the result of a survey conducted in seven different regions gave the figure of 31.6 per thousand.[53] But in our opinion, those figures do not give a true picture of the reality. In rural areas, particularly upland and ethnic minority regions, people consider new-born mortality very bad luck. They do not register nor wish to recall those deaths. So it is hard to get the precise statistics even if quantitative or qualitative surveys are conducted. People called death of the newly born and children (under the working age) a "wasteful death." This is because all efforts and investment in nurturing, education, and training such children brings about no result, as the children die before reaching working age and starting production in society.

Low educational and cultural levels are also a cause of the high birth rate. A survey conducted among people aged between 41 and 50 during the 1980s showed that 66% of respondents with primary education said more children would give them more work hands, and assumed the family would be better off economically. Some 33% of interviewed farmers with a primary education said that a family with three or four children is small.[54]

All these social and economic factors—new born deaths, the desire for more children, low educational attainment of women—are inter-related. Social and economic factors are often very important, as shown by the fact that a large proportion of child-bearing mothers over 40 are illiterate, have many children, and have low incomes.[55] Surveys conducted in some communes on the outskirts of Hanoi and Hai Phong show that only 4% of the respondents aged 15 and above went to school. Of the total number aged between 6 and 14, only 80% are able to go to school. The number of illiterates and semi-illiterates has been increasing rapidly.[56] Surveys conducted in the mountainous provinces, such as Son La (Moc Chau district), found that nearly all of the Hmong women are illiterate; in Lao Cai and Yen Bai, 93% of the Hmong women and 80% of the Yao women are illiterate; in Gia Lai province, 83.6% of the Gia Rai women are illiterate.

Of the total adult population (aged 15 and over), only 20–30% (20% of women) sometimes read. The remaining 70–80% do not know what books and newspapers are; 4.5% (53% of women) have never watched films; 62% (69% of women) have never seen a theatrical performance.[57] Obviously, this situation limits the effectiveness of communication and education, with regard to state policies, especially concerning family planning. We must look forward to a time when women achieve higher levels of education and a better place in society (through their activities in social organizations), and when their sense of responsibility towards their work makes them think that a large family would be a hindrance. These changes would bring about a reduction in the birth rate.

One factor of the high birth rate is that care for the elderly, particularly where chronic illness and very old age are concerned, is not yet properly provided by society. Therefore, the psychology of desire for more children, both male and female, to support people in their old age is very widespread.

In rural areas, particularly in the upland regions, many people firmly believe that the strength of the family and clan is measured by the number of its members, particularly the number of sons in each family clan. Surveys show that 79.8 % of interviewees said that they must have sons, 80% said that having no sons is the greatest unhappiness.[58]

According to statistics released by the National Committee for Population and Family Planning through surveys in the summer of 1988, more than 17% of married women with children did not have sons. This situation clearly affects the birth rate. Due to the fact that they must have more births to hope to have sons as they wish, in places where the birth rate is high, the proportion of women having no sons is low. For this reason, in rural areas, the proportion of married women having no sons is lower than in urban areas.[59]

NORTH VIETNAM'S POPULATION PYRAMID IN 1960

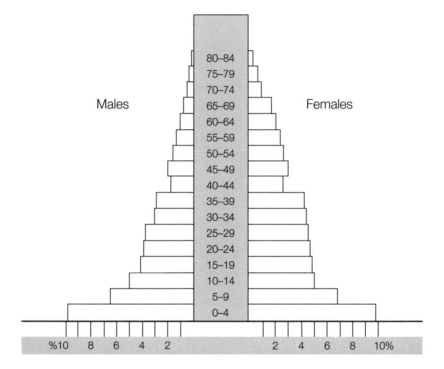

VIETNAM'S POPULATION PYRAMID IN 1979

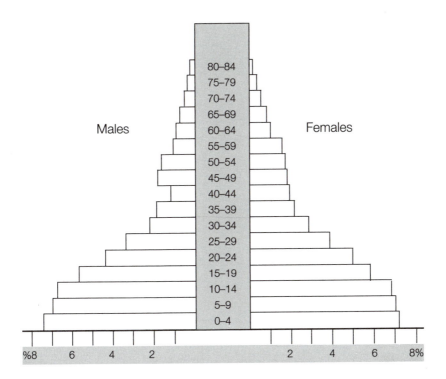

VIETNAM'S POPULATION PYRAMID IN 1989

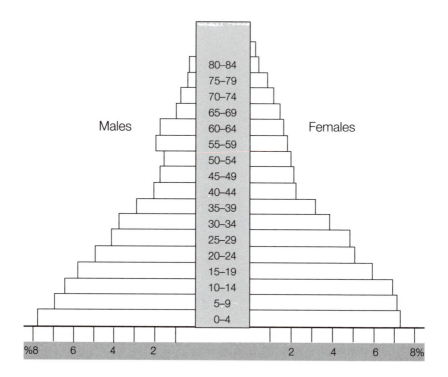

CONCLUSION

THE MOST important task in any analysis of the development of population and society is to comprehend the extent and manner by which the socio-economic situation affects the natural reproduction of the population, in both the areas of fertility and mortality. Biologically speaking, there are features of this process which are common to all humans, but different groups, categorized in terms of race, language, ethnicity, and even geographical region, show different characteristics. The study of these characteristics from the perspectives of ethnology and demography is the challenge of ethno-demography.

To study demographic characteristics of ethnic groups, the researchers have to understand what an ethnic group is and, in the territory under analysis, how many ethnic groups live there. The greatest achievement of Vietnamese ethnologists in the recent decades was the introduction of a system of classification to define the composition of ethnic groups. Based on that system, social scientists in general and ethnologists in particular have concluded that in Vietnam there are fifty-four ethnic groups. Even though there remains a certain amount of controversy around the sub-groups within certain ethnic groups, it is acknowledged that this process of classification has made a remarkable contribution, in both theory and practice, to the resolution of a number of ethnic problems and to the implementation of policies on ethnic groups by the Vietnamese Communist Party and State.

However, the composition of ethnic groups is constantly evolving and developing. This may be due to normal ethnic changes, or to the fact that classifications made in the past were not completely accurate.

It is necessary, as a result, to reconsider the issue once in a while. This task should be carried out objectively, with coordination between different branches and sectors with relevant responsibilities to ensure that reconsideration is appropriate, and to avoid radical shifts in perspective, from one extreme to another, from one unreasonable position to another, which only serve to complicate matters. Success in this task is an achievement which allows for the implementation of policies on ethnic groups and population issues by the Vietnamese State.

Population policies have been implemented to a limited extent, with a view to improvements in the size, structure, and distribution of the population, as well as its characteristics. Vietnam is a country with a high population, the thirteenth largest in the world. The population growth rate has been high, particularly in the second half of the twentieth century. Among some ethnic groups, notably the San Chay, Gie-Trieng, Pa Then, population growth has been very rapid indeed. But while some ethnic groups have grown rapidly, even abnormally so, others have not grown at all, and have even experienced reductions in their population. Many such cases were the results of ethnic changes rather than natural population growth or loss. But comparison with the national average shows that population growth among ethnic minority groups, particularly those living in the northwest and Central Highlands regions has been higher. The cause of this is a high birth rate; although the general mortality rate has been reduced, infant mortality remains high, the age of first marriage is low, and most people's socio-economic and cultural status is poor.

Analysis of population structure, especially the sex ratio, shows that most ethnic minority groups have higher male/female ratios than the majority Kinh. The figure is low only among the Khmer (male/female 90%). Regarding age structure, the proportion of children under working age is higher among ethnic groups living in the mountainous regions than the average for the whole country, while the proportion of the elderly is somewhat lower. This shows that the birth rate among ethnic minorities in Vietnam remains high, while the active proportion of their population is low.

The redistribution of the population has been a major element in Party and State policy. Since the 1960s, a campaign has been under way to encourage people from the plains to move to mountainous regions to clear land and build new economic zones in an attempt to reduce the population pressures in the lowlands and limit the growth of cities and towns. So far, some five million people from the plains have been mobilized to settle in sparsely populated areas as part of the State's efforts to redistribute the population and move labor evenly throughout the country.

However, the general territorial distribution of Vietnam's population remains, as yet, little changed. Imbalances remain between the land available in different regions and the population living there. While the Kinh were being mobilized to move from the lowlands to the mountainous areas to make a living, the minority inhabitants of these mountains themselves started moving elsewhere. Our comparative studies of the ethnic groups of the northwest region reveal that the Muong people have traditionally been the least inclined to migrate. There is a saying among the Muong "If you move a short distance, a chicken will be lost; if you move a long distance, humans will be lost." But over the past few years, thousands of Muong have been leaving for the central highland provinces to settle down and live. In particular, other ethnic minority groups such as the Hmong, Tay, Nung, and Yao have traditionally moved only short distances. Now, because of population pressure, a degraded environment, and other reasons, these ethnic groups are starting to move over long distances, often freely migrating in north-south and east-west directions. This trend continues today and, if no appropriate measures and policies are adopted, the political, social, economic, and cultural situation of the ethnic groups living in the mountainous regions in the north, the Central Highlands, and southeastern Vietnam will be badly affected.

The Vietnamese Party and State have issued a number of policies on population. The most important of these was announced in 1963. The campaign focused on family planning in the north, with a target of reducing the birth rate from 3.5% to 2.5% and then 2%. The policy strove to achieve the target of two to three children per married couple and spacing between births of between five and six years.

In May 1970, the Council of Ministers issued Decision 94–CP on family planning, with the target of reducing the birth rate in the north to between 2.2% and 2.4%. The targets for urban areas were 1.8-2 %, and lowland provinces 2.3–2.5%. With regard to ethnic minority groups living in the midlands and highlands, they were encouraged to increase their population levels.

In 1976, among the tasks and targets set for the 1976–1980 five-year plan to be submitted to the Fourth National Party Congress was the following instruction: "The family planning campaign should be further stepped up, to reduce the annual population growth rate, striving to achieve the population growth rate of just over 2% by 1980."

In August 1981, the Council of Ministers issued Directive No. 29/ HDBT for the promotion of the family planning campaign from 1981 to 1985. It set a target of two children for each married couple, and a five year spacing between births. It was planned that by 1985, the average population growth rate would be reduced to 1.7% .

At the Fifth National Party Congress (held in August 1982), it was pointed out, among the various tasks and main targets for socio-economic development, that the government should, "Step up the education, mobilization and application of administrative and economic measures and create all favourable conditions for the people to carry out the family planning campaign to reduce the average population growth rate from 2.4% to 1.7% by 1985."

The Sixth National Party Congress (in December 1986) continued to stress: "The socio-economic situation of the country requires the reduction of the current population growth rate of 2.2% to 1.7% by 1990."

In October 1988, the Council of Ministers issued Decision No. 162/ HDBT, which set the age for a couple's first birth as follows: 22 years for females and 24 years for males living in cities, provincial towns, and economic zones; 19 years for females and 24 years for males in other regions. Married couples were restricted to two children, while the figure for couples living in the northern mountainous regions, Central Highlands and the southeast was set at three.[1]

At the Fourth Plenum of the Party Central Committee (seventh tenure in January 1993), a separate resolution was passed on population and family planning policies. The resolution stressed "Population and family planning is an important part of the country's development strategy: a first and primary economic issue for the country, and a fundamental factor in the improvement of the quality of life for each citizen, each family, and the whole society. The specific target for each family is one or two children so that by 2015 the average number of children for each married couple will be two, advancing towards a stabilized population structure by the twenty-first century. Effort should be concentrated on creating a drastic change in the 1990s."[2]

It is clear that over the last thirty years, the Vietnamese Party and State have issued and implemented many resolutions and policies concerning family planning. But, in fact, no comprehensive population policy has ever been issued and the government's focus has been restricted to the reduction of births. Even here, policies and measures to reduce birth rates have not been uniform and concrete. For example, for many decades, housing was distributed according to the number of family members. Allowances were given to parents with many children, and land was allotted according to the number of family members. No special measures were taken in regards to ethnic minorities and people living in the mountainous regions. In those directives and resolutions, ethnic minorities were mentioned only once (in 1970), saying they are encouraged to increase their population. Two mountainous regions were also mentioned once (in 1988), saying married couples were allowed to have a third child. No attention was paid to other aspects, such as the quality and distribution of the population.

In our opinion, the issue is not to encourage or control births. Rather, it is the quality of the Vietnamese population that is the important issue. Population and socio-economic development are quite clearly inter-related. Specific policies and comprehensive, timely measures must be taken to raise the economic, cultural, and social conditions of life of the people throughout the country, and especially in upland, remote, and inaccessible areas. If they are not, it will be difficult to fulfill the set targets for the population.

ANNEX 1

POPULATION BY ETHNIC GROUP IN 1960 IN NORTH VIETNAM*

(unit: persons)

No.	Ethnic Group	Males	Females	Total	Compared with total (%)
(1)	(2)	(3)	(4)	(5)	(6)
	TOTAL	7,687,814	8,229,141	15,916,955	100.0
1	Kinh	6,521,901	7,031,845	13,553,746	85.2
2	Tay (Tho)	247,435	256,560	503,995	3.1
3	Muong	200,147	215,511	415,658	2.6
4	Thai	190,269	194,922	385,191	2.6
5	Nung	153,619	160,379	313,998	2.0
6	Meo	105,521	113,993	219,514	1.4
7	Man	92,373	93,698	186,071	1.2
8	Hoa	91,850	82,794	174,644	1.1
9	San Diu	17,349	16,564	33,913	0.2
10	Cao Lan	11,122	11,421	22,543	0.1
11	Xa	11,121	11,379	22,500	0.1
12	Nhang	8,082	8,347	16,429	0.1
13	San Chi	7,224	7,158	14,382	0.1
14	Lo Lo	3,331	3,567	6,898	
15	Van Kieu	2,815	2,671	5,486	
16	U Ni	2,569	2,690	5,259	
17	Puoc	2,191	2,320	4,511	
18	Sa Phang	1,484	1,610	3,094	
19	Khu Sung	1,259	1,218	2,477	
20	Sa Pho	649	714	1,363	
21	Lu	647	614	1,261	
22	Qui Chau	523	593	1,116	
23	Day	533	530	1,063	
24	Khua	496	509	1,005	
25	May	449	415	864	
26	Thu Lao	363	389	752	
27	Others	12,492	6,730	19,222	

* Population in North Vietnam (Data of the population census 1 March 1960), General Statistical Office, 1962, 35. Statistics 1961, General Statistic Office, (Hanoi: Su That Publishing House, 1963), 31.

ANNEX 2

POPULATION BY ETHNIC GROUP IN NORTH VIETNAM, 1 APRIL 1974*
(unit: persons)

No.	Ethnic Group	Total	Males	Females	Proportion of females of the total population %	Proportion of ethnic groups of total (%)
(1)	(2)	(3)	(4)	(5)	(6)	(7)
	Total	22,561,829	10,520,856	12,040,973	53.37	100.00
1	Kinh	18,925,839	8,763,378	10,162,461	53.70	83.88
2	Tay	744,351	353,850	390,501	52.46	3.30
3	Thai	631,753	305,866	325,887	51.58	2.80
4	Muong	596,191	278,000	318,191	53.37	2.64
5	Nung	472,750	226,100	246,650	52.17	2.10
6	Meo	348,722	170,708	178,014	51.05	1.55
7	Dao	290,792	144,178	146,614	50.42	1.29
8	Hoa	256,534	131,416	125,118	48.77	1.13
9	San Diu	57,440	28,235	29,205	50.84	0.25
10	Cao Lan	41,910	20,051	21,859	52.16	0.19
11	Kho Mu	30,990	15,273	15,717	50.72	0.14
12	Tho	26,976	12,966	14,010	51.94	0.12
13	San Chi	25,817	12,590	13,227	51.23	0.11
14	Giay	25,754	12,696	13,058	50.70	0.11
15	Lao	11,394	6,712	4,682	41.09	
16	Ha Nhi	8,897	4,389	4,508	50.67	
17	Xinh Mun	7,621	3,766	3,855	50.58	
18	Van Kieu	7,228	3,688	3,540	48.98	
19	La Chi	5,450	2,663	2,787	51.14	
20	Phu La	4,419	2,147	2,272	51.41	
21	La Hu	4,204	2,066	2,138	50.86	
22	Lu	2,456	1,204	1,252	50.98	
23	Lo Lo	2,219	1,049	1,170	52.73	
24	Khang	1,938	947	991	51.14	
25	Mang	1,780	867	913	51.29	
26	Chut	1,767	918	849	48.05	
27	Pa Then	1,476	763	713	48.31	
28	Tu Di	1,085	524	561	51.71	
29	Ba Na	969	575	394	40.66	
30	E De	958	511	447	46.66	
31	Bru	957	490	467	48.80	
32	Khmer	949	567	382	40.25	
33	Co Lao	929	458	471	50.70	
34	Si La	927	404	523	56.42	
35	Pu Na	859	416	443	31.37	
36	Hre	830	553	277	33.37	
37	Cong	807	386	421	52.17	
38	Gia Rai	582	400	182	31.27	
39	Pu Peo	525	248	277	52.76	
40	Co	517	238	279	53.59	
41	Others	5,852	3,304	2,548	43.54	

* Population of the Socialist Republic of Vietnam, General Statistical Office, Hanoi 1976, 28, 29.

ANNEX 3

POPULATION BY ETHNIC GROUP IN SOUTH VIETNAM, 5 FEBRUARY 1976*

(unit: persons)

No.	Ethnic Group	Total	Males	Females	Proportion of females of the total population %	Proportion of ethnic groups of total (%)
(1)	(2)	(3)	(4)	(5)	(6)	(7)
	Total	23,664,591	11,208,722	12,455,869	52.63	100.00
1	Kinh	21,091,919	9,954,039	11,137,880	52.81	89.13
2	Hoa	939,978	465,975	474,003	50.43	3.97
3	Khmer	676,795	318,364	358,431	52.96	2.86
4	Gia Rai	161,790	80,879	80,911	50.11	0.86
5	E De	141,077	71,978	69,099	48.98	0.60
6	Ba Na	79,005	39,471	39,534	50.04	0.33
7	Gie	67,834	32,289	35,545	52.40	0.29
8	Cham	65,294	31,087	34,207	52.39	0.28
9	Co Ho	63,521	29,703	33,818	53.24	0.27
10	Mnong	53,908	26,102	27,806	51.58	0.23
11	Xo Dang	47,212	23,582	23,630	50.05	0.20
12	Raglai	39,333	18,113	21,220	53.95	0.17
13	Stieng	35,107	16,244	18,863	53.73	0.15
14	Ma	23,815	11,200	12,615	52.97	0.10
15	Van Kieu	22,160	10,947	11,213	50.60	
16	Ha Lang	21,897	10,938	10,959	50.60	
17	Ca Tu	21,780	11,040	10,740	49.31	
18	Ta Oi	18,517	9,040	9,477	51.18	
19	Co	14,078	7,239	6,839	48.58	
20	Nung	13,582	6,953	6,629	48.81	
21	Tay	10,480	5,318	5,162	49.26	
22	Chu Ru	7,989	3,749	4,240	53.08	
23	Trieng	5,037	2,492	2,545	50.52	
24	Tho	4,659	2,337	2,322	49.84	
25	Thai	3,574	1,806	1,768	49.46	
26	Muong	2,225	1,028	1,197	53.80	
27	Hroi	1,325	542	783	59.09	
28	Dao	1,001	525	476	47.55	
29	Ve	856	420	436	50.93	
30	Hre	515	245	270	52.51	
31	Sre	429	193	236	54.97	
32	Giay	70	38	32	45.71	
33	Cao Lan	44	20	24	54.54	
34	Bru	28	13	15	53.57	
35	San Chi	13	9	4	30.77	
36	San Diu	9	3	6	66.67	
37	Lao	9	3	6	66.67	
38	Meo	3	3	-	-	
39	Other ethnic group	11,103	5,867	5,236	47.16	
40	Others Nationalities	16,620	8,928	7,692	46.92	

* Population of the Socialist Republic of Vietnam, General Statistical Office, Hanoi, 1976, 339–340.

ANNEX 4

POPULATION BY ETHNIC GROUP FOR THE ENTIRE COUNTRY, 1 OCTOBER 1979*

(unit: person)

No.	Ethnic Group	Total	Females	% of Females	Ethnic group structure
	Total	52,741,766	27,161,184	51.50	100.00
1	Kinh	46,065,384	23,735,196	51.53	87.34
2	Hoa	935,074	472,522	50.53	1.77
3	Tay	901,802	462,784	51.32	1.71
4	Thai	766,720	392,063	51.14	1.45
5	Khmer	717,291	378,167	52.72	1.36
6	Muong	686,082	359,461	52.39	1.30
7	Nung	559,702	286,997	51.28	1.06
8	Hmong	411,074	209,084	50.86	0.78
9	Dao	346,785	174,175	50.23	0.66
10	Gia Rai	184,507	96,208	52.14	0.35
11	E De	140,884	73,726	52.33	0.27
12	Ba Na	109,063	54,708	50.16	0.21
13	San Chay	77,104	39,552	51.39	0.15
14	Cham	77,012	39,871	51.77	0.15
15	Xo Dang	73,092	37,274	51.00	0.14
16	Co Ho	70,470	36,825	52.26	0.13
17	Hre	66,884	34,302	51.29	0.13
18	San Diu	65,808	32,966	50.09	0.12
19	Raglai	57,984	30,059	51.84	0.11
20	Mnong	45,954	24,122	52.49	
21	Stieng	40,763	21,562	52.90	
22	Bru (Van Kieu)	33,090	16,441	49.69	
23	Kho Mu	32,136	16,146	50.24	
24	Giay	27,913	14,140	50.66	
25	Co Tu	26,993	13,299	49.27	
26	Tho	24,839	12,565	50.59	
27	Ta Oi	20,517	10,074	49.10	
28	Ma	20,264	10,491	51.77	
29	Co	16,828	7,926	47.10	
30	Gie-Trieng	16,824	8,599	51.11	
31	Ha Nhi	9,444	4,806	50.89	
32	Xinh Mun	8,986	4,587	51.05	
33	Chu Ru	7,738	4,121	53.26	
34	Cho Ro	7,090	3,858	54.41	
35	Phu La	6,872	3,539	51.50	
36	Lao	6,781	3,367	49.67	
37	La Chi	5,855	3,047	52.04	
38	La Hu	4,270	2,048	47.96	
39	La Ha	3,174	1,611	50.76	
40	Chut	2,984	1,529	59.24	
41	Lu	2,952	1,505	50.98	
42	Mang	2,434	1,239	50.90	

* Vietnam's Population 1 October 1979, Hanoi, 1983

No.	Ethnic Group	Total	Females	% of Females	Ethnic group structure
43	Lo Lo	2,371	1,212	51.12	
44	Khang	2,327	1,129	48.52	
45	Pa Then	2,181	1,030	47.23	
46	Bo Y	1,342	660	49.18	
47	Ngai	1,318	630	47.80	
48	Co Lao	1,185	580	48.95	
49	Cong	843	427	50.65	
50	Si La	404	191	47.28	
51	Pu Peo	264	132	50.00	
52	Ro Mam	143	81	56.64	
53	O Du	137	13	9.49	
54	Brau	95	25	26.32	
	- Unidentified	8,830	4,471	50.63	
	- Foreigners	32,903	14,041	42.67	

ANNEX 5

POPULATION BY ETHNIC GROUP AND SEX FOR THE ENTIRE COUNTRY
1 APRIL 1989*

(unit: person)

No.	Ethnic Group	Total	Males	Females	Ratio % male/female
(1)	(2)	(3)	(4)	(5)	(6)
	Total	64,375,762	31,230,737	33,145,025	94,22
1	Kinh	55,900,224	27,056,673	28,843,551	93,80
2	Tay	1,190,342	589,922	600,420	98,25
3	Thai	1,040,549	517,619	522,930	98,98
4	Muong	914,596	447,384	467,212	95,76
5	Hoa	900,185	446,068	454,117	98,23
6	Khmer	895,299	424,331	470,968	90,10
7	Nung	705,709	348,656	357,053	97,64
8	Hmong	558,053	276,870	281,183	98,46
9	Dao	473,945	236,991	236,954	100,01
10	Gia Rai	242,291	117,838	124,453	94,68
11	E De	194,710	94,533	100,177	94,36
12	Ba Na	136,859	68,110	68,749	99,07
13	San Chay	114,012	56,834	57,178	99,40
14	Cham	98,971	48,608	50,363	96,51
15	Xo Dang	96,766	47,902	48,864	96,34
16	San Diu	94,630	47,925	46,705	102,61
17	Hre	94,259	46,427	47,832	97,06
18	Co Ho	92,190	44,655	47,535	93,94
19	Raglai	71,696	34,686	37,010	93,72
20	Mnong	67,340	32,483	34,857	93,19
21	Tho	51,274	25,581	25,693	97,56
22	Stieng	50,194	23,911	26,283	90,97
23	Kho Mu	42,853	21,679	21,174	102,38
24	Bru (Van Kieu)	40,132	20,198	19,934	101,32
25	Giay	37,964	18,884	19,080	98,97
26	Co Tu	36,967	18,809	18,158	103,58
27	Gie-Trieng	26,924	13,251	13,673	96,91
28	Ta Oi	26,044	13,126	12,918	101,61
29	Ma	25,436	12,290	13,146	93,49
30	Co	22,649	11,716	10,933	107,16
31	Cho Ro	15,022	7,232	7,790	92,84
32	Ha Nhi	12,489	6,297	6,192	101,69
33	Xinh Mun	10,890	5,373	5,517	97,39
34	Chu Ru	10,746	5,112	5,634	90,73
35	Lao	9,614	4,863	4,751	102,36
36	La Chi	7,863	3,873	3,990	97,07
37	La Hu	5,319	2,766	2,553	108,34
38	Khang	3,921	1,946	1,975	98,53

* Vietnam's Population Census. Result of the general population census, Vol. I, Hanoi, 1991, 66–67. The order in which the ethnic groups were originally listed have been reversed.)

No.	Ethnic Group	Total	Males	Females	Ratio % male/female
(1)	(2)	(3)	(4)	(5)	(6)
39	Lu	3,684	1,845	1,839	100,33
40	Pa Then	3,680	1,839	1,841	99,89
41	Lo Lo	3,134	1,505	1,629	92,39
42	Co Lao	1,473	742	731	101,50
43	Bo Y	1,420	700	720	97,22
44	Cong	1,261	626	635	98,58
45	Si La	594	298	296	100,68
46	Pu Peo	382	200	182	109,89
47	Brau	231	110	121	90,91
48	Ro Mam	227	99	128	77,34
	- Others	13,680	6,887	6,793	101,38
	- Foreigners	5,749	3,093	2,656	116,45
	- Unidentified	21,320	11,371	9,949	114,29

ANNEX 6

LIST OF ETHNIC GROUPS AND POPULATION IN VIETNAM*

No.	Ethnic group	Population	Other names	Locations and provinces
(1)		(2)	(3)	(4)
A. THE AUSTRO-ASIATIC LANGUAGE FAMILY **74,416,894**				
a. The Viet-Muong Group 67,005,456				
1	Viet	65,795,718	Kinh	Living in all provinces and cities of Vietnam
2	Muong	1,137,515	Mon, Moan, Moal, Au Ta	Hoa Binh, Thanh Hoa, Phu Tho, Son La, Ninh Binh
3	Tho	68,394	Keo, Mon, Cuoi, Ho, Tay Pong, Dan-Lai, Ly Ha	Nghe An, Thanh Hoa
4	Chut	3,829	Xo Lang, Tu Vang, Sach, May, Ruc, ARem, Ma Lieng	Quang Binh, Ha Tinh
b. The Mon-Khmer Group 2,101,203				
5	Khmer	1,055,174	Cur, Cul, Tho, Crom	Soc Trang, Tra Vinh, Kien Giang, An Giang, Bac Lieu, Ca Mau
6	Ba Na	174,456	Ro Ngao, Gio-Lang, Go La, To Lo, Bang Huong	Gia Lai, Kon Tum, Binh Dinh, Phu Yen
7	Xo Dang (Sedang)	127,148	Xo Teng, To Dra, Mnam, Ca Dong, Ha Lang, Tra Tri	Kon Tum, Quang Nam, Quang Ngai
8	Hre	113,111	Re, Cre, Luy, Da Vach	Quang Ngai, Binh Dinh, Kon Tum
9	Co Ho	128,723	Xre, Nop, Chil, Lat, Tring, Co Don	Lam Dong, Binh Thuan, Ninh Thuan, Dong Nai
10	Mnong	92,451	Pnong, Kil, Gar, Preh, Rlam, Panor, Biat, Kuyenh	Dac Lac, Binh Phuoc, Lam Dong
11	Stieng	66,788	Xa Dieng, Bu De, Bu Lo, Bu Dip, Bu Lach	Binh Phuoc, Dong Nai
12	Kho Mu	56,542	Xa, Xa Cau, Pu Thenh, Tay Hay, Mun Xen, Kha Cau	Nghe An, Lai Chau, Son La, Yen Bai
13	Bru-Van Kieu	55,559	Van Kieu, Khua, Tri, Ma Coong	Quang Tri, Quang Binh, Dac Lac, Thua Thien
14	Co Tu	50, 458	Ca Tu, Cao, Ha, Phuong	Quang Nam, Thua Thien
15	Gie-Trieng	30,243	Ta Re, Bri La Pnong Gie, Trieng, Ve	Kon Tum, Quang Nam

* Population of Vietnam, 1 April 1999

No.	Ethnic group	Population	Other names	Locations and provinces
(1)	(1)	(2)	(3)	(4)
16	Ta Oi	34,960	Toi Oi, Pa Co, Ta Uot, Can Tua, Pa Hi	Thua Thien, Quang Tri
17	Ma	33,338	Chau Ma, Ngan, Xop, Crung, To	Lam Dong, Dac Lac, Dong Nai
18	Co	27,766	Cor, Col, Cua, Trau	Quang Ngai, Quang Nam
19	Cho Ro	22,567	Do Ro, Chau Ro	Dong Nai, Binh Thuan
20	Xinh Mun	18,018	Puoc, Pua, Xa, Da, Nghet	Son La, Lai Chau
21	Khang	10,272	Xa, Mang, Mo Hang, Bren	Lai Chau, Son La
22	Mang	2,663	Xa Mang, Mang Lu, He, Gung, Nieng O, Xa La Vang	Lai Chau
23	Brau	313	Brao	Kon Tum
24	Rmam	352		Kon Tum
25	O Du	301	Tay Hat	Nghe An

c. The Hmong-Yao Group
1,413,711

No.	Ethnic group	Population	Other names	Locations and provinces
26	Hmong	787,604	Meo, Na Meo, Man Trang	Ha Giang, Lai Chau, Lao Cai, Son La, Yen Bai, Cao Bang, Nghe An, Tuyen Quang, Hoa Binh, Thai Nguyen, Lang Son
27	Dao	620,538	Man, Dong, Trai, Xa, Diu Mien, Kim Mien, Tong, Dai Ban, Tieu Ban	Ha Giang, Cao Bang, Tuyen Quang, Lao Cai, Yen Bai, Quang Ninh, Lai Chau, Lang Son, Thai Nguyen, Son La, Bac Can, Hoa Binh, Phu Tho, Bac Giang, Thanh Hoa, Vinh Phuc
28	Pa Then	5,569	Pa Hung, Thuy	Ha Giang, Tuyen Quang

d. The Tay-Thai Group
3,877,503

No.	Ethnic group	Population	Other names	Locations and provinces
29	Tay	1,477,514	Tho, Ngan, Phen, Thu Lao, Pa Di, Tho Da Bac	Cao Bang, Lang Son, Tuyen Quang, Ha Giang, Thai Nguyen, Yen Bai, Bac Can, Lao Cai, Bac Giang, Quang Ninh
30	Thai	1,328,725	Tay, Tay Muoi, Tay Thanh, Hang Tong, Pu Thay	Son La, Nghe An, Thanh Hoa, Lai Chau, Lao Cai, Yen Bai, Hoa Binh
31	Nung	856,412	Xuong, Giang, Phan Xinh, Qui Rin	Lang Son, Cao Bang, Bac Giang, Ha Giang, Thai Nguyen, Lao Cai, Yen Bai, Dac Lac, Bac Can, Tuyen Quang, Lam Dong, Gia Lai

No.	Ethnic group	Population	Other names	Locations and provinces
(1)		(2)	(3)	(4)
32	San Chay	147,315	Hon Ban, Son Tu, Cao Lan, San Chi	Tuyen Quang, Thai Nguyen, Bac Giang, Quang Ninh, Yen Bai, Cao Bang, Lang Son, Phu Tho, Vinh Phuc
33	Giay	49,098	Xa, Nhang, Dang, Pu Na, Qui Chau	Lao Cai, Ha Giang, Lai Chau, Yen Bai, Cao Bang
34	Lao	11,611	Lao Boc, Lao Noi	Lai Chau, Son La, Lao Cai
35	Lu	4,964	Nhuon, Duon	Lai Chau
36	Bo Y	1,864	Chung Cha, Tu Di	Lao Cai, Ha Giang, Tuyen Quang
e. The Ca Dai Group 19,021				
37	La Chi	10,765	Tho Den, Man, Xa, Cu Te, La Qua	Ha Giang, Lao Cai, Tuyen Quang
38	Co Lao	1,865	Quoc Lao	Ha Giang, Tuyen Quang
39	La Ha	5,686	Xa Khao, Kh'Lao, Ph'Lao	Son La
40	Pu Peo	705	Ca Peo, La Qua, Pen Ti, Lo Lo	Ha Giang, Tuyen Quang

B. THE MALAYO-POLYNESIAN LINGUISTIC FAMILY
832,687

No.	Ethnic group	Population	Other names	Locations and provinces
41	Gia Rai	317,557	Cho Rai, Ro Ray, Chor, Hdrung, ARap, Mthur, Tbuam	Gia Lai, Kon Tum, Dac Lac
42	E De	270,348	Ra De, De, Kpa, Adham, Ktul, Epan, Blo, Bih	Dac Lac, Gia Rai
43	Cham	132,873	Cham, Chiem Thanh, Hoi, Hroi	Ninh Thuan, Binh Thuan, Phu Yen, An Giang, Ho Chi Minh, Binh Dinh, Tay Ninh, Dong Nai
44	Rag Lai	96,931	Noang, La Oang, Rang Lai, Rai	Ninh Thuan, Khanh Hoa, Binh Thuan
45	Chu Ru	14,978	Chu, Cru, Cho Ru	Lam Dong

No.	Ethnic group	Population	Other names	Locations and provinces
(1)	(2)	(3)	(4)	
C. THE SINO-TIBETAN LINGUISTIC FAMILY **1,032,727**				
a. The Chinese Group 993,449				
46	Hoa	862,371	Han, Sa Phang, Ha	Ho Chi Minh, Dong Nai, Soc Trang, Bac Lieu, Kien Giang, Can Tho, An Giang, Song Be, Bac Giang, Bac Lieu,Tra Vinh, Binh Thuan, Lam Dong, Tuyen Quang, Ca Mau
47	San Diu	126,237	San Deo, Trai, Trai Dat, Man Quan Coc	Thai Nguyen, Vinh Phuc, Bac Giang, Quang Ninh, Tuyen Quang
48	Ngai	4,841	Sin, Le, Dan, Hac Ca	Thai Nguyen, Cao Bang, Tuyen Quang, Quang Ninh, Lang Son
b. The Tibeto-Burma Group 39,278				
49	Ha Nhi	17,535	Uni, Xa, La Mi, Co Cho	Lai Chau, Lao Cai
50	Phu La	9,046	Bo Kho Pa, Xa Pho, Lavat-xo, Pu Dang	Lao Cai, Yen Bai, Ha Giang, Lai Chau
51	La Hu	6,874	Xa Tong Luong, Kha Qui, Khu Sung	Lai Chau
52	Lo Lo	3,307	O Man, Mun Di, La Qua, La La	Cao Bang, Ha Giang, Lai Chau, Tuyen Quang
53	Cong	1,676	Xa, Xam Khong, Phua	Lai Chau
54	Si La	840	Cu De Su, Kha Pe	Lai Chau
TOTAL 76,282,308				

NOTES

INTRODUCTION

1. S. I. Bruk, *Issues on Ethno-Geography* (Moscow: Science Publishing House, 1973).

2. V. I. Kozlov, *Ethno-Demography* (Moscow: The Statistical Publishing House, 1977).

3. See D. I. Valentei, *Basis of Population Theory* (Moscow: Moscow College Publishing House, 1977).

4. *Marx-Engels Collection*, Volume II (Hanoi, 1981), 614.

CHAPTER I

1. Constitution of the Socialist Republic of Vietnam (Hanoi: Su That and Phap Ly Publishing House, 1992), 14.

2. M.G. Levin, N. N. Tsebocsarov, "Races, Languages and Ethnic Groups" in *General Ethnology*.

3. N. N. Tsebocsarov, "The Question of Classification of Ethnic Communities in the Works of Soviet Scholars," *Soviet Ethnological Magazine*, No. 4, 1967.

4. V. I. Kozlov, *Ethno-Demography* (Moscow: The Statistical Publishing House, 1977), 22.

5. V. I. Kozlov, "Ethnic Group and Ethnic Economics Soviet," *Ethnological Magazine*, No. 6, 1970.

6. V. I. Kozlov, *Ethno-Demography*, 23.

7. N. N. Tseboksarov, *Issues of the Origin of Ancient and Modern Ethnic Groups* Moscow: Science Publishing House, 1964.

8. Y. V. Bromlei, "Ethnic Groups and Ethnology," *Soviet Ethnological Magazine*, 1973, 92.

9. V. I. Kozlov, *Ethno-Demography*, 25–26.

10. A. F. Dashdamirov, "On Research Methodologies on Ethnic Psychology," *Soviet Ethnological Magazine*, No. 2, 1983, 62–74.

11. Y. V. Bromlei, "On the Impacts of the Characteristic of Cultural Environment on Psychology," *Soviet Ethnological Magazine*, No. 3, 1983, 7–75.

12. V. P. Levkovich, "Aspects of Social Psychology of Ethnic Consciousness," *Soviet Ethnological Magazine*, No. 4, 1983, 75–78.

13. Y. V. Bromlei, "Ethnic Group and Intra-marriage," *Soviet Ethnological Magazine*, No. 6, 1969.

14. Y. V. Bromlei, "Ethnic Group and Ethnology," ibid., 116.

15. V. I. Kozlov, *Ethno-Demography*, 28–29.

16. Mac Duong, "On the Principles of Classification and Defining of Ethnic Composition in North Vietnam," *Ethnological Bulletin*, No. 3, 1973, 46–51.

17. Azema, A. and R. Henri, *Les Stieng de Bro Lam, Excursion et Reconnaissances* T. XII, No. 27–28, 1986.

18. Bonifacy, "Etude des Caolan, 1907," *T'oung Pao*, Vol. II.

19. Dieguet, E. *Les Montagnards du Tonkin*, 1908.

20. Maitre, H. *Les Rund les Moi*, Paris, 1912.

21. Maspero, G. *Groupe Ethnique, Une Empire Coloniale Française: L'Indochine*, 1929.

22. Rozarie, D., *Groupes Ethniques de l'Indochine*, 1935.

23. Vuong Hoang Tuyen, "The Issue of Surveys to Define the Ethnic Composition of the Ethnic Minorities in North Vietnam," *National Unity Review*, No. 4, 1962; "Some Opinions on the Question of Nationalities in Vietnam," *Ethnological Review*, No. 35, 1962; "Some Documents on Ethnological Language to Classify Ethnic Minority Groups in Vietnam," *Ethnological Review*, No. 36, 1962.

24. Mac Duong, "Basic Issues in Defining Ethnic Groups," *Ethnological Review*, No. 35, 1962.

25. La Van Lo, "Further Discussions on Criteria for Defining the Composition of Ethnic Minorities," *Ethnological Review*, No. 36, 1962.

26. Hoang Thi Chau and Nguyen Linh, "Some Opinions on Defining Ethnic Minorities in North Vietnam," *Ethnological Review*, No. 38, 1963.

27. Be Viet Dang, "Some Opinions on Defining the Ethnic Composition in North Vietnam," *Ethnological Bulletin*, No. 1, 1972, 11.

28. Institute of Ethnology, *The Issue of Defining the Composition of Ethnic Minorities in Northern Vietnam* (Hanoi: Social Science Publishing House, 1975).

29. Be Viet Dang, "Some Opinions on Defining Ethnic Composition . . . ," 10–25.

30. "Defining Ethnic Composition in North Vietnam" (Account of the conference held in June, 1973), *Ethnological Bulletin*, No. 2, 1973, 121.

31. Nguyen Duong Binh, "Some Thinking on the Task of Defining Ethnic Composition," *Ethnological Bulletin*, No. 3, 1973, 55–56.

32. Hoang Hoa Toan, "Some Opinions on the Criteria on Defining Ethnic Composition in North Vietnam," *Ethnological Bulletin*, No. 3, 1973, 55–56.

33. See the summary of speeches at the conference, *Ethnological Bulletin*, No. 3, 1973, 103–132.

34. Summary of speeches at the conference, *Ethnological Bulletin*, No. 3, 1973, 103–132, Lam Thanh Tong, 103–105, Hoang Thi Chau and Nguyen Linh, 105–107, Trieu Huu Ly, 107–110, Bui Khanh The, 113–116, Lam Xuan Dinh, 120.

35. *Ethnic Minorities in Vietnam* (Hanoi: Culture Publishing House, 1959), 241–248.

36. Vuong Hoang Tuyen, *Ethnic groups of Austro-Asiatic Language Family in North Vietnam* (Hanoi: Education Publishing House, 1963); *Distribution of Ethnic Groups and Population in North Vietnam* (Hanoi: Education Publishing House, 1966); Mac Duong, *Ethnic minorities in North central Vietnam* (Hanoi: History Publishing House, 1964); La Van Lo and Dang Nghiem Van, *Brief Introduction of the Tay-Nung-Thai Ethnic Groups in Vietnam* (Hanoi: Social Science Publishing House, 1968); Cuu Long Giang and Toan Anh, *Upper High Plateaux* (Saigon: 1969); Be Viet Dang, et al, *The Yao in Vietnam* (Hanoi: The Social Science Publishing House, 1971); Bui Van Kin, Mai Van Tri, Nguyen Phung, *Contribution to Research on Hoa Binh Province*; Dang Nghiem Van, et al, *Ethnic groups of the Austro-Asiatic Language Family in Northwestern Vietnam* (Hanoi: The Social Science Publishing House, 1972); Ha Van Vien and Ha Van Phung, *Ethnic Minorities in Tuyen Quang Province* (Nationalities Committee of Tuyen Quang Province, 1973).

37. This list follows that published in, *Ethnic Minorities in Vietnam (North Provinces)*. (Hanoi: 1978) and *Ethnological Review*, No. 1. 1974, 57–63.

38. People of the Xa group were divided into other ethnic groups. Most of the other small groups were merged into larger groups as, for example, the Cao Lan and San Chi, which have been merged into the Cao Lao-San Chi or San Chay ethnic group.

39. *Ethnological Review*, No. 1, 1979, 59–63.

40. See Nguyen Duong Binh, "On the Composition of the Nguon," in *The Issue on the Defining of Compositions . . .* , 472; Nguyen Khac Tung, "Contributing to Studying the Composition of the Nguon through Assessments on their Housing," in *The Issue on the Defining of Compositions . . .* , 492; Khong Dien, "On Ethnic Groups in Central Provinces," *Ethnological Review*, No. 4, 1993.

41. Pham Duc Duong, "On the Close Relationship between Different Languages in the Viet-Muong Linguistic Group, Western Quang Binh Province," in *The Issue on the Defining of Compositions . . .* , 500–517; Ta Long, "On the Ethnic Community Relationship between the Three Groups of May, Ruc and Sach," in *The Issue on the Defining of Compositions . . .* , 518–530.

42. Nguyen Quoc Loc et al, *Ethnic Minority Groups in Binh Tri Thien* (Thuan Hoa: Hue Publishing House, 1984), 40–41.

43. Representing the Committee for Social Sciences were participants from the Institute of Ethnology and the Institute of Linguistics. Representing Hanoi University were participants from the Ethnology Division of the History Faculty and the Linguistics Division of the Linguistics Faculty.

44. See *Ethnic Minorities in Vietnam (Southern Provinces)* (Hanoi: Social Sciences Publishing House, 1984), 108.

45. "Stieng Ethnic Group," in *Ethnic Minorities in Vietnam (Southern Provinces)*, 142.

46. M. B. Kriukov and Tran Tat Chung, "The Issue of Origin of the Ta Mun Group," *Ethnological Review*, No. 2, 1990, 36–39.

47. Ngo Duc Thinh, "Some Opinions Contributing to Defining the Pa Di Group in Muong Khuong (Lao Cai Province)," in *The Issue of Defining the Composition . . .* , 287–305.

48. Ngo Duc Thinh, "The Pa Di Group in Lao Cai Province," *Ethnological Bulletin*, No. 3, 1973, 72–76.

49. Ngo Duc Thinh and Chu Thai Son, "The Thu Lao Group in Lao Cai Province," *Ethnological Bulletin*, No. 3, 1973, 77–81.

50. Be Viet Dang, "Initial Results of the Defining of Ethnic Groups," *Ethnological Bulletin*, No. 3, 1973, 17–18.

51. Bui Kin, Mai Van Tri and Nguyen Phung, *Contributing to Research on Hoa Binh Province* (Hoa Binh: Hoa Binh Department of Culture and Information, 1972).

52. Chu Thai Son, Nguyen Chi Hyen, "Composition of the Tho Group in Da Bac District (Hoa Binh Province)," *Ethnological Review*, No. 2, 1974, 42–52.

53. Nguyen Nam Tien, "On the Relationship Between the Two Groups of Cao Lan and San Chi," *Ethnological Bulletin*, No. 1, 1972, 59–75.

54. Nguyen Nam Tien, "On the Relationship between the Two Groups of Cao Lan and San Chi," *Ethnological Bulletin*, No. 1, 1972, 59–75; "On the Origin and the Process of Migration of the Cao Lan-San Chi," *Ethnological Bulletin*, No. 1, 1973, 41. Further discussion on the relationship between the two groups of Cao Lan-San Chi is published in *The Issue of Defining the Composition . . .* , 274–286. See also the Cao Lan-San, *Chi Group in Ethnic Minorities in Vietnam (Northern Provinces)*, 219–233.

55. Chu Thai Son, "The Tu Di in Lao Cai province," *Ethnological Bulletin*, No. 3, 1973, 82–86. See also *The Issue of Defining the Composition . . .* , 317–330 for current cultural activities of the Boy in Ha Giang province and *The Issue of Defining the Composition . . .* , 331–364 for a history of the migration and cultural activities of the Tu Di in Lao Cai.

56. Khong Dien, *On the Cham Group in Nghia Binh Province*, Report at the Conference on Ethnological Report, 1978.

CHAPTER II

1. *Statistical Year Book, 1990* (Hanoi: Statistical Publishing House, 1992), 5–6.

2. *Some Issues of the Population Situation of North Vietnam* (according to statistics of the 1960 population census), (Hanoi, 1961).

3. See Khong Dien, "Ethnic Groups in the Truong Son-Tay Nguyen Region," *Ethnological Review*, No. 1, 1984, 41–47, 60.

4. Khong Dien, "On the Issue of Residence of Ethnic Groups in Our Country," *Ethnological Review*, No. 3, 1993, 41–42.

5. See Diep Dinh Hoa et al, *Studies of Vietnamese Villages* (Hanoi: Social Science Publishing House, 1990), 20.

6. See Nguyen Van Huy, "Some Issues on the Studies of the Viet in Tay Nguyen at Present," *Ethnological Review*, No. 1, 1984, 49.

7. Mac Duong et al, *The Issue of Ethnic Groups in Lam Dong* (Lam Dong Provincial Department of Culture, 1983), 18.

8. Statistics of the Population Census of 1989.

9. La Van Lo, Nguyen Huu Thau et al, *Ethnic Minorities in Vietnam* (Hanoi: Culture Publishing House, 1959), 85.

10. See Thi Nhi and Tran Manh Cat, *"Some Aspects on the Tho in Nghe An,"* in *The Issue of Defining the Composition . . .* , 444–455.

11. Nguyen Duong Binh, "Overview on Economic Activities and Primitive Vestiges of Some Ethnic Minorities in North Truong Son Range," *Science Report*, Vol. 1, History Faculty of Hanoi University, 1962, 31.

12. Ta Long, "On the Relationship between Ethnic Communities Between Three Groups of May, Ruc and Sach," in *The Issue of Defining the Composition . . .* , 518–530.

13. According to the population census of 1979, the Gie-Trieng population was only 2,196 in Dien Khanh district, Phu Khanh province, and in 1989 there were 2,623 people in Khanh Vinh district, Khanh Hoa province. Although studies have yet to be conducted, it is our opinion that these people may belong to the T'Ring sub-group of the Co Ho ethnic group.

14. *Ethnic Minorities in Vietnam, (Southern Provinces),* 117.

15. According to the population census of 1979, there were some 1,054 Mnong people in the districts of Phuoc Son and Tra My of Quang Nam-Da Nang province. In 1989 there were 10,083 people. In our opinion, these people belong to the Pnong group or Pa Noong group of the Gie-Trieng ethnic group.

16. In the population census of 1960, the Kho Mu were included in the Sa ethnic group. This means that no statistics are available for this group specifically.

17. In the population lists of 1989, this group was not included in the Gie-Trieng ethnic group.

18. See Dang Nghiem Van, Nguyen Truc Binh, Nguyen Van Huy, Thanh Thien, *Ethnic Groups Belonging to the Austro-Asiatic Language Family in Northwestern Vietnam*, (Hanoi: Social Science Publishing House, 1972), 253–254.

19. *Ethnic Groups Belonging . . .* , 315.

20. Be Viet Dang, et al, *The Yao in Vietnam*, 16.

21. *The Ethnic Minorities in Vietnam (Southern Provinces)*, 120.

22. Ngo Duc Thinh, Chu Thai Son, "The Thu Lao in Lao Cai," *Ethnological Bulletin*, No. 3, 1973, 77–81.

23. Ngo Duc Thinh, "The Pa Di in Lao Cai," *Ethnological Bulletin*, No. 3, 1973, 72–76.

24. *Ethnic Minorities in Vietnam (Southern Provinces)*, 104–105.

25. Cam Trong, *The Thai in Northwestern Vietnam* (Hanoi: Social Sciences Publishing House. 1978), 25–26.

26. *Ethnic Minorities in Vietnam (Northern Provinces)*, 145.

27. La Van Lo, Dang Nghiem Van, *Brief Introduction of the Ethnic Groups of the Tay, Nung and Thai in Vietnam* (Hanoi: Social Science Publishing House, 1968), 31–32; *Ethnic Minorities in Vietnam (Northern Provinces)*, 200–201.

28. Nguyen Nam Tien, "On the Origin and the Process of Migration of the Cao Lan-San Chi," *Ethnological Bulletin*, No. 1, 1973, 42–43.

29. *Ethnic Minorities in Vietnam (Southern Provinces)*, 251–252.

30. See Ma Khanh Bang, *The San Diu in Vietnam* (Hanoi: Social Science Publishing House, 1983), 8–9.

31. *Ethnic Minorities in Vietnam (Northern Provinces)*, 343.

32. According to Nguyen Van Huy, *Culture and Life of the Ha Nhi-Lo Lo* (Hanoi: Culture Publishing House, 1985), 10.

33. Institute of Ethnology, *Booklet on Ethnic Minorities in Vietnam* (Hanoi: Social Science Publishing House, 1983), 224.

34. According to Nguyen Van Huy, *Culture and Life of the Ha Nhi-Lo Lo*, 6.

35. *Ethnic Groups Belonging . . .* , 211.

CHAPTER III

1. Daniel Noin, *Géographie de la population* (Masson, Paris, 1988), 273 and 274.

2. See Khong Dien, "The Process of Demographic Movement and Distribution of Population and Labour Force in the Whole Country," *Ethnology Magazine* No. 1, 1986, 55–64 and 71.

3. P. Gourou, *Les Paysans du delta Tonkinois* (Paris, 1936).

4. Phanh Khanh et al, *Sketch of Vietnam Irrigation History*, Vol. 1 (Hanoi: Social Science Publishing House, 1981), 11.

5. Phanh Khanh et al, *Sketch of Vietnam Irrigation History*, Vol. 1, 11.

6. Truong Huu Quynh. *The Agrarian Regime in Vietnam in the 11th–17th Century* (Hanoi: Social Science Publishing House, 1982), 31–32, 38–39 and 78–79.

7. Vietnam Commission for Social Sciences, *Vietnam's History*, Vol. 1 (Hanoi: Social Science Publishing House, 1971), 272.

8. See Phan Huy Le, *The Agrarian Reform and Agricultural Economy of the Le Dynasty* (Hanoi: Literature, History and Geography Publishing House, 1959).

9. *Vietnam's History*, Vol. 1, 293–294.

10. Nguyen Dinh Dau, *The Feudal State Rice Fields and Feudal State Land in the History of Land Reclamation in the Six Provinces of Nam Ky* (Hanoi: Vietnam Historians' Association, 1992), 30–32.

11. Nguyen Dinh Dau, *The Feudal State Rice Fields . . .* , 30–32.

12. Phan Dai Doan, "An Overview on Que Hai Canton (Ha Nam Ninh) from Its Founding until the Middle of the Twentieth Century," in *Vietnamese Peasants and Countryside in Modern Times*. Vol. 1 (Hanoi: Social Science Publishing House, 1990), 123–127.

13. Vu Huy Phuc, *Studies of the Agrarian Regime in Vietnam in the First Half of the Nineteenth Century* (Hanoi: Social Science Publishing House, 1979), 83, 136.

14. Dau Quy Ha, *A Hitting Strategic Issue*, included in the records of the "Symposium on Emigration to Build New Economic Zones," The Ministry of Labor, Invalids and Social Affairs, March 1990.

15. Nguyen Khanh Toan et al, *Vietnam's History*, Vol. II (Hanoi: Social Science Publishing House, 1985), 24.

16. Vu Huy Phuc, *Studies of the Agrarian Regime . . .* , 85, 136.

17. Le Duan, *The Proletarian Class and the Question of Peasantry in the Vietnamese Revolution* (Hanoi: Su That Publishing Houses, 1965), 24.

18. Duong Kinh Quoc, *Some Regulations on Land in Vietnam in the Modern History*, in *Vietnamese Peasants and Countryside in Modern Times*, Vol. 1 (Hanoi: Social Science Publishing House, 1990), 29–32.

19. Nguyen Khanh Toan et al, *Vietnam's History*, Vol. II, 10, and 103.

20. Duong Kinh Quoc, "Some Regulations on Land in Vietnam in Modern History," in *Vietnamese Peasants ...* , 39.

21. See Cao Van Bien, *The Working Class in Vietnam in the 1936–1939 Period* (Hanoi: Social Science Publishing House, 1979), 127–128.

22. Tran Van Giau, *Vietnam's Working Class* (Hanoi: Su That Publishing House, 1958), 17.

23. Ngo Van Hoa, Duong Kinh Quoc, *Vietnam's Working Class in the Years Prior to the Founding of the Party* (Hanoi: Social Science Publishing House, 1978), 36–39.

24. Tran Van Giau, *Vietnam's Working Class*, 169–70.

25. Ngo Van Hoa, Duong Kinh Quoc, *Vietnam's Working Class in the Years Prior to the Founding of the Party*, 57.

26. By 1907, in the northern mountainous provinces alone there were 97 plantations: 6 in Lang Son, 25 in Tuyen Quang, 3 in Ha Giang, 8 in Lao Cai, 10 in Ben Yai, 19 in Thai Nguyen, 12 in Quang Ninh, and 14 in Hoa Binh province.

27. According to Nguyen Duy Xuan (in the *An Binh Journal*, Can Tho, No. 4, 1974), around 250,000 people moved each year from the north and central regions to settle in areas of the south.

28. The Party Central Committee History Research Board, *The History of the Communist Party of Vietnam* (draft), Volume I, 1920–1954 (Hanoi: Su That Publishing House, 1984), 39.

29. Truong Trung Thu, Nguyen Manh De, *The US Neo-colonialist Economic Policies in South Vietnam* (Hanoi: Su That Publishing House, 1962), 3.

30. Nguyen Xuan Nghia, "Initial Assessment on the Structure and Movement of Population in South Vietnam under the US Puppet Regime," *Ethnology Review*, No. 1, 1978, 10–12.

31. Do Khac Tung, "On Urban Areas and the Urbanisation in South Vietnam under the US Puppet Regime," *Ethnology Review*, No. 4, 1977, 96–106.

32. Nguyen Huu Dao, "Review of Development of the Working Class in Vietnam in the Last 40 Years," *History Research Review*, No. 4, 1985, 20–23.

33. Van Tao, Dinh thu Cuc, "The Working Class in North Vietnam" in the *Period of Economic and Cultural Restoration, Reform and Development 1955–1960* (Hanoi: Social Science Publishing House, 1974), 49–64.

34. See Khong Dien, "Processes of Migration and Redistribution of Population and Labour Force in the Whole Country," *Ethnology Review*, No. 1, 1986, 62.

35. Tran Dinh Hoan, "Thirty Years of Emigration for New Economic Development and the Fundamental Change in the Coming Period," in the *Special Journal of the Ministry of Labor, Invalids and Social Affairs* (Hanoi, 1991), 7, 8.

36. *Population of the Socialist Republic of Vietnam 1974–1976* (Hanoi: General Statistics Office 1976), 347.

37. According to Nguyen Huu Dao, *Looking Back at Development of the Vietnamese Working Class Over the Past Forty Years* (already cited).

38. Pham Do Nhat Tan, *Orientations of Emigration of people to build new economic zones in the coming time*, Workshop on emigration to build new economic zones, Hanoi, March 1990.

39. The Department of Labor Distribution, *Review of Some Issues Relating to Labor and Population Mobilization to Build New Economic Zones (1981–1988)*, Symposium on migration (already cited).

40. According to Tran Dinh Hoan, *Inter-provincial Migration in 1976–1980*.

41. Pham Do Nhat Tan, *Orientation of Migration* (already cited).

42. Nguyen Van Thanh, "Renewal of Management Mechanism of Migration and Building New Economic Zones", in *Thirty years of the cause of land reclamation and building of new economic zones 1961–1991*, 16.

43. Le Manh Khoa, Nguyen Duc Hung, Do Tien Dung, "Migration, the Formation of Labour Sources for Socio-economic Development in Tay Nguyen," in *Population—The Labour Source-Migration for Socio-economic Development in Tay Nguyen* (Hanoi: Centre for Population and Labour Sources Studies, 1988), 15, 16.

44. Nguyen Trong Le, "Some socio-economic characteristics and organisation of defence of the Vietnam-China border" in the records of the Second Conference of Social Sciences on Socio-economic Situation of Mountainous Provinces in North Vietnam (Hanoi, 1985), 216–217.

45. Le Dang Giang, "Forms of emigration among ethnic minority groups along the northern border regions," in the Records of the Symposium on Population and Labor Sources organized by the Research Centre on Population and Labor Sources under the Ministry of Labor, Invalids, and Social Affairs (Hanoi, March 1988), 159, 160.

46. Nguyen Manh Hung, "From spontaneous emigration to understanding more about the rules of migration" in *Thirty Years of Land Reclamation and Building of New Economic Zones 1961–1991*, 43–45.

47. Vong Thai Bieu, *Quan Doi Nhan Dan* Newspaper, (September 27, 1994).

48. Nguyen Manh Hung, "From spontaneous emigration to understanding more about the rules of migration" (already cited), 40–44.

CHAPTER IV

1. Be Viet Dang and Khong Dien, "Some Characteristics of the Process of Population Development in Vietnam," *Ethnological Review*, No. 4, 1984, 2.

2. Nguyen Xuan Nghia, "Initial Comment on the Population Structure and Change in the South under the US puppet Regime," *Ethnological Review*, No. 1, 1978, 101–121.

3. Vietnam's Population October 1, 1979 (already cited), 34–74.

4. According to statistics of the 1989 population census released by the Central Population Census Committee.

5. Statistics of the surveys conducted in 1991.

6. See also Do Thinh, "Elderly people of ethnic groups," *Ethnological Review*, No. 1, 1993, 41–42.

7. Nguyen Duc Uyen, "Population and Family Planning in Vietnam in Recent Years," *Population Bulletin*, No. 3, 1991, 25.

8. Hoang Tich Giang, "Elderly People in Vietnam," *Population Bulletin*, No. 5, 1991, 11–12.

9. According to the Report of the National Committee on Population and Family Planning (April 1990), the average crude birth rate in 1989 was 31.3 per thousand, 23.4 per thousand in urban areas, and 34.4 per thousand in rural areas.

10. Ha Tuyen's Statistics in 1976, 1980–1984, Ha Tuyen Provincial Statistical Office, 1985, 29.

11. *Statistical Year Book 1986* (Hanoi, 1988), 13.

12. *Statistical Year Book 1987* (Hanoi, 1989), 15.

13. According to Le Duy Dai, "Tay Nguyen Population from the Angle of Ethno-demographic Research," Doctoral thesis, Institute of Ethnology archives.

14. Le Dinh Ky, "The Birth Rate and Its Trend in Vietnam: Optimism and New Challenges, *Ethnological Bulletin* No. 1, 1992, 6.

15. According to Dang Thu, the TFR in the regions are as follows: Eastern Nam Bo 3.23 children, the Red River Delta 3.67, the Mekong River Delta and the Central Coastal region 4.2, the remaining three regions have the highest TFR: Tay Nguyen 5.87, Northern mountainous and midland region 4.95, former Zone 4, 4.74. (Assessment of fertility rate and changes of fertility rate in some regions, provinces, districts and ethnic groups, Hanoi: Social Science Publishing House, 1993, 10).

16. Le Dinh Ky (already cited), 11–12.

17. Nguyen Thieu Lau, *La mortalité dans le Quang Binh, Bulletin* Paris: Imprimerie Nationale, 1951, 141.

18. Le Dinh Ky, "A Demographic Trend in Vietnam," *Population Bulletin,* No. 5, 1992, 6.

19. General Statistical Office, *Vietnam Figures and Events 1945–1989* (Hanoi: Su That Publishing House, 1990), 19.

20. General Statistical Office, *Situation of the Population Growth in North Vietnam* (through sample surveys), archive of the Institute of Economics.

21. General Statistical Office, *Situation of the Population Growth in North Vietnam* (through sample surveys), archive of the Institute of Economics.

22. General Statistical Office, *Situation of the Population Growth in 1963*, No. 97/TCTK-VK, Hanoi, November 14, 1964.

23. According to the Statistical Yearbooks from 1960 to 1975 in North Vietnam and from 1976 to the present for the whole country.

24. According to the *Statistical Year Books from 1979–1988.*

25. Le Van Duy, "Three Basic Factors Affecting the Birth Rate on the National Scale," *Population Bulletin,* No. 6, 1990, 8–12.

26. Le Van Duy, "Factors Affecting Mortality of Vietnamese Population," *Population Bulletin,* No. 5, 1992, 1–5.

27. Dang Nghia Phan, "Situation of Vietnamese Population in the 1979–1989 Period," *Population Bulletin,* 1991, 3–8.

28. According to Dang Thu and Doan Mau Diep (already cited), Hanoi 1998, 9–15.

29. Le Duy Dai, *Population in Tay Nguyen from the Angle of Ethno-demography Research* (already cited).

30. *Population Bulletin,* No. 3, 1984, 28.

31. Statistics supplied by the Central Population Census Committee.

32. Dang Nghiem Van et al, *Ethnic Groups of the Autro-Asiatic Linguistic Group in Northwestern Vietnam*, 211.

33. Khong Dien, Ngo Vinh Binh, Pham Quang Hoan, "Distribution of Population in the Mountainous Region of Binh Tri Thien Province," *Ethnological Review*, No. 1, 1977, 11, The Chut population at that time was only 1,415 people.

34. Khong Dien, "Ethnic groups in Central Provinces," *Ethnological Review*, No 4, 5.

35. According to the field survey of Dr. Vu Dinh Loi, Institute of Ethnology.

36. See Luong Xuan Quy, Nguyen Dinh Cu, *Population Boom, Consequence and Solution* (Hanoi: Su That Publishing House, 1992), 54.

37. According to Le Phuong Mai, "Brief introduction on the impacts of population growth on socio-economic development in Vietnam," *Population Bulletin*, No. 5, 1991.

38. Luong Xuan Quy, Nguyen Dinh Cu, *Population Boom...* , 57.

39. Nafis Sadik, "Population, Health, Environment and Women," *Population Bulletin*, No. 6, 1991.

40. *Statistical Year Book 1988, 1990*.

41. *Statistical Year Book 1990*.

42. *Report of the Steering Committee of the Population Census of Ha Tuyen Province*, September 4, 1989.

43. Le Phuong Mai, "Some Social and Cultural Issues Through the Sociological Sample Survey of Mountainous Ethnic Ggroups in Lang Son Province in 1992," *Population Bulletin*, No. 3, 1993, 7–12.

44. Tran Si Nguyen, Dinh Xuan Ha, "On the Building and Development of Education in Mountainous Regions and Ethnic Minority Groups," *Education Studies*, No. 12, 1989, 9–10.

45. Do Ngoc Bich, "Some Measures to Promote Education Among the H'Mong Ethnic Minority Group," *Education Studies*, No. 12, 1989, 11.

46. Tu Dien, "Issue of Population and Food," *Population Information*, No 4, 1991, 9–12.

47. *Population Education in School* (Hanoi: Education Publishing House, 1984), 90.

48. Minh Huong, *Lao Dong Newspaper*, March 1986.

49. Le Ngoc Van, "Impacts of the Feudal Viewpoints on Family Planning," *Sociological Review*, No. 4, 1985, 38–41.

50. General statistics of the whole country, also covering the separately surveyed groups.

51. According to Nguyen Minh Thang, "Quantitative Analysis of Factors Affecting the Birth Rate in Our Country," *Population Bulletin*, No. 4, 1990.

52. Le Ngoc Lam, "Why Annual Population Growth Rate in Our Country Remains High," *Population Bulletin* No. 5, 1989.

53. Ministry of Public Health, *Development of Healthcare for the People from Now Till 2000,* report presented at the Fouth Plenum of the Party Central Committee, Seventh Tenure, Hanoi, September 1992, 7.

54. Do Long, "Traditional Social Psychology and Population Planning in Vietnam," *Sociological Review,* No. 4, 1985.

55. Le Dinh Ky, "Relationship Between Infant Mortality and Birth Rate," *Population Bulletin,* No. 5, 1988.

56. Le Ngoc Lam, *Population Bulletin,* No. 5, 1989.

57. Do Thuy Binh, "Some Issues When Studying the Situation of Ethnic Minorities: Women's Lives and Contributions towards Implementing Social Policies," *Ethological Review,* No. 2, 1993, 39.

58. Le Ngoc Lam, *Population Bulletin* No. 5, 1989.

59. Nguyen Minh Thang, "Quantitative Analysis ...".

CONCLUSION

1. *Population Bulletin* (special issue), 1992.

2. Vietnam Communist Party, Document of the Fouth Plenum of the Party Central Committee.

REFERENCES
(TRANSLATED INTO ENGLISH)

BOOKS

Be Viet Dang, Nguyen Khac Tung, Nong Trung, Nguyen Nam Tien. *The Yao in Vietnam*. Hanoi: Social Science Publishing House, 1971.

Be Viet Dang, Chu Thai Son, Vu Thi Hong, Vu Dinh Loi. *Overview on the E De, Mnong in Dac Lac*. Hanoi: Social Science Publishing House, 1982.

Brook, S. I. *Issues on Ethno-Geography* (in Russian). Moscow: Science Publishing House, 1973.

Bui Xuan Dinh. *Village Rules and State Law*. Hanoi: Justice Publishing House, 1985.

Cam Trong. *The Thai in the Northwestern Region of Vietnam*. Hanoi: Social Science Publishing House, 1978.

Cao Van Bien. *The Vietnamese Working Class in the 1936–1939 Period*. Hanoi: Social Science Publishing House, 1979.

Cuu Long Giang, Toan Anh. *Upper High Plateaux*. Saigon, 1969.

Some Basic Issues on Ancient Socio-economic History of the Thai in the Northwestern Region of Vietnam. Hanoi: Social Science Publishing House, 1987.

Constitution of the Socialist Republic of Vietnam. Hanoi: Justice-Truth Publishing House, 1992.

Diep Dinh Hoa et al. *Studies of Vietnamese Village*. Hanoi: Social Science Publishing House, 1990.

Diep Trung Binh. *The San Diu Folk Singing*. Hanoi: Nationality Culture Publishing House, 1987.

Duong Kinh Quoc. *The Colonial Regime in Vietnam Prior to the August 1945 Revolution*. Hanoi: Social Science Publishing House, 1988.

Dao Van Tap et al. *Thirty years of Vietnam's Economy*. Hanoi: Social Science Publishing House. 1980.

Dang Nghiem Van, Nguyen Truc Binh, Nguyen Van Huy, Thanh Thien. *Ethnic Groups of the Austro-Asiatic Language Family*. Hanoi: Social Science Publishing House, 1972.

Dang Nghiem Van, Dinh Xuan Lam. *Dien Bien in History*. Hanoi: Social Science Publishing House, 1979.

Dang Nghiem Van, Cam Trong, Tran Manh Cat, Le Duy Dai, Ngo Vinh Binh. *Ethnic Groups in Gia Lai-Kon Tum Province*. Hanoi: Social Science Publishing House, 1981.

Dang Nghiem Van. *Relationship between Ethnic Groups in a Country*. Hanoi: National Political Publishing House, 1993.

Dang Thu et al. *Assessment of the Birth Rate and the Birth Rate Variations in Regions, Provinces, Districts and Ethnic Groups*, Hanoi: Social Science Publishing House, 1993.

Ethnic Minorities in Vietnam. Hanoi: Culture Publishing House, 1959.

Ha Van Vien, Ha Van Phung. *Ethnic Minorities in Tuyen Quang Province*. Nationalities Committee of Tuyen Quang Province, 1973.

General Statistical Office. *Vietnam Figures and Events 1945–1989*. Hanoi: Su That Publishing House, 1990.

Institute of Agricultural Planning and Designing. *Agriculture in the midland and mountainous regions, real state and prospects*. Hanoi: Agriculture Publishing House, 1993.

Institute of Ethnology. *Archive Documents on the Thai History and Society*. Hanoi: Social Science Publishing House, 1977.

_____. *The Issues of Defining the Composition of Ethnic Minorities in North Vietnam*. Hanoi: Social Science Publishing House, 1975.

_____. *Ethnic Minorities in Vietnam (Northern provinces)*. Hanoi: Social Science Publishing House, 1978.

_____. *Handbook on Ethnic Groups in Vietnam*. Hanoi: Social Science Publishing House, 1983.

_____. *Ethnic Minorities in Vietnam* (Southern provinces). Hanoi: Social Science Publishing House. 1984.

_____. *Contribution to Studying the National Identities in Vietnam*. Hanoi: Social Science Publishing House, 1980.

_____. *Some Socio-economic Issues in Northern Mountainous Provinces*. Hanoi: Social Science Publishing House, 1987.

_____. *The Tay, Nung Ethnic Groups in Vietnam*. Hanoi, 1992.

_____. *Economic and Cultural Changes in Northern Mountainous Provinces*. Hanoi: Social Science Publishing House, 1993.

Institute of History. *Farmers and Rural Vietnam in the Modern Time*. Hanoi: Social Science Publishing House, 1990.

Issue of Ethnic group nationalities in the Mekong River Delta. Hanoi: Social Science Publishing House, 1991.

Kozlov, V. I. *Ethno-Demography* (in Russian). Moscow: Statistics Publishing House, 1977.

La Van Lo, Nguyen Huu Thau, Mai Van Tri, Ngoc Anh, Mac Nhu Duong. *Ethnic minority groups in Vietnam*. Hanoi: Culture Publishing House, 1959.

La Van Lo, Dang Nghiem Van, *Brief Introduction of the Tay-Nung, Thai ethnic groups in Vietnam*. Hanoi: Social Science Publishing House, 1968.

La Van Lo. *Initial Studies on Ethnic Minority Groups in Vietnam in the Cause of Building and Defending the Country*. Hanoi: Social Science Publishing House, 1973.

Le Thi Nham Tuyet, *Vietnamese Women Through Different Eras*. Hanoi: Social Science Publishing House, 1975.

Luc Van Pao. *The Tay-Nung Idioms*. Hanoi: Social Science Publishing House. 1991.

————. *Put Tay*. Hanoi: Social Science Publishing House, 1992.

Luong Xuan Quy, Nguyen Dinh Cu. *Population Boom, Consequences and Solutions*. Hanoi: Su That Publishing House, 1992.

Ma Khanh Bang, *The San Diu in Vietnam*. Hanoi: Social Science Publishing House. 1983.

Mac Duong. *Ethnic Groups in the Northern Mountainous Areas of Central Vietnam*. Hanoi, 1964.

Mac Duong. *Ethnic Minorities in North Central Vietnam*. Hanoi: History Publishing House, 1964.

Mac Duong et al. *The Question of Nationality in Lam Dong*. Hanoi: Department of Culture and Information of Lam Dong, 1983.

————. *The Question of Nationality in Song Be*. Tong Hop, 1985.

Nguyen Dinh Dau. *The Feudal State Rice-fields and Feudal State Land Regime in the History of Land Reclamation to set up Hamlets in the Six Provinces of Nam Ky*. Hanoi: Vietnam Historians' Association, 1992.

Nguyen Huy Phuc. *Studies on the Agrarian Regime in Vietnam in the First Half of the Nineteenth Century*. Hanoi: Social Science Publishing House, 1979.

Nguyen Khanh Toan et al. *Vietnam's History*. Vol. II, Hanoi: Social Science Publishing House, 1981.

Nguyen Khac Tung, Ngo Vinh Binh. *The Great Family of Vietnamese Nationalities*. Hanoi: Education Publishing House, 1981.

Nguyen Khac Tung et al. *The Rong (Communal) House of the Ethnic Minority Groups in Tay Nguyen*. Hanoi: Social Science Publishing House.

Nguyen Van Huy. *Culture and the life style of the Ha Nhi Lo Lo*. Hanoi: Culture Publishing House, 1985.

————. *The Traditional Culture of the La Chi Ethnic Group*. Hanoi: Nationality Culture Publishing House, 1991.

Phan Huy Le. *The Agrarian Reform and Agricultural Economy of the Le Dynasty*. Hanoi: Literature, History and Geography Publishing House, 1959.

Phan Huy Le, Chu Thien, Vuong Hoang Tuyen, Dinh Xuan Lam. *Vietnam's Feudal History*. Hanoi: Education Publishing House, 1965.

Phan Khanh et al. *Overview on the History of Irrigation in Vietnam*, Vol, I. Hanoi: Social Science Publishing House, 1981.

Phan Xuan Bien, Phan An, Phan Van Dop. *The Cham Culture*. Hanoi: Social Science Publishing House, 1991.

Phuong Bang, La Van Lo. *Luon Sluong*. Hanoi: Nationality Culture Publishing House, 1992.

Population Bulletin, No. 3, 1984.

Population Bulletin (special issue), 1992.

Result of the General Population Census in 1989. Central Steering Committee of Population Census. Hanoi, 1991 (Vol. I).

Statistical Data 1961. Hanoi: Su That Publishing House, 1963.

Statistical Year Book, 1986. Hanoi: Statistical Publishing House, 1988.

Statistical Year Book, 1987. Hanoi: Statistical Publishing House, 1989.

Statistical Year Book, 1990. Hanoi: Statistical Publishing House, 1992.

Tran Van Giau. *Vietnam's Working Class*. Hanoi: Su That Publishing House, 1958.

Truong Huu Quynh. *The Agrarian Regime in Vietnam in the 11th–18th Century*, Vol. I. Hanoi: Social Science Publishing House, 1982.

Valentei, D. I. *Basis of the Population Theory* (In Russian). Moscow: Moscow College Publishing House, 1977.

Van Tao, Dinh Thu Cuc, *North Vietnam's Working Class*. Hanoi: Social Science Publishing House, 1974.

Vietnam Commission for Social Sciences, *Vietnam's History*, Vol. 1. Hanoi: Social Science Publishing House, 1971.

Vietnam's Population October 1, 1979. Central Steering Committee of Population Census. Hanoi, 1983.

Vietnam Social Science Committee. *Vietnam's History*, Vol. I. Hanoi: Social Science Publishing House, 1971.

_____. *Some Socio-economic Issues in Tay Nguyen*. Hanoi: Social Science Publishing House, 1986.

_____. *Tay Nguyen on the Road of Development*. Hanoi: Social Science Publishing House, 1989.

Vietnam Social Science Committee and Dac Lac Provincial People's Committee. *Socio-Economic Development of Ethnic Minority Groups in Dac Lac*. Hanoi: Social Science Publishing House, 1990.

Vietnam Social Science Institute and Van Lang district People's Committee. *Van Lang, A Border District of Lang Son*. Hanoi: Social Science Publishing House, 1990. *Population of the Socialist Republic of Vietnam 1974–1976*. General Statistical Office, Hanoi, 1976.

Vu Huy Phuc, *Studies of the Agrarian Regime in Vietnam in the First Half of the Nineteenth Century*. Hanoi: Social Science Publishing House, 1979.

Vuong Hoang Tuyen. *Ethnic groups of Austro-Asiatic Language Family in North Vietnam*. Hanoi: Education Publishing House, 1963.

_____. *Distribution of Ethnic Groups and Population in North Vietnam*. Hanoi: Education Publishing House, 1966.

ARTICLES

Be Viet Dang, "Some Opinions on Defining the Ethnic Composition in North Vietnam," *Ethnological Bulletin*, No. 1, 1972.

_____, "Initial Results of the Defining of Ethnic Groups," *Ethnological Bulletin*, No. 3, 1973.

_____, and Khong Dien, "Some Characteristics of the Process of Population Development in Vietnam," *Ethnological Review*, No. 4, 1984.

Bonifacy, "Etude des Caolan, 1907," *T'oung Pao*, Vol. II.

Bromlei, Y. V., "Ethnic Group and Intra-marriage," *Soviet Ethnological Magazine*, No. 6, 1969.

_____, "Ethnic Groups and Ethnology," *Soviet Ethnological Magazine*, 1973.

_____, "On the Impacts of the Characteristic of Cultural Environment on Psychology," *Soviet Ethnological Magazine*, No. 3, 1983.

Chu Thai Son, Nguyen Chi Hyen, "Composition of the Tho Group in Da Bac District (Hoa Binh Province)," *Ethnological Review*, No. 2, 1974.

Dang Nghia Phan, "Situation of Vietnamese Population in the 1979–1989 Period," *Population Bulletin*, 1991.

Dashdamirov, A. F. "On Research Methodologies on Ethnic Psychology," *Soviet Ethnological Magazine*, No. 2, 1983.

Do Khac Tung, "On Urban Areas and the Urbanisation in South Vietnam under the US-Puppet Regime," *Ethnology Review*, No. 4, 1977.

Do Long, "Traditional Social Psychology and Population Planning in Vietnam," *Sociological Review*, No. 4, 1985.

Do Thinh, "Elderly people of ethnic groups," *Ethnological Review*, No. 1, 1993.

Do Ngoc Bich, "Some Measures to Promote Education Among the H'Mong Ethnic Minority Group," *Education Studies*, No. 12, 1989.

Do Thuy Binh, "Some Issues When Studying the Situation of Ethnic Minorities Women's Lives and Contribution towards Implementing Social Policies," *Ethological Review*, No. 2, 1993.

Hoang Hoa Toan, "Some Opinions on the Criteria on Defining Ethnic Composition in North Vietnam," *Ethnological Bulletin*, No. 3, 1973.

Hoang Thi Chau and Nguyen Linh, "Some Opinions on Defining Ethnic Minorities in North Vietnam," *Ethnological Review*, No. 38, 1963.

Hoang Tich Giang, "Elderly People in Vietnam," *Population Bulletin*, No. 5, 1991.

Kozlov, V. I. "Ethnic Group and Ethnic Economics Soviet," *Ethnological Magazine*, No. 6, 1970.

Khong Dien, "On Ethnic Groups in Central Provinces," *Ethnological Review*, No. 4, 1993.

----------. "Ethnic Groups in the Truong Son-Tay Nguyen Region," *Ethnological Review*, No. 1, 1984.

----------. "On the Issue of Residence of Ethnic Groups in Our Country," *Ethnological Review*, No. 3, 1993.

----------. "The Process of Demographic Movement and Distribution of Population and Labour Force in the Whole Country," *Ethnology Magazine* No. 1, 1986.

----------. "Processes of Migration and Redistribution of Population and Labour Force in the Whole Country," *Ethnology Review*, No. 1, 1986.

----------, Ngo Vinh Binh, Pham Quang Hoan, "Distribution of Population in the Mountainous Region of Binh Tri Thien Province," *Ethnological Review*, No. 1, 1977.

Kriukov, M. B. and Tran Tat Chung, "The Issue of Origin of the Ta Mun Group," *Ethnological Review*, No. 2, 1990.

La Van Lo, "Further Discussions on Criteria for Defining the Composition of Ethnic Minorities," *Ethnological Review*, No. 36, 1962.

Le Dinh Ky, "Relationship Between Infant Mortality and Birth Rate," *Population Bulletin*, No. 5, 1988.

----------. "The Birth Rate and Its Trend in Vietnam: Optimism and New Challenges," *Ethnological Bulletin* No. 1, 1992.

----------. "A Demographic Trend in Vietnam," *Population Bulletin*, No. 5, 1992.

Le Ngoc Lam, "Why Annual Population Growth Rate in Our Country Remains High," *Population Bulletin* No. 5, 1989.

Le Ngoc Van, "Impacts of the Feudal Viewpoints on Family Planning," *Sociological Review*, No. 4, 1985.

Le Phuong Mai, "Brief introduction on the impacts of population growth on socio-economic development in Vietnam," *Population Bulletin*, No. 5, 1991.

----------. "Some Social and Cultural Issues Through the Sociological Sample Survey of Mountainous Ethnic Ggroups in Lang Son Province in 1992," *Population Bulletin*, No. 3, 1993.

Le Van Duy, "Three Basic Factors Affecting the Birth Rate on the National Scale," *Population Bulletin*, No. 6, 1990.

----------. "Factors Affecting Mortality of Vietnamese Population," *Population Bulletin*, No. 5, 1992.

Levkovich, V. P. "Aspects of Social Psychology of Ethnic Consciousness," *Soviet Ethnological Magazine*, No. 4, 1983.

Mac Duong, "On the Principles of Classification and Defining of Ethnic Composition in North Vietnam," *Ethnological Bulletin*, No. 3, 1973.

----------. "Basic Issues in Defining Ethnic Groups," *Ethnological Review*, No. 35, 1962.

----------. "The Pa Di Group in Lao Cai Province," *Ethnological Bulletin*, No. 3, 1973.

Ngo Duc Thinh and Chu Thai Son, "The Thu Lao Group in Lao Cai Province," *Ethnological Bulletin*, No. 3, 1973.

Nguyen Duc Uyen, "Population and Family Planning in Vietnam in Recent Years," *Population Bulletin*, No. 3, 1991.

Nguyen Duong Binh, "Some Thinking on the Task of Defining Ethnic Composition," *Ethnological Bulletin*, No. 3, 1973.

―――――. "Overview on Economic Activities and Primitive Vestiges of Some Ethnic Minorities in North Truong Son Range," *Science Report*, Vol. 1, History Faculty of Hanoi University, 1962.

Nguyen Huu Dao, "Review of Development of the Working Class in Vietnam in the Last 40 Years," *History Research Review*, No. 4, 1985.

Nguyen Minh Thang, "Quantitative Analysis of Factors Affecting the Birth Rate in Our Country," *Population Bulletin*, No. 4, 1990.

Nguyen Nam Tien, "On Relationship Between the Two Groups of Cao Lan and San Chi," *Ethnological Bulletin*, No. 1, 1972.

―――――. "On the Origin and the Process of Migration of the Cao Lan-San Chi," *Ethnological Bulletin*, No. 1, 1973.

―――――. and Chu Thai Son, "The Tu Di in Lao Cai province," *Ethnological Bulletin*, No. 3, 1973.

Nguyen Van Huy, "Some Issues on the Studies of the Viet in Tay Nguyen at Present," *Ethnological Review*, No. 1, 1984.

Nguyen Xuan Nghia, "Initial Assessment on the Structure and Movement of Population in South Vietnam under the US-Puppet Regime," *Ethnology Review*, No. 1, 1978.

Nguyen Xuan Nghia, "Initial Comment on the Population Structure and Change in the South under the US puppet Regime," *Ethnological Review*, No. 1, 1978, 101–121.

Sadik, Nafis, "Population, Health, Environment and Women," *Population Bulletin*, No. 6, 1991.

Tran Si Nguyen, Dinh Xuan Ha, "On the Building and Development of Education in Mountainous Regions and Ethnic Minority Groups," *Education Studies*, No. 12, 1989.

Tsebocsarov, N. N, "The Question of Classification of Ethnic Communities in the Works of Soviet Scholars," *Soviet Ethnological Magazine*, No. 4, 1967.

Vuong Hoang Tuyen, "The Issue of Surveys to Define the Ethnic Composition of the Ethnic Minorities in North Vietnam," *National Unity Review*, No. 4, 1962.

―――――. "Some Opinions on the Question of Nationalities in Vietnam," *Ethnological Review*, No. 35, 1962.

―――――. "Some Documents on Ethnological Language to Classify Ethnic Minority Groups in Vietnam," *Ethnological Review*, No. 36, 1962.

INDEX